The Rights Paradox

The US Supreme Court is the chief institution responsible for guarding minority rights and equality under the law, yet, in order to function authoritatively, the Court depends on a majority of Americans to accept its legitimacy and on policymakers to enforce its rulings. *The Rights Paradox* confronts this tension, offering a careful conceptualization and theory of judicial legitimacy that emphasizes its connection to social groups. Zilis demonstrates that attitudes toward minorities and other groups are pivotal for shaping popular support for the Court, with the Court losing support when it rules in favor of unpopular groups. Moreover, justices are aware of these dynamics and strategically moderate their decisions when concerned about the Court's legitimacy. Drawing on survey and experimental evidence, as well as analysis of Court decision-making across many recent high-profile cases, Zilis examines the implications for 'equal justice under the law' in an era of heightened polarization and conflict.

MICHAEL A. ZILIS is Associate Professor of Political Science at the University of Kentucky. His research on political resistance to the US Supreme Court has been supported by the National Science Foundation. He is the author of *The Limits of Legitimacy*, which was named a 2015 Exemplary Law Book.

The Rights Paradox
How Group Attitudes Shape US Supreme Court Legitimacy

MICHAEL A. ZILIS
University of Kentucky

CAMBRIDGE
UNIVERSITY PRESS

University Printing House, Cambridge CB2 8BS, United Kingdom

One Liberty Plaza, 20th Floor, New York, NY 10006, USA

477 Williamstown Road, Port Melbourne, VIC 3207, Australia

314–321, 3rd Floor, Plot 3, Splendor Forum, Jasola District Centre, New Delhi – 110025, India

79 Anson Road, #06–04/06, Singapore 079906

Cambridge University Press is part of the University of Cambridge.

It furthers the University's mission by disseminating knowledge in the pursuit of education, learning, and research at the highest international levels of excellence.

www.cambridge.org
Information on this title: www.cambridge.org/9781108832090
DOI: 10.1017/9781108937764

© Michael A. Zilis 2021

This publication is in copyright. Subject to statutory exception and to the provisions of relevant collective licensing agreements, no reproduction of any part may take place without the written permission of Cambridge University Press.

First published 2021

A catalogue record for this publication is available from the British Library.

Library of Congress Cataloging-in-Publication Data
NAMES: Zilis, Michael A., author.
TITLE: The rights paradox : how group attitudes shape U.S. Supreme Court legitimacy / Michael A. Zilis, Associate Professor, Department of Political Science, University of Kentucky.
DESCRIPTION: New York : Cambridge University Press, [2020?] | Includes bibliographical references and index.
IDENTIFIERS: LCCN 2020046837 (print) | LCCN 2020046838 (ebook) | ISBN 9781108832090 (hardback) | ISBN 9781108927697 (paperback) | ISBN 9781108937764 (epub)
SUBJECTS: LCSH: Minorities–Legal status, laws, etc.–United States. | Minorities–Civil rights–United States. | United States. Supreme Court–Public opinion. | Legitimacy of governments–United States. | School integration–Law and legislation–United States. | Aversion–Political aspects–United States.
CLASSIFICATION: LCC KF4755 .Z55 2020 (print) | LCC KF4755 (ebook) | DDC 342.7308/7–DC23
LC record available at https://lccn.loc.gov/2020046837
LC ebook record available at https://lccn.loc.gov/2020046838

ISBN 978-1-108-83209-0 Hardback

Cambridge University Press has no responsibility for the persistence or accuracy of URLs for external or third-party internet websites referred to in this publication and does not guarantee that any content on such websites is, or will remain, accurate or appropriate.

*To Katrina and Chelsea
and the years to come*

Contents

List of Figures	*page* xi
List of Tables	xiii
Acknowledgments	xv
Table of Cases	xvii

1 Legitimacy and Minority Rights   1
   Foundations and Limits of Supreme Court Authority   2
   Supreme Court Legitimacy and Its Relationship with Minority Rights   3
   The Argument   4
   Why Care about Group-Based Legitimacy? Implications on the Bench   6
   The Plan of the Book   6

2 The Group Antipathy Theory of Supreme Court Legitimacy   11
   Institutional Legitimacy as the Supreme Court's Foundational Resource   12
   Existing Models of Institutional Legitimacy   15
   Research on Group-Based Attitudes   17
   The Group Antipathy Model of Legitimacy   18
       Contextualizing the Model   23
       Alternative Explanations and Threats to Inference   25
       Long-Term Implications and Contributions   30
   Research Design Strategy   32

3 Under Siege: Gay Rights and Immigration at the Supreme Court   34
   Signals from the Court   36
       Applying the Group Antipathy Model   38
   Study A: Landmark Court Decisions   39

	Measures	40
	Analysis	41
	Discussion	49
4	Opening the Floodgates: Big Business, Citizens United, and Evaluations of the Court	51
	Perceptions of a Pro-business Court	52
	Applying the Group Antipathy Hypothesis	54
	Study B: Survey Evidence	55
	Analysis	55
	Study C (Big Business): Experimental Evidence	58
	Design	59
	Analysis	62
	Discussion	64
5	Experimental Tests of the Group Antipathy Model	66
	Overview and Methodology	67
	Study C (All Groups): Identical Decisions and Group Antipathy	68
	Design	69
	Analysis	70
	Disaggregated Legitimacy	76
	Group-Specific Effects	79
	Additional Institutional Perceptions: Politicization	81
	Study D: Additional Identical Decision Study	82
	Analysis	84
	Study E: Multiple Decisions	86
	Design	87
	Analysis	88
	Study F: A Pending Case concerning the "Muslim Ban"	91
	Analysis	92
	Summary and Discussion	95
6	How Citizens Use Groups to Evaluate Judicial Preferences	97
	Studies C and D: The Identical Decision Studies Revisited	98
	Analysis	99
	Study G: Conjoint Analysis	101
	Analysis	102
	The Compound Influence of Group Cues on Institutional Legitimacy	104
	Discussion	105
7	Group Antipathy and Strategic Behavior on the Supreme Court	108
	Types of Strategic Adjustment	110
	Testing the Argument	111
	Understanding Patterns in Group-Rights Rulings	114
	Study H: Judicial Strategy and Group-Rights Rulings	117
	Discussion and Future Directions	122

8 Conclusion	126
Summary of Findings	127
Implications Regarding Attitudes toward the Court, Nominations, and Politicization	128
Relationship with the Supreme Court Media Literature	130
General Implications Regarding Public Opinion	131
Implications Regarding Strategic Behavior and Minority Rights	132
Limitations, Unanswered Questions, and Future Directions	133
Appendix	137
References	161
Index	173

Figures

3.1	Predicted legitimacy change as a function of gay antipathy	page 46
3.2	Predicted legitimacy change as a function of immigrant antipathy	47
3.3	Cumulative changes in legitimacy, simulated	48
4.1	News coverage linking the Court with big business, by month	54
4.2	Variations in business affect and predicted legitimacy	57
4.3	Experimental results	63
5.1	The effect of group attitudes on institutional legitimacy	74
5.2	The interaction between groups and knowledge vis-à-vis legitimacy	75
5.3	The effect of group attitudes on institutional legitimacy, disaggregated	78
5.4	Disaggregated by group	80
5.5	The effect of group attitudes on legal perceptions	82
5.6	The effect of group attitudes on institutional legitimacy, additional model	85
5.7	The interactive effect of favoritism condition and group dislike	90
5.8	The heterogeneous effect of antipathy and expectations	94
6.1	Conjoint analysis of social groups and Supreme Court ideology	103
6.2	The compound influence of social group cues on legitimacy	106
7.1	Proportion of Supreme Court rulings that concern social groups over time	115
7.2	Effect on decision direction of group-rights cases (broad measure)	121
7.3	Effect on decision direction of group-rights cases (intermediate measure)	122
7.4	Effect on decision direction of group-rights cases (narrow measure)	123
A.1	Conditioning effects of knowledge, by gay antipathy	151

xi

A.2 Conditioning effects of knowledge, by immigrant antipathy   152
A.3 Knowledge interaction, Study D   153
A.4 Knowledge interaction, Study E   155
A.5 The effect of group antipathy on legal acceptance   159

Tables

2.1	Effects of group antipathy on legitimacy across scenarios	page 22
3.1	Diffuse support at before and after minority rights rulings	42
3.2	The influence of group dislike on dynamics in legitimacy	45
4.1	Dislike for big business and Supreme Court legitimacy	56
4.2	Vignette for campaign finance experiment	60
4.3	Predicting institutional legitimacy, business experiment	62
5.1	Summary of experimental evidence	68
5.2	Full experimental stimuli	71
5.3	Predicting institutional legitimacy, identical decision experiment	73
5.4	Predicting institutional legitimacy, disaggregated	77
5.5	Predicting institutional legitimacy, disaggregated by group	79
5.6	Predicting perceptions of the Supreme Court as a legal institution	81
5.7	Predicting institutional legitimacy, additional identical decision experiment	84
5.8	Legitimacy as a function of group favoritism	89
5.9	Legitimacy and exposure to minority-targeted policies	93
6.1	Ideological perceptions of the Supreme Court	99
6.2	Possible ruling profiles presented to respondents	102
6.3	Example pair of rulings presented to respondents	102
6.4	Alternative specification controlling for ideological disagreement	106
7.1	Measures of group-rights rulings at the Supreme Court	113
7.2	Validating group-rights cases with division, salience, and content	114
7.3	Proportion of Supreme Court social group rulings, by Chief Justice	115
7.4	Descriptive patterns	116
7.5	Frequency of liberal decisions	117
7.6	Predicting decision direction	119
A.1	Descriptive statistics for Study A	140

A.2	Descriptive statistics for Study C	142
A.3	Descriptive statistics for Study D	143
A.4	Descriptive statistics for Study E	144
A.5	Descriptive statistics for Study F	145
A.6	Possible ruling profiles presented to respondents	149
A.7	Ruling-pairs presents to respondents	150
A.8	Knowledge interaction, Study A	150
A.9	Knowledge interaction, Study D	152
A.10	Knowledge interaction, Study E	154
A.11	Legitimacy disaggregated, Study D	155

Acknowledgments

I am indebted to the many people who provided support and inspiration over the past few years. I would like to begin by thanking my colleagues and friends at the University of Kentucky. Rick Waterman, Steve Voss, Ellen Riggle, Emily Bacchus, Abby Cordova, Horace Bartilow, and Dan Morey provided valuable comments on the project during seminars. Betül Demirkaya joined the department after these seminars, and I am happy to be her colleague. Jesse Johnson, Tiffany Barnes, and Jill Haglund offered valuable feedback and their friendship, and I am thankful for them. Clayton Thyne makes the department a wonderful place to work. He offered consistent support (and many IRB application signatures!) throughout the course of the project. This book would not exist without the detailed feedback from Mark Peffley and Justin Wedeking. Mark provided thought-provoking comments on many occasions, greatly improving the project in the process. And I am most lucky to work with Justin, a friend and outstanding judicial scholar. His comments and mentorship were the single greatest influence on this work.

The small seeds for this work were planted during my Ph.D. studies at Michigan, and I am grateful for the people I met there. In particular, Chuck Shipan and Nancy Burns are first-rate mentors and genuine people from whom I learned so much. I am also thankful for comments and advice from Ted Brader, Phoebe Ellsworth, and Vince Hutchings. The book would also not exist were they not for pioneering work on group attitudes by Don Kinder and Phil Converse. And finally, I am lucky to have my once-Michigan colleague and still-best friend Hyeonho Hahm. It has been a long time since that first after-class coffee.

Intellectually, I owe a debt to many. Brandon Bartels has been tremendously generous and supportive. His comments greatly improved the project. And his own work is a major influence, shaping our understanding of the Supreme Court in the modern era. My sincere appreciation also goes to Larry Baum, whose detailed comments helped improve the work in many ways. Larry's work and research from Lee Epstein, Jeffrey Segal, and Christopher Parker were also invaluable as they developed the main arguments of the book. I also received helpful comments on portions of the work contained here from Jamie Druckman, Mike Nelson, Ali Masood, and Matt Hitt. Many others supplied the shoulders on which this project stands. In particular, Jim Gibson's legitimacy research remains a dominant influence on not only my only thinking but the field as a whole, and this book would not exist without it.

My family is the most wonderful source of support, the best that I could ask for. I am thankful for my aunt and uncle and an exceptional set of in-laws, most especially Harper and Olivia. I owe everything I am to my parents, the way they raised me, and who they are. I understand that even more now than I once did. I am lucky that my sister, Molly, is also my friend, now and always. Thank you.

To my wife, Katrina, whom I've known since kindergarten. It's amazing that you're even more right for me with every year that goes by. You are the most supportive person, the best wife that I could ask for. I wish I had better words to express what you mean to me and how grateful I am for you. I love you so much.

At the start of drafting this book, my wife and I learned we were expecting. As I finished the manuscript, our baby came along, cutting down on my sleep and making the project seem unimportant in the best kind of way. Chelsea, I hope you may one day read this dedication and understand how much you mean to me and your mom.

Table of Cases

Arizona v. United States 2012. 567 U.S. 387. 7, 31, 35–8, 43, 49–50, 66, 112, 124, 130

Bowers v. Hardwick. 1986. 478 U.S. 186. 21
Brown v. Board of Education. 1954. 347 U.S. 483. 1, 4, 11–14, 24, 30, 109, 111–12, 117, 126–8, 131, 133–5

Citizens United v. Federal Election Commission. 2010. 558 U.S. 310. 8, 24, 33, 50–9, 66, 97, 111, 130, 141
Cooper v. Aaron. 1958. 358 U.S. 1. 11

Dred Scott v. Sandford. 1857. 60 U.S. 393. 21

Employment Division v. Smith. 1990. 494 U.S. 872. 66

Fisher v. University of Texas. 2016. 579 U.S. ___. 86

Green v. New Kent County. 1968. 391 U.S. 430. 1, 3–6, 11, 17, 22, 24, 26, 110, 126, 135
Grutter v. Bollinger. 2003. 539 U.S. 306. 4

Hollingsworth v. Perry. 2013. 570 U.S. 693. 7, 23, 34–6, 38, 43, 49–50, 107

Knox v. Service Employees International Union, Local 1000. 2012. 567 U.S. 310. 23, 38–9, 43, 50
Korematsu v. United States. 1944. 324 U.S. 214. 4, 21, 24, 32, 134

Lawrence v. Texas. 2003. 539 U.S. 558. 31, 111, 126
Loving v. Virginia. 1967. 388 U.S. 1. 11

Marbury v. Madison. 1803. 5 U.S. 137. 13
Milliken v. Bradley. 1974. 418 U.S. 717. 2, 6

Obergefell v. Hodges. 2015. 576 U.S. 644. 4, 6, 13, 24, 50, 135

Regents of the University of California v. Bakke. 1978. 438 U.S. 265. 11, 24, 134

Sessions v. Dimaya 2018. 544 U.S. ___. 134
Shelby County v. Holder. 2013. 570 U.S. 2. 21, 23–4, 37, 39, 43, 91, 134
Shelley v. Kraemer. 1948. 334 U.S. 1. 4
Swann v. Charlotte-Mecklenberg Board of Education. 1971. 402 U.S. 1. 11

Texas v. Johnson. 1989. 491 U.S. 397. 97
Trump v. Hawaii. 2018. 585 U.S. ___. 21, 66
Trump v. International Refugee Assistance Project. 2017. 582 U.S. ___. 66

United States v. Carolene Products. 1938. 304 U.S. 144. 109
United States v. Windsor. 2013. 570 U.S. 144. 7, 23–4, 34–6, 38, 43, 49–50, 65, 107, 126, 130

1

Legitimacy and Minority Rights

The morning of April 3, 1968, was fraught with tension. Nearly a decade and a half after *Brown v. Board of Education* (1954), racial integration had proved elusive. At first, the resistance was overt and powerful, echoing the words of a Mississippi judge who had taunted, "it will take an army of one hundred million men" to enforce desegregation (see Brandenburg 2004; Klarman 2006; Ross 2002; Sunstein 2004). But as time passed, segregation became a more insidious problem. Most southern districts adopted "freedom of choice" plans that offered minorities a say in the schools they would attend. But theory was not matched by reality. In one Virginia county, for example, 85% of African American students – and zero whites – attended the once all-black school (Stancil 2018). Against this backdrop, attorney Samuel W. Tucker stepped before the US Supreme Court. Tucker represented the petitioners challenging Virginia's "part white part Negro" system of "dual schooling." The case was *Green v. New Kent County* (1968). Free choice plans, Tucker argued, had little practical effect. Schools remained overwhelmingly segregated by race. He called on the justices to address the problem.

One month later, a unanimous Supreme Court offered one of the strongest frameworks for protecting minority rights ever endorsed by the US judiciary (Stancil 2018). Its ruling called for the "dismantling" of dual systems. It was not enough to simply offer school choice, the Court found. The government had a responsibility to proactively bring about integration.

Green ushered in a new era of backlash. On the night the ruling was announced, a cross was burned on the lawn of New Kent's all-black school (Allen and Daugherity 2006). New segregation academies – private institutions created to evade desegregation mandates – sprung up.[1] The North also became

---

[1] For more information, see "Segregation Academies and State Action," *Yale Law Journal* 82(7): 1436–1461.

a venue for powerful resistance. Rather than referencing race overtly, northern communities attacked policies that would benefit African Americans, leading to the ultimate failure of court-ordered busing (Hannah-Jones 2019; Perlstein 2012). Nor was resistance confined to policy alone. The judiciary itself came under siege. To provide one example, detractors aimed to limit the power of the Supreme Court many times in the decade that followed *Green* by restricting its jurisdiction to weigh in on key policy matters (Nichols, Bridge, and Carrington 2014). Within a few years, the Supreme Court would issue *Milliken v. Bradley* (1974), backtracking on the most proactive efforts to combat segregation.

Long overshadowed by other civil rights decisions, *Green* highlights a basic tension that faces the US Supreme Court. While a fundamental responsibility of the institution is to protect the rights of vulnerable minorities, the Court depends on political leaders to carry out and the public to comply with its decisions. But in civil rights cases, the factor driving resistance was the public's animus toward the very group the Court intended to safeguard.

FOUNDATIONS AND LIMITS OF SUPREME COURT AUTHORITY

Alexander Bickel considered the Supreme Court "the most extraordinarily powerful court of law the world has ever known" (1986, 1). In no small part, the power stems from judicial review as a check on the will of the majority in order to protect fundamental rights of the minority. Indeed, Alexander Hamilton advocated judicial independence for this very reason: "to guard the Constitution and the rights of individuals from ... *serious oppressions of the minor party in the community*" (*Federalist 78*, emphasis added). The Court has often taken the charge seriously. Some of its most notable rulings exercised judicial review in order to protect the rights of political minorities and disliked groups. According to Justice Robert Jackson, "One's right to life, liberty, and property, to free speech, a free press, freedom of worship and assembly, and other fundamental rights may not be submitted to a vote; they depend on the outcome of no elections" (quoted in Sandalow 1977, 1164).

Because the Court lacks the power to enforce, its ability to protect fundamental rights depends on the basic pillar of institutional legitimacy. Legitimacy, or diffuse support, consists of a long-standing, durable attachment to an institution on the part of the public (Easton 1965, 1975). It signals, in other words, the public's willingness to acknowledge institutional authority even in the wake of controversial actions. Absent legitimacy, the Court may fear that politicians and the public will ignore or undercut its decisions.

Questions about the Supreme Court's legitimacy have become common in recent years. Following the Court's landmark same-sex marriage ruling in 2015, Justice Antonin Scalia bemoaned a "decree" that made an "unelected committee of nine" relying on the "mystical aphorisms of the fortune cookie" into the "Ruler of 320 million Americans." Such language was not an expression of simple disagreement with an outcome, but rather suggested that the decision lacked a legitimate basis. A year later, Scalia passed away, setting off a highly politicized battle over the future of the Court. Then, in 2018, the nomination of Judge Brett Kavanaugh to the Court sparked a firestorm when he was accused of sexual assault. The institution, some commentators suggested, faced a "crisis of legitimacy" (Continetti 2019). Political leaders offered proposals to restructure the Court, arguing that the modern institution could no longer claim to represent the American public. The developments raise troubling questions about Supreme Court legitimacy in the twenty-first century.

SUPREME COURT LEGITIMACY AND ITS RELATIONSHIP WITH MINORITY RIGHTS

James Gibson and colleagues continue to refine our understanding of Supreme Court legitimacy, or diffuse support, since publishing initial work on the concept over two decades ago. While acknowledging that diffuse support may shift gradually over time, work in this vein primarily emphasizes the obdurate nature of legitimacy as rooted in the democratic norms and political values held by the public. "Diffuse support," Caldeira and Gibson write, "flows from those who are sympathetic to the function of the Court," which includes "the protection of liberty and democracy" (Caldeira and Gibson 1992, 649; see also Gibson, Caldeira, and Spence 2003a, 2003b; Gibson and Nelson 2014, 2015; Nelson and Tucker in press).

From a different perspective, others identify threats to legitimacy in a polarized era. Bartels and Johnston (2013, 2020) argue that legitimacy may wither when citizens disagree with the policy direction and ideological preferences of the Court (see also Christenson and Glick 2015; Johnston, Hillygus, and Bartels 2014). Another study, buttressing this perspective, finds evidence of a "negativity bias," or the idea that negative reactions to displeasing decisions tend to have a greater effect on Court legitimacy than positive ones (Christenson and Glick 2019). This stands in contrast to "positivity theory," a long-standing view of how the Court is able to replenish its support even when enmeshed in political controversy (Gibson, Caldeira, and Spence 2003b). Two other areas attracting recent attention concern the ability of political elites to manipulate support for the Court (Armaly 2018; Nelson and Gibson 2019) and debate over key measurement issues in the study of legitimacy (Badas 2019; Bartels and Johnston 2020; Nelson and Gibson 2020).

In spite of a robust and lively literature on legitimacy, the *Green* case suggests a critical but overlooked consideration. Recall that backlash to the ruling appeared not to derive from displeasure with the institution's insufficient commitment to democratic norms nor, even, its ideological direction. It came instead from potent group-based attitudes: the strong negative feelings that many citizens held toward African Americans.

The *Green* case is no exception. The Supreme Court has explicitly and continually emphasized the importance of group-based considerations. This jurisprudence nods back to Madison's words in *Federalist 10*, which expressed concern that rights were "too often decided, not according to the rules of justice and the rights of the minor party, but by the superior force of an interested and overbearing majority." In other words, small and vulnerable groups require careful protection to secure their rights and liberties, a perspective adopted and expanded upon by the Supreme Court over the years. Justice Harlan Fiske Stone's famous "footnote four" in *United States v. Carolene Products* (1938) set the stage for "searching judicial inquiry" when it came to the rights of religious groups, racial minorities, and others. Within two decades of Stone's writing, the institution had issued landmark decisions concerning Japanese internment in World War II (*Korematsu v. United States* [1944]), racial covenants in real estate (*Shelley v. Kraemer* [1948]), and racial segregation. Rulings concerning equality before the law have continued into the modern era, including some of the most important cases of the twenty-first century, such as *Grutter v. Bollinger* (2003), *United States v. Windsor* (2013) and *Obergefell v. Hodges* (2015). Simply put, the protection of minority rights has found a central place in the jurisprudence of the modern Supreme Court.

Rights rulings have clear implications for the Court's legitimacy and, in turn, its ability to balance majority will and minority rights. Singular among its caseload, decisions that safeguard unpopular groups have the potential to displease large segments of the population. By definition, these decisions protect the few at the expense of policies adopted by the many. Recognizing this fact, the Court has taken steps to shore up popular support in their wake. For example, in *Brown v. Board of Education*, Justice Felix Frankfurter and Chief Justice Earl Warren expended significant effort to secure a unanimous outcome (Tushnet and Lezin 1991, 1869–1880). The potential for public backlash significantly burdened the Warren Court, and the justices had concern that protecting minority rights would damage their legitimacy.

Were their fears justified? When citizens perceive the Supreme Court to favor unpopular social groups, does the Court's legitimacy suffer? And how pressing is this concern for the modern Court? These questions cut at the heart of what may be considered the *rights paradox*: whether the Supreme Court, whose authority depends on acknowledgment of its legitimacy, endangers this resource when it protects the rights of narrow or unpopular segments in society.

THE ARGUMENT

This manuscript introduces a novel perspective for understanding the institutional legitimacy of the US Supreme Court. Drawing on an extensive body of work that suggests the important role played by strategic social groups in shaping public opinion (e.g., Brady and Sniderman 1985; Conover 1988; Conover and Feldman 1984; Converse 1964; Green, Palmquist, and Schickler 2004; Tajfel and Turner 1979), as well as research showing the increasing importance of social identity as it becomes more closely connected to political identities (Huddy 2001; Mason 2015, 2018), I formulate a theory that explains how citizens use their views about disliked social groups to evaluate the judiciary. In this account, groups provide citizens a means to assess the Supreme Court by simplifying the standard of judgment. Citizens who evaluate the institution using their attitudes toward social groups consider two basic questions: To what extent is the Supreme Court an ally of various groups in society? And how do I feel about these groups? The major implication is that Americans translate their dislike for specific groups into judgments about judicial illegitimacy when the Court protects fundamental rights.

The argument takes seriously the idea that citizens are only moderately sophisticated, possess opinions on issues that shift over time, and commonly eschew ideological judgments for less abstract forms of thinking about political affairs (Converse 1964; Kinder and Kalmoe 2017). This is important when it comes to the judicial context, where there is evidence that group-based considerations are, for certain issues, more important than policy concerns for even the justices themselves (Baum 2017; Epstein, Parker, and Segal 2018). Moreover, the Court regularly reaches decisions regarding the rights afforded to various groups in society, and these rulings receive substantially more attention than others (Collins and Cooper 2012; Flemming, Bohte, and Wood 1997). As *Green* illustrates, the connection between various groups and the Court may be quite salient and potent. It may be visible for citizens who pay even a modest degree of attention to the institution.

Group antipathy theory makes a number of contributions to our understanding of the Court today. First, it connects debates concerning legal legitimacy to a wider dialogue about public opinion. This demonstrates that citizens do not entirely evaluate the Supreme Court as a unique or standalone entity but instead use their perceptions of how the institution connects to highly visible segments in political society. Second, the group antipathy account adds nuance to our understanding of judicial legitimacy. The manuscript demonstrates, both theoretically and empirically, that group antipathy and adherence to democratic values operate as distinct influences on judicial support. In other words, when citizens perceive the judiciary to favor groups they dislike, the abstract value of tolerance is not enough to prevent them from penalizing the Court. In addition, the manuscript shows that group antipathy independently shapes legitimacy even after accounting for ideological and policy-based judgments about the Court. Learning about a Court decision, citizens make distinct evaluations depending on whether it benefits groups they dislike, *even holding the substance of the ruling itself constant*. So, for example, free speech protections lead to more positive assessments of the Court when they involve a well-liked group, but a loss in legitimacy when they involve a disliked group. These group-based assessments influence perceptions of the Court's ideological preferences as well.

Another advancement points to how Americans make judgments about the Court given their limited knowledge of political affairs. Many Americans pay attention to the Court only in the wake of high-profile rulings, such as *Obergefell*, or during contentious nomination battles, such as the one that erupted over Brett Kavanaugh. Consonant with this insight, the group antipathy model demonstrates that Americans can evaluate the Court even if they do not possess the ability to make abstract assessments of its ideological direction or the extent to which it is fulfilling its democratic function. Rather, they can simply assess whether they perceive it to favor groups about which they already possess strong attitudes. While the manuscript focuses on controversial rulings throughout, its insights about public opinion have implications for recent controversies concerning the Court's membership and direction, particularly given the high-profile role that social groups and lobbying organizations have during nomination battles.

Finally, the model makes a significant normative contribution in pointing to the tension between the Court's protection of unpopular groups and the basic legitimacy required for decisions to be accepted and implemented. This speaks directly to backlash in the modern era.

WHY CARE ABOUT GROUP-BASED LEGITIMACY? IMPLICATIONS ON THE BENCH

Legitimacy, as the acknowledgment of an institution's authority to render decisions for political society (see Easton 1965, 1975) is, in some sense, an intangible resource. Does it matter whether minority rights decisions imperil popular support for an unelected institution?

Undoubtedly, the answer is yes. Justices are strategic actors (Epstein and Knight 1997) who prefer to see their decisions implemented. When its legitimacy is threatened, the Court adjusts both its decisions and opinions in order to bring about implementation and compliance (e.g., Black et al. 2016a, 2016b; Hall 2014). If the protection of minority rights can imperil the Court's legitimacy, this provides incentives for the Court to modify its behavior. Specifically, the Court may become a less demanding guarantor of minority rights. The aftermath of *Green* provides an example. Observing the backlash to its integration framework, the Supreme Court voted in 1974 to curtail proactive integration efforts (*Milliken v. Bradley*). In the final chapter, I subject this contention – that a group-based component of legitimacy leads the Court to become a less aggressive protector of minority rights – to systematic empirical testing. I demonstrate that group-based legitimacy alters the behavior of the Court, rebalancing the scales between majority will and minority rights in favor of the former.

THE PLAN OF THE BOOK

I test key insights of the theory with a multiple method approach, using evidence from representative surveys, including panel data, as well as numerous

The Plan of the Book

experimental tests. The tests involve a wide range of social groups, including racial, religious, and ethnic minorities, political protestors, and distinct socioeconomic strata. The groups also vary in their ideological characteristics across the left and right.

The book proceeds as follows. In Chapter 2, I discuss the theoretical framework, describing a model of Supreme Court legitimacy rooted in attitudes toward strategic social groups. This is the *group antipathy model*. I begin by reviewing two well-developed literatures on which the model builds. First, I consider existing theories of Supreme Court legitimacy, which generally focus on the obdurate nature of diffuse support (Caldeira and Gibson 1992; Gibson, Caldeira, and Spence 2003b; Gibson and Nelson 2014, 2015) or, more recently, its ideological, political, and partisan bases (Bartels and Johnston 2013; Christenson and Glick 2015; Johnston, Hillygus, and Bartels 2014). While these theories significantly advance our understanding of institutional support, they do not explicitly grapple with whether a fundamental judicial responsibility – the protection of unpopular groups – has implications for attitudes toward the Court. Second, I turn to the behavioral literature concerning social groups. The fundamental insight of this work is that Americans' understanding of politics is group-centric. As one study notes, "citizens can draw an impressively accurate map of politics ... by relying on their political affect, their likes and dislikes of politically strategic groups" (Brady and Sniderman 1985, 1061; see also Conover 1988; Converse 1964; Iyengar, Sood, and Lelkes 2012; Nelson and Kinder 1996). Building on these insights, I detail the novel model of Supreme Court legitimacy in which many citizens evaluate the institution based on the extent to which they perceive it as an ally of groups they dislike. I generate hypotheses about how the Court's support for important social groups will impact its legitimacy under theoretically specified conditions. To illustrate these insights more fully, I offer a typology of judicial actions based on the group antipathy model, detailing their implications for legitimacy.

In Chapter 3, I begin my empirical examination of the group antipathy account, focusing on how the Court's protection of gay and immigrant rights affected its legitimacy over the course of 2012 and 2013. This time frame allows me to examine cases in which the theory predicts a link between group antipathy and institutional legitimacy, as the Court issued three high-profile rulings concerning these groups (*Arizona v. United States* [2012], *Hollingsworth v. Perry* [2013], and *United States v. Windsor* [2013]). I examine the salience of the rulings and the substance of the group cues they provide to the public, which indicate that the Court was expanding its protection of certain minority rights. I then leverage survey data to explore whether and how antipathy toward gays and immigrants shapes Supreme Court legitimacy. Robust evidence demonstrates that the Court's rulings damaged its legitimacy among citizens with negative feelings toward gays and immigrants and that these effects were not the product of ideological considerations alone.

In Chapter 4, I subject the group antipathy model to an additional empirical examination, this time focused on a very different group: big business organizations. While certainly not a traditional "minority group," big business represents a salient social grouping that many Americans use to organize their understanding of the political world and, as I demonstrate, one that they view in quite unfavorable terms. I am therefore able to test the model in a different context from that in the prior chapter. I examine legitimacy in the post–*Citizens United* (2010) era, following a ruling that Justice John Paul Stevens criticized as failing to "prevent corporations from undermining self-government." Using survey data, I show that Americans' negative attitudes toward big business predict opposition to the Court – and specifically its institutional legitimacy – in the modern era. Are perceptions of the Court's "pro-business" orientation driving this pattern? I gain further empirical traction on this question using a survey experiment administered to a national sample of US adults, randomly varying exposure to information that the Court is "pro-business" and finding support for my argument. I discuss a unique implication of this finding: the fact that the Court's standing suffers when it rules in favor of groups disliked by liberals (as well as those disliked by conservatives).

Chapter 5 complements and expands upon the empirical evidence presented in Chapters 3 and 4. Building on the previous cross-sectional and panel analyses, Chapter 5 uses four experiments, using representative and convenience samples, to isolate group-specific effects. This allows me to manipulate rather than measure the Court's support for a wide variety of social and political groups in society. These studies vary in the groups they concern: I aim for a diverse set of racial, ethnic, religious, and political segments from both sides of the political aisle. The studies also vary in the manipulations they employ: in one, I present subjects with information about the *proportion of decisions made by the Court* to favor a particular group, while in others, I describe *identical decisions*, varying only the groups they stand to benefit. With this diversity – in samples, groups, and manipulations – I am able to offer robust evidence for the group-based model.

Chapter 6 explores the ideological implications of the group antipathy model, demonstrating how citizens utilize group cues to infer the Supreme Court's ideological preferences. In a series of experiments, I demonstrate that citizens will infer that the Court is either liberal or conservative from a single decision depending upon the groups that benefit. For example, conventional wisdom is that the protection of free speech suggests a liberal Court, but I show that this perception only occurs when the speech comes from prochoice protestors, religious minorities, and the like. The same speech decisions, when they involve prolife groups or other conservative organizations, lead to the *opposite* perception of a conservative Court. Chapter 6 concludes by examining the complex relationship between groups, ideological perceptions, and legitimacy to show how the Court builds support.

The Plan of the Book

In Chapter 7, I explore additional implications of the group antipathy model as it relates to judicial behavior. Since the Court cares deeply about its legitimacy, it has reason to strategically adjust its behavior in cases that could negatively impact diffuse support. I derive empirical indicators of group-based cases, demonstrating that the Court puts only a small number of these on its docket at any given time. Moreover, the Court more frequently rules in line with majority preferences when a case is salient and concerns an important social group, indicating a measure of strategic behavior. The implication: the Court's willingness to protect so-called fundamental rights actually hinges on a strategic calculus concerning its legitimacy. I discuss future directions for research on strategic responsiveness in light of the group antipathy model.

The concluding chapter continues this discussion, this time focusing on the counter-majoritarian dilemma, or the trade-offs faced by courts that protect minority rights but depend on popular support, in principle and practice. I proffer the book's central contributions in light of enduring debates in this literature (e.g., Bickel 1986; Hall 2016; Rosenberg 2008). I also explore the contributions to research on political behavior, institutional legitimacy, and judicial decision-making.

One important implication of my findings is that they offer a clear incentive for Supreme Court justices to de-emphasize their traditional role as a guardian of minority rights. When Americans penalize the modern Court for protecting the rights of unpopular groups, and these penalties come in the form of institutional *illegitimacy* – which can undermine decision implementation and make the Court vulnerable to politicized attacks – the institution may be forced to abandon this crucial role. I close with a discussion of other implications and future directions for research.

***

Some seven decades after Alexander Hamilton defended the judiciary as an essential safeguard of rights and liberties, the United States Congress considered supplying the courts an even more powerful tool to protect these privileges. A series of raucous debates had erupted over a proposal that would ultimately become the Fourteenth Amendment to the United States Constitution. Senator Jacob Howard of Michigan rose to introduce the Amendment. He depicted the proposal as one that, with the help of the courts, "forever disable[d] every [state] from passing laws entrenching upon those fundamental rights and privileges which pertain to citizens of the United States, and to all persons who may happen to be within their jurisdiction" (quoted in Judd 1905, 339–340). Howard noted how the Amendment targeted disadvantaged groups in society for protection – namely African Americans and former slaves, but perhaps others as well. "It establishes," he praised, "equality before the law, and it gives to the humblest, the poorest, the most despised of the race, the same rights and the same protection before the law as it gives to the most powerful, the most wealthy, or the most haughty."

In spite of the Amendment's ultimate ratification, Howard's proposal met with derision in some quarters. Senator Edgar Cowan of Pennsylvania responded with vitriol. Concerned about the proposal's citizenship provision, he listed the potential beneficiaries. "Is the child of the Chinese immigrant in California a citizen? Is the child of a Gypsy born in Pennsylvania a citizen?" Moreover, Cowen asked, are US citizens

to remain quiescent while they are overrun by a flood of immigration of the Mongol race? ... There is a race in contact with this country which, in all characteristics except that of simply making fierce war, is not only our equal, but perhaps our superior. I mean the yellow race; the Mongol race ... Therefore I think that before we assert broadly that everybody who shall be born in the United States shall be taken to be a citizen of the United States, we ought to exclude others besides Indians. (quoted in Library of Congress n.d., 2890)

Cowan's charged racial language is not the only remarkable aspect of this exchange. Notice that both supporters and opponents of the Fourteenth Amendment specifically emphasized disadvantaged or disliked segments of society. For Cowan, the Amendment did not present a problem because of the ideals it effectuated nor its protection of African American rights. Rather, it was troublesome because it would allow the judiciary to protect other groups not fit to be a part of the American experiment – Mongols, immigrants, gypsies, and the like.

The Pennsylvania Senator did not speak for all Americans, and many of his views have faded into irrelevance. But the Supreme Court has, at least to an extent, proven willing to protect the rights of all manner of unpopular groups in the subsequent century and a half. The question that this book seeks to answer is whether Americans shape their attitudes toward the modern institution as a result.

2

The Group Antipathy Theory of Supreme Court Legitimacy

Brown v. Board of Education and *Green v. New Kent County* established the lengths to which the Supreme Court would go to safeguard the rights of African Americans. In the years after *Brown*, when the justices took a dim view of "specific benefits enjoyed by white students [that] were denied to Negro students of the same educational qualifications," the Court became a strong guardian of civil rights.[1] But even as they fortified Equal Protection guarantees, the justices had very real reason to fear for the health of their institution. Fewer than one in four Southerners approved of the *Brown* ruling throughout the decade that followed, and a vast majority objected to sending their children to integrated schools (Rosenberg 2008, 127). From Virginia's massive resistance campaign to the election of pro-segregation, anti-Court governors throughout the South, *Brown* sparked a firestorm. Statements like that from Governor Ross Barnett of Mississippi – who spat that he would "rot in a federal jail before he will let one nigra cross the sacred threshold of our white schools" (Sarratt 1966, 7) – did not just exemplify displeasure with a Court ruling. They showed citizens questioning the basic authority of the institution itself.

While anecdotal evidence suggests that group-based attitudes played an essential role in the aftermath of *Brown* and *Green*, it is a different proposition to consider whether they hold similar sway in other contexts. After all, the cases occurred in a distant historical era and involved one of the more fractious issues the Court has faced. But while the depth of passion the case invoked may be unique, the *ingredients* driving the backlash continue to matter. Research on

---

[1] The Supreme Court twice called for rapid progress toward desegregation (*Brown II* [1955] and *Cooper v. Aaron* [1958]), struck down bans on miscegenation (*Loving v. Virginia* [1967]), permitted busing to achieve racial parity (*Swann v. Charlotte-Mecklenburg Board of Education* [1971]), and approved the use of affirmative action (*Regents of the University of California v. Bakke* [1978]).

political behavior suggests the powerful resonance of group-based attitudes in American politics into the modern era (e.g., Jardina 2019). Coupled with the information citizens learn about the Court, these attitudes have clear implications when it comes to institutional support.

This chapter offers a rigorous theoretical framework on the group-basis of judicial legitimacy. In the coming pages, I review the concept of legitimacy, or diffuse support, and discuss the theoretical frameworks scholars use to understand it. I then integrate a new perspective. Building on classic research in political behavior, which emphasizes that Americans utilize strategic social groups to formulate their opinions about political affairs, I point to the role that these groups play in shaping assessments of the Supreme Court. Specifically, I offer a framework that explains how the Court's protection of particular groups influences its legitimacy. One key component of this framework involves the scenario where citizens believe that the Court favors disliked groups. The *Brown* example illustrates the basic idea. In the aftermath of the controversial ruling, many Americans newly perceived the Court as a guardian of African American rights. For some citizens – namely blacks themselves – this was a welcome development, but for others such as white Southerners, who held very negative feelings toward African Americans, the decision called the Court's legitimacy into question. I close by explaining the contributions and implications of the group antipathy account of legitimacy in light of existing research on institutional support.

INSTITUTIONAL LEGITIMACY AS THE SUPREME COURT'S FOUNDATIONAL RESOURCE

To start at the beginning: What is the nature of Supreme Court legitimacy, and why is it so important in the modern era? After all, the institution weathered the *Brown* crisis in spite of the massive controversy the ruling generated. The Court generally enjoys a higher degree of confidence than other federal institutions – even though, in a concerning trend, this support has declined in recent years (Slattery 2014). It is being tested anew as the Court finds itself drawn into politicized battles over its decisions and membership, including a severe partisan conflict that erupted in the wake of sexual assault allegations against nominee Brett Kavanaugh, raising questions about the long-term health of the institution (Gawthorpe 2018).

Although the Court has historically enjoyed a degree of confidence from the American public, this is not the same as legitimacy. David Easton's seminal work draws a distinction between specific and diffuse support for political institutions. "The uniqueness of specific support," he writes, "lies in its relations to the satisfactions that members of a system feel they obtain from the perceived outputs and performances of the political authorities" (Easton 1975, 437). On the other hand, diffuse support consists of a "reservoir of favorable attitudes or goodwill that helps members accept or tolerate outputs to which they are opposed" (Easton 1965, 273). In this formulation, specific support is a form of short-term approval (or confidence) that may fluctuate in response to particular institutional actions, whereas diffuse support obtains when citizens make a more nuanced calculation as to whether an institutional exerts *rightful* authority, even in the face of displeasing decisions.

Diffuse support is critical for courts and the Supreme Court in particular. Because its justices are chosen through appointment and granted lifetime tenure, the institution is insulated from political pressure and granted a measure of independence. This also means, however, that the Court lacks the consent of the governed as ratified through elections, a basic ingredient that helps to build legitimacy of democratic institutions. The Court also faces a well-known enforcement problem. Although the institution claims the authority to resolve fundamental conflicts in American politics, it lacks the power to carry out its decisions. For this, it must depend on other political actors. The dilemma is best exemplified by *Marbury v. Madison* (1803). The Court claimed a tremendous authority in its decision, the power to strike down legislation incompatible with the Constitution. Yet, the Court recognized the limits of its power at the same time, and it was forced to craft its decision in order to safeguard against noncompliance from the administration of President Thomas Jefferson, a staunch opponent.

Enmeshed in political controversy, then, the Supreme Court depends heavily on diffuse support. "People who believe specific decisions are wrong, even wrongheaded," one study notes, will continue to accept rulings "if they respect the court as an institution that is generally impartial, just, and competent" (Murphy and Tanenhaus 1969, 275). Over time, the idea of diffuse support has become synonymous with *legitimacy* and *loyalty* in the literature (Gibson, Caldeira, and Spence 2003a; Gibson and Nelson 2014). One key question: Whether the public will remain loyal to the institution, acknowledging its rightful authority, even in the face of displeasing decisions? Tyler (2006) considers this a basic psychological property of an institution that "leads those connected to it to believe that it is appropriate, proper, and just" (375).

The divergent reactions to a pair of highly politicized rulings – *Brown* and *Bush v. Gore* (2000) – help to illustrate why the public's acknowledgment of rightful authority matters, even for an unelected Court. The former case saw overt resistance and a stunning lack of progress on desegregation efforts in the wake of a decision that many Southerners considered illegitimate. Yet, in the wake of the latter, the public generally acknowledged and accepted the institution's legitimacy (Gibson, Caldeira, and Spence 2003b). This is not always the case. In the years following the Obamacare ruling (*National Federation of Independent Business v. Sebelius* [2012]), for example, some citizens resisted the Court's authority (Christenson and Glick 2015; Johnston, Hillygus, and Bartels 2014) while a segment of political elites aimed to curtail judicial independence (e.g., Cruz 2015). Similarly, the Court's ruling in the same-sex marriage case *Obergefell v. Hodges* (2015) also met with pockets of resistance, most notably from a Kentucky county clerk who defied the order under "God's authority" (Ohlheiser 2015).

To be sure, these cases are exceptions. In many instances, the legitimacy of the modern institution goes unchallenged (or at least unnoticed). Yet, the exceptions have significant consequences for our political system. If highly controversial cases cause citizens to question their loyalty to the Court, which lacks the ability to enforce its rulings, this may precipitate further developments that undercut its authority. As a result, the Court may be forced to strategically modify its decision-making so as to maintain or rebuild its legitimacy (see Gibson and Nelson 2014, 203). In this scenario, the Court abandons its counter-majoritarian function and instead acts in the interests of the majority to shore up support. Indeed, the scholarly evidence indicates that the fear of non-implementation causes the Court to moderate its use of judicial review and rule in favor of current political majorities (Hall 2011, 2014) and renders the Court vulnerable to politicized attacks that aim to strip it of authority and independence (Engel 2011). While few of these attacks have been put into law in recent decades (Farganis 2009), they send a powerful signal to the institution that its public support is waning (Clark 2009, 2011).

Next, note that it is not of too much interest whether citizens consider the Court as legitimate when they are predisposed to support its actions. This is due to the fact that deference and compliance are very likely among supporters. For example, Northern proponents of desegregation had little reason to question the Court's authority following *Brown*. Non-compliance, rather, came from political elites and segments of the public, largely but not exclusively concentrated in the South, that contended that the justices had rendered an illegal or illegitimate decision when they chose to interfere with the states. In other words, these opponents questioned the Court's rightful authority to rule. The focus on a decision's opponents has given rise to two essential threads of the legitimacy literature. First, there are questions about the relationship between diffuse support (legitimacy) and specific support (opposition to rulings such as *Brown*). How closely connected are the two? The Court's specific support may suffer from partisan, ideological, and policy disagreements, but it becomes much more concerning for the institution if long-term loyalty to it suffers as well (see Bartels and Johnston 2013; Gibson and Nelson 2015). Second, the well-known quip that "legitimacy is for losers" encapsulates the idea that the reactions of citizens in the wake of *displeasing* decisions are most important when it comes to understanding legitimacy (Gibson 2015).

These conceptual issues have implications for measurement. Gibson, Caldeira, and Spence (2003a) develop a set of items to get at the joint ideas of loyalty and rightful authority. Following in this vein, standard legitimacy batteries consist of items measuring support for structural and jurisdictional changes to the institution, judicial favoritism, and judicial politicization (see also Caldeira and Gibson 1992; Gibson and Nelson 2015). The key feature of these measures involves their ability to separate institutional commitments from more short-term forms of support such as confidence or approval. More recently, however, Bartels and Johnston (2020) argue that these items encapsulate a variety of concepts that include procedural perceptions, trust, and institutional restructuring. Their preferred measurement strategy focuses on opposition to Court curbing as an indirect indicator with implications for legitimacy, which minimizes contamination from procedural considerations. Measurement questions aside, there is widespread consensus about the concept of institutional legitimacy, or diffuse support, as encompassing citizens' acknowledgment of the Court's rightful authority to resolve controversies within the American political system.

Simply put, institutional legitimacy acts as the foundational resource for the Supreme Court. It allows the institution to maintain its independence, ensure enforcement of its rulings, and decide as it sees fit. Though overt resistance to the Court is not common, this apparent tranquility should not mask the justices' deep concern over their popular support. The importance of legitimacy thus established, the question then becomes whether the Supreme Court's standing is relatively secure in the eyes of the public.

EXISTING MODELS OF INSTITUTIONAL LEGITIMACY

The literature has produced a diverse array of insights about public assessments of the Supreme Court. One longstanding perspective sees legitimacy as relatively obdurate. This view is advocated most notably by Gibson and colleagues in a series of studies (e.g., Caldeira and Gibson 1992; Gibson, Caldeira, and Spence 2003b; Gibson and Nelson 2015). The perspective suggests that a predominant portion of the Court's legitimacy derives from Americans' adherence to traditional norms of democracy, including support for the rule of law, the liberty of political minorities, and political tolerance. Not coincidentally, these norms are ones that the Court has a primary responsibility to protect. Norm-support is an orientation formulated early in life and one that endures over time. As a result, assessments of institutional legitimacy for most Americans track closely their adherence to democratic norms, with stronger proponents of these values viewing the judiciary as more legitimate. The pattern tends to persist even in the face of disliked Court decisions (Gibson, Caldeira, and Spence 2003b; Nelson and Tucker in press), as citizens put aside policy-specific disagreements and instead rely on more obdurate values to evaluate the Court.[2]

A second perspective, a result of recent theoretical advancements, sees legitimacy as conditioned on the way in which citizens perceive the institution's decision-making. Bartels and Johnston (2013, 2020; see also Johnston,

---

[2] However, the patterns are distinct when it comes to the attitudes of African Americans toward the Court (Gibson and Nelson 2018).

Hillygus, and Bartels 2014) argue that citizens' perceived ideological agreement with the institution shapes their legitimacy assessments. In other words, citizens formulate assessments of the institution's ideological preferences and then compare these to their own ideological predilections to determine their level of support for the Court. When they perceive the Court as ideologically distant, they tend to see the institution as less legitimate. Building on this perspective, Christenson and Glick (2019) demonstrate not only that policy and ideological disagreement shape legitimacy in the wake of high-profile rulings, but also that a displeasing decision damages legitimacy to a greater degree than a pleasing one buttresses it. In other words, "the dramatic drops among those with positions contra the Court's decisions point to asymmetrical" effects, at least in the most salient and polarizing cases, which represents a form of "negativity bias" (649).

A number of disagreements persist. Critics of the subjective ideological disagreement model contend that many Americans are unequipped to make the ideological assessments it requires to evaluate the institution (Gibson, Pereira, and Ziegler 2017). Instead, the (relatively small) portion of legitimacy determined by specific support for the institution's decisions is best conceptualized through a simple model of "liking" decisions (Gibson and Nelson 2015). Citizens may extend less support to the Court when it issues high-profile rulings they dislike, irrespective of their ideological content.

A related model suggests that citizens condition their assessments of the Court on the degree to which they perceive it as politicized. Disliked decisions harm Court legitimacy only among those citizens who view the Court as a political institution or see its decision-making as driven by politics. So, for instance, Christenson and Glick (2015) find that "legalistic priors" – the pre-existing view that the Court operates primarily as a legal, not political, institution – helped safeguard institutional support in the wake of the Obamacare decision. On the other hand, exposure to the information that Chief Justice John Roberts switched his vote in the case for strategic purposes activates a politicized behavior framework, which damages legitimacy (see also Christenson and Glick 2019). In a related vein, work by Gibson, Lodge, and Woodson (2014) shows that legal symbolism – pictures of the Court building or the Lady Justice, for example – can activate the view that "courts are different," in turn facilitating compliance with rulings (see also Gibson and Caldeira 2009; Gibson and Nelson 2018).

A series of significant questions remain. First and most basically, debate persists about the extent to which citizens distinguish between diffuse and specific support in their evaluations of the Court. Put differently, to what extent is legitimacy insulated from specific displeasure with the institution's policy output? This represents a basic disagreement between the democratic value and ideological support models of diffuse support. It also has implications for a fundamental question: Can the Court issue rulings without fear of public reprisal? Another question concerns the limits of Americans' political awareness about the Court, with critics of ideological disagreement model suggesting that it sees the public as overly sophisticated. Finally, existing models have little to say about how specific beneficiaries affect attitudes toward the Supreme Court. Yet, this may be a fundamental ingredient given the Court's historical role in protecting the rights of unpopular segments.

RESEARCH ON GROUP-BASED ATTITUDES

Should the judiciary fear illegitimacy if it protects the rights of unpopular social groups? Although this question has received little attention in the legitimacy literature, a more general research program in political behavior suggests that views about social groups strongly influence a range of popular attitudes, including issue positions (Conover 1988; Converse 1964) and partisan identities (Green, Palmquist, and Schickler 2004). These accounts define social groups as collections of individuals who have objective or perceived criteria that causes them to be perceived as members of that particular group (e.g., Conover 1988). In general, these studies agree that "public opinion on matters of government policy is *group-centric*: Shaped in powerful ways by the attitudes citizens possess toward the social groups they see as the principle beneficiaries (or victims) of the policy" (Nelson and Kinder 1996, 1055–1056, emphasis in original).

The original statement of the role that social groups play in structuring political opinion was made by Philip Converse (1964) in the essay, "The Nature of Belief Systems in Mass Publics." Converse's examination of the American public found that a relatively small number of citizens conceptualized politics using abstract judgments such as ideological evaluations, and fewer still applied these with a degree of consistency and accuracy. Rather, the most prominent tool that citizens used to make sense of political affairs involved "visible social groupings" such as racial and socioeconomic segments of the population. Citizens, and particularly non-elites, use these groups as a reference point when formulating their attitudes toward political issues and institutions. Instead of making abstract ideological judgments, citizens formulate opinions on the basis of their feelings about the groups involved in a controversy.

In the years since, a considerable array of evidence has illustrated the potency of group-based attitudes. Social groups function as a heuristic that allows both knowledgeable (Cohen 2003) and less well-informed (Arceneaux and Kolodny 2009) citizens to make sense of a complex political world by reducing political controversies to a simple standard of judgment (Lupia 1994; Popkin 1991; Sniderman, Brody, and Tetlock 1991). In essence, to formulate views about political affairs, citizens may consider a relatively simple question: How do I feel about the various groups involved in the controversy? Group affect can thus act as a mental shortcut that allows Americans to make sense of a complicated political reality. To reiterate one landmark finding, "citizens can draw an impressively accurate map of politics ... by relying on their political affect, their likes and dislikes of politically strategic groups" (Brady and

Sniderman 1985, 1061). The extent to which citizens feel favorably toward salient or strategic groups may serve as an organizing principle for the ways in which social groups influence political judgments in general (see also Iyengar, Sood, and Lelkes 2012; Iyengar and Westwood 2015).

Negative attitudes toward groups are particularly powerful antecedents of opinion. As Jardina (2014, 27) explains, when out-groups make political gains, it represents a threat to the in-group, tying in-group identity to out-group hostility (see also Jardina 2019). This "increases the link between an identity and politics. It does this first by increasing the salience of the identity in the public domain, and then by orienting the group toward political solutions to the threat." In other words, when disliked groups make political gains, it can initiate a two-step response. First, seeing disfavored groups as beneficiaries of policy raises the *salience* of group identity. Second, the assessment of group identity becomes *linked* with plausible responses to mitigate the threat. The danger represented by out-group gains increases the role that negative assessments play in structuring opinion. Consistent with this perspective, Banks and Hicks (2015), Banks and Valentino (2012), and Brader, Valentino, and Suhay (2008) emphasize that negative emotional responses play an important role in tying attitudes toward social groups with feelings about policy.

The corresponding role of group threat is visible in multiple contexts. For instance, negative racial cues activate racial attitudes and buttress their influence on opinion (Valentino, Hutchings, and White 2002). To wit, civil rights gains often correspond with negative feelings toward black influence (Giles and Evans 1985), much as a focus on immigration sharpens the influence that negative attitudes toward immigrants have on policy opinion (Valentino, Brader, and Jardina 2013).

Feldman and Stenner (1997) detect an asymmetry in the relationship between perceptions of threat and other political attitudes. As they explain, "greater perceptions of threat are associated with more ethnocentric and punitive attitudes [but] it is only among those high in authoritarianism that threat has this effect" (761; see also Soroka 2014). In research more specific to the realm of judicial politics, Clark et al. (2018) demonstrate that anger was particularly pronounced among policy opponents in the wake of recent same-sex marriage rulings, and Christenson and Glick (2019) find evidence of a negativity bias when citizens evaluate the Court. Overall, this research makes clear that negative evaluations of groups have a powerful effect on opinion and a wide variety of political opinions have group-centric antecedents. Yet, a group-centric model of public opinion has seldom been applied in order to understand support for the US Supreme Court.

THE GROUP ANTIPATHY MODEL OF LEGITIMACY

Before formalizing theoretical expectations, it is important to consider the value of a group-inflected account of legitimacy. Such an account takes seriously the idea that citizens are only moderately sophisticated, possess opinions on issues that shift over time, and commonly eschew ideological judgments for less abstract forms of thinking about political affairs (Converse 1964). This is important when it comes to the context of the Supreme Court, where there is evidence that group-based considerations are, for certain issues, more important than policy concerns for even the justices themselves (Baum 2017; Epstein, Parker, and Segal 2018). By moving the focus away from policy support, a group-based account acknowledges that policy opposition to specific decisions may have a limited effect on legitimacy, at least prior to the accumulation of *numerous* policy-specific grievances (Gibson and Nelson 2015; but see the experiment in Bartels and Johnston 2013). Policy-based accounts also may require considerable sophistication from the public – a demanding standard for evaluating the Court (Gibson, Pereira, and Ziegler 2017) – while overlooking the fact that policy attitudes themselves may be colored by group affect (Nelson and Kinder 1996).

With this in mind, citizens face a relatively complex set of informational challenges in assessing the Court. As Bartels and Johnston (2013) suggest, Americans have a difficult time agreeing on any "objective" standard of Court ideology, instead cueing off of factors such as salient cases and news media coverage to formulate their assessments.[3] Yet, the institution is covered only to a limited degree, oftentimes quite inaccurately (Slotnick 1991), and detailed knowledge about counter-majoritarian decision-making may be lacking (Gibson and Caldeira 2009, 439). In this environment, attitudes toward important social groups allow citizens to evaluate the judiciary by using judgments about salient groups that its decisions involve. Indeed, the Court regularly reaches decisions regarding the rights afforded to various groups in society, and these rulings receive substantially more attention than others (Collins and Cooper 2012; Flemming, Bohte, and Wood 1997). Public reactions may be a response to new rights-conferrals as well as particularly pronounced among opponents of a group's gains (Clark et al. 2018). In other words, the connection between various groups and the Court is clear for those who pay even a modest degree of attention to the institution.[4]

With these fundamentals in place, I theorize that affective attachments to strategic social groups perceived as the beneficiaries of Court decision-making will shape the level of legitimacy that citizens afford the Court. In other words, opinion about the Court is group-centric (see also Zilis 2018; Zilis in press). This observation does not require that citizens perceive the entirety of the Court's jurisprudence regarding a group with accuracy, but I do suggest that

---

[3] More recently, Nelson and Gibson (2019) introduce the role of elite cues.
[4] Of course, the predictive power of these feelings themselves can vary depending upon a variety of factors. "Group centrism is not the only thing going on in [the judgment and policy attitudes of many] cases, but it is always present and of all the various ingredients that go into opinion, it is often the most powerful" (Nelson and Kinder 1996, 1056).

formulating such perceptions is a more straightforward process than making more abstract judgments (see Gibson, Pereira, and Ziegler 2017 for a related discussion).

At the same time, citizens have a number of considerations at hand when evaluating the Court. Not all rulings involve social group attitudes. Rather, high-profile cases that have clear implications for groups, and tend to attract disproportionate media coverage (O'Callaghan and Dukes 1992), are most likely to influence public opinion. Since social group attachments consist of potent feelings that influence a range of political attitudes, citizens can draw on them to make sense of Court decision-making. Doing so allows citizens to formulate their attitudes toward the institution, extracting meaning from its perceived support of various groups in order to evaluate its legitimacy.

A second consideration that is relevant to the group-based support model involves a simple form of variance in judicial behavior: the choice to grant or deny a group's rights-claim. The Court has the ability to protect or limit rights with its rulings, and the groups that are the objects of these decisions can themselves vary in their level of popular support.[5] I posit that one specific action – the decision to protect the rights of a disliked group – is particularly consequential from a legitimacy-maintenance perspective. When the Court does so, it offers a signal about its support for the group in question. The protection of a right, or conferral of a "new" right, is among the most powerful actions the Court may take.

Furthermore, protecting the rights of a disliked group is likely to activate concerns among citizens about the threat represented by the group. There are reasons to expect negative attitudes toward the group will bleed over into more general assessments of the Court itself. For instance, Jardina's (2014) account suggests that citizens will search for a "political solution" to the threat represented by minority gains. A simple yet powerful solution is to withhold support for the Court itself.

In short, the group antipathy model hinges on the interaction between perceptions that the Supreme Court favors specific social groups and popular feelings toward these groups. In instances where Americans perceive the Court to strongly favor specific groups, citizens will use their feelings toward the group as a means to assess the Court. Therefore, I hypothesize the following:

Group Antipathy Hypothesis: As dislike of social groups that are perceived as the primary beneficiaries of Supreme Court rulings increases, citizens will report lower levels of diffuse support for the Court.

The above hypothesis details a straightforward relationship between group-centric attitudes and opinion about a Court that protects the rights of a social

---

[5] To this point, we have mentioned a number of notable cases in which the Court supported equal protection claims, but it has of course ruled in the opposite direction in other high-profile cases. I review some of these in detail in the coming pages and chapters.

group. On the other hand, consider that even though the judiciary is often seen as the guardian of minority rights, courts may not always protect these rights. Some of the most notorious decisions in history – e.g., the *Dred Scott* (1857) ruling and *Korematsu v. United States* (1944) – illustrate this contention. Even in the current era, the Court has ruled against claimants seeking protection. For instance, the Court famously turned back an equal protection claim in *Bowers v. Hardwick* (1986), rolled back safeguards to combat black disenfranchisement in *Shelby County v. Holder* (2013), and denied an Establishment Clause challenge in *Trump v. Hawaii* (2018). These actions raise questions about the influence of group-centric attitudes on legitimacy when the institution is perceived as unsympathetic to minority groups.

Two potential public responses are possible. On the one hand, citizens may "reward" the judiciary with an additional measure of legitimacy when it denies the claims of disfavored groups or is otherwise seen as unsympathetic to them. This suggests a simple model of liking decisions, whereby the Court is penalized for unwanted rulings and rewarded for desirable ones. However, this model conflicts with much of what is known about how group-centric attitudes shape political behavior. In fact, there are reasons to expect that courts may not enjoy increased legitimacy when they deny rights-claims. The activation of group attitudes occurs more readily when feelings of threat brought about by the political gains of negatively viewed groups are aroused (Jardina 2014). More generally, negative information tends to exert more a substantial impact on judgments and behavior than positive information, which may be the result of people's tendency to perceive it as more salient and their stronger motivation to "avoid costs than to approach gains" (Lau 1985, 122; see also Baumeister et al. 2001). In the Court literature, there is also evidence of "negativity bias" (Christenson and Glick 2019; Mondak and Smithey 1997) or the idea that negative reactions to rulings are more powerful than positive ones (e.g., Clark et al. 2018).

These findings suggest that when unpopular social groups receive *unfavorable* outcomes, the influence of group attitudes on political evaluations should prove less potent than when disliked groups make political gains. In short, courts that deny the claims of unpopular minority groups are not likely to be substantially "rewarded" by the public.

> *Rights Limitation Hypothesis*: When the Supreme Court is perceived as unsympathetic to a group's claims, there will be little or no association between dislike for the group and judicial legitimacy.

To summarize, the group antipathy model rests on the insight that citizens use strategic social groups as a means to formulate attitudes toward the judiciary. In fact, some factors make group-based evaluations more common when it comes to the Supreme Court – the fact that it issues contradictory ideological signals, oftentimes within the space of a single term, as well as the fact that the institution has the basic task of protecting the rights of unpopular segments.

When it does so, the model anticipates a relationship between dislike for the groups it protects and declines in its legitimacy.

What the model does *not* assume, however, is that citizens carefully monitor the balance of the Court's jurisprudence and respond to each ruling that involves a prominent social grouping. Not only is this a wholly unrealistic standard for citizens, whose knowledge about the institution is modest (Gibson, Pereira, and Ziegler 2017), but it also conflicts with one of the main contributions of the model, which recognizes the limits of popular political awareness. It is important to emphasize that Americans likely pay attention only to prominent developments that strongly influence the extent to which they perceive the Court to favor certain groups. This means that some (though not all) high-profile decisions may shape the influence of group-based considerations on legitimacy, but there is little reason to expect that low salience holdings would do the same. The reason is simple: because Americans pay attention to the Court only sporadically, and most commonly following high-profile developments that send strong signals about its preferences, little-known cases do not enter into evaluations. In these cases, which occur on dozens of occasions per term, signals about the Court's preferences fail to penetrate public discussions of the institution, limiting their impact. This leads to our final hypothesis:

Weak Signal Hypothesis: Following low salience rulings, there will be no association between dislike for the group and judicial legitimacy.

Table 2.1 organizes the insights of the group antipathy model into a simple typology. Again, two factors are essential: the extent to which citizens perceive the Supreme Court to favor specific social groups and their feelings toward these groups. In instances in which citizens receive a strong signal about the Court's preferences, support for the institution depends upon how an unpopular social group fares before the justices. For example, the *Green* case sent a clear indication that the Court would protect the rights of African Americans, which caused civil rights opponents to question and resist the institution's authority. Yet, it is also important to acknowledge the limits of political awareness. In lower salience cases, there is no reason to expect the public to react.

TABLE 2.1 *Effects of group antipathy on legitimacy across scenarios*

	Strong signal about Court	Weak signal about Court
Rights protection (Court favorable to group)	Negative	Null
Rights limitation (Court unfavorable to group)	Null	Null

The Group Antipathy Model of Legitimacy

To further illustrate the insights of the group antipathy model, we can consider decisions from two recent terms of the Court.[6] One high-profile set of cases concerned the rights of gays and same-sex couples. The Court released opinions in both *United States v. Windsor* (2013) and *Hollingsworth v. Perry* (2013) on the same day, drawing front-page coverage across the nation. This coverage trumpeted the rulings as a victory for gay rights in America. Because many citizens perceived the rulings to benefit lesbian, gay, bisexual, and transgender (LGBTQ) groups, the model anticipates a link between negative attitudes toward gays and the legitimacy of the Court in their aftermath (the Group Antipathy Hypothesis).[7] A second high-profile case involved voting rights protections. In *Shelby County v. Holder* (2013), the justices struck down key portions of the Voting Rights Act, which led to an outcry from critics that the Court had dealt a blow to the rights of African Americans. The model anticipates that this example would not precipitate changes in the institution's legitimacy (the Rights Limitation Hypothesis). Finally, a third case, *Knox v. Service Employees International Union, Local 1000* (2012), concerned another prominent and controversial group: labor unions. The case attracted almost no popular attention due to the technical legal issues involved, and there is little reason to expect that citizens would condition their evaluation of the institution on their feelings toward labor unions (the Weak Signal Hypothesis).

Contextualizing the Model

Assume, for a moment, that the group antipathy model reasonably characterizes a portion of Supreme Court legitimacy. We should then ask, *So what?* To put this differently, consider one insight of the model – that high-profile rulings that protect the rights of unpopular segments will affect legitimacy. In order to fairly evaluate the implications, we must have some understanding of how common such rulings are.

We can assess the prominence of group-rights cases at the Court in at least three ways: by evaluating their absolute number, their relative salience, and their capacity to attract additional attention. Using the first metric, we can say that such cases make up a small yet meaningful portion of the modern Court's docket.[8] One study of the early Rehnquist Court found that civil rights

---

[6] This paragraph provides a brief summary to illustrate the model's insights. I review in much more detail the cases that I discuss here and their media coverage as well as empirically assess public responses to them in Chapter 3.

[7] A word on terminology. Cases such as *Windsor* implicate attitudes toward same-sex couples and LGBTQ groups more generally, attitudes which tend to covary with one another. However, in the pre-existing survey data I am able to employ, beginning Chapter 3, the available measures specifically tap into Americans' feelings toward "gays" and "gay rights activists." I therefore use this terminology in order to provide the best link with the available evidence, even as I acknowledge the value of other language and ways to conceptualize these groups.

[8] In Chapter 7, I develop a novel measure of group-rights cases and find consistent insights.

cases – perhaps the quintessential example of disputes that involve visible social groups – made up approximately 9% of the docket (O'Callaghan and Dukes 1992). If we broaden this to include First Amendment cases, which often feature unpopular groups exercising free speech rights or religious organizations drawing on free exercise rights, the number rises to 19% of cases. More recently, between the 2000 and 2016 terms, the Court averaged 13 cases per term dealing with civil rights matters (calculated from Spaeth et al. 2017). This represents a minority of the Court's overall docket (approximately 16% in all) but a substantial number of cases (some 221 total) to potentially provide the public with signals about the Court's orientation toward specific groups.[9] Overall, some of the more widely covered and closely watched rulings are those that rearrange the distribution of political benefits among social groups (Flemming, Bohte, and Wood 1997).

Of course, the salience of these signals also matters. The evidence suggests that group-based claims receive strong attention. The same study that found that civil rights cases made up 9% of the docket in one term also found that these rulings attracted disproportionate media coverage. They were the subject of 22% of all published reports on cases in newspapers and 58% in newsmagazines (O'Callaghan and Dukes 1992). More recent research finds further evidence of this pattern. For example, a study of news coverage in the Court's 2014–2015 term, which gathered reports from 29 outlets, found that the civil rights case *Obergefell v. Hodges* was, by far, the most covered ruling – nearly 14% of stories concerned this one case (Zilis, Wedeking, and Denison 2017). To take another example, I also supply an analysis of coverage of the Court's ties with big business in Chapter 4, showing persistent and powerful media attention related to *Citizens United* in the half decade that followed.

In fact, cases that involve visible social groupings may have an additional capacity to attract media attention – precisely *because* they involve segments about which the public feels strongly. It may not be an accident that equal rights cases constitute some of the most significant and high-profile judicial rulings ever released. These include the rights of Japanese Americans (*Korematsu v. United States*), African Americans (*Brown*, *Green*, *Bakke*, and *Shelby County*), and same-sex couples (*United States v. Windsor* and *Obergefell*), to name just a few. Overall, the influence of group antipathy may be in play in a number of, though far from all, high-profile controversies. Group-based considerations have a central role to play in the small but important set of cases that attract public attention, particularly when media coverage highlights their group-centric considerations.

With attention to group claims established, it next becomes important to contextualize the model's implications. A basic contradiction becomes

---

[9] Of course, the public did not follow all of these cases closely, but a number of them did in fact attract considerable attention.

apparent. Because the Supreme Court is tasked with protecting minority rights and yet depends on legitimacy to function effectively, it is of substantial consequence if public evaluations of the institution hinge on its social group rulings. This is the heart of the *rights paradox*. Even if it is the case that only a handful of rulings each year attract public notice, the Court finds itself in a vulnerable position if these rulings imperil its legitimacy.

In sum, group antipathy theory offers a simple account of judicial support that has substantial consequences for our understanding of minority rights. In this account, citizens may penalize the Court when they perceive it as an ally of disliked social groups, but fail to reward it when the Court denies rights-claims.[10] The group-based roots of judicial legitimacy have clear implications for judicial responsiveness, calling into stark relief the dangers when Court displeases a popular majority.[11]

Alternative Explanations and Threats to Inference

Given that the group antipathy model offers a novel approach to understanding judicial legitimacy, it is worth considering further how the model fits within the existing literature as well as threats to inference as we evaluate its insights from an empirical perspective. In the next section, I evaluate four important considerations.

The Obdurate Legitimacy Perspective

The most well-known account of legitimacy emphasizes its obdurate nature (see Caldeira and Gibson 1992; Gibson and Nelson 2015). It suggests that adherence to democratic values such as the rule of law drive support for the institution; that specific displeasure with rulings has a limited effect on legitimacy, in part because symbols of judicial authority help inoculate the Supreme Court against the most damaging effects of decisional disappointment (Gibson, Caldeira and Spence 2003b; Gibson, Lodge, and Woodson 2014); and that disappointing rulings can negatively impact legitimacy, but only after a substantial string of them has accumulated (Gibson and Caldeira 1992).

On these last points, the group antipathy model stands in contrast. Under this model, specific displeasure with discrete actions *can* translate into declining support, so long as these actions affect the extent to which citizens perceive the

---

[10] One reading of this account may imply a negative spiral in which the Court's legitimacy would inevitably dry up over time. This is not realistic. I note here that this is inconsistent with some empirical evidence on legitimacy, but I also consider the possibility in much more detail later in the manuscript, finding that the most alarmist negative spiral accounts are unfounded. In part, this may be due to the fact that the Court strategically adjusts its behavior in group-rights cases when it is most concerned about its legitimacy (see Chapter 7).

[11] These dangers are perhaps greatest if media coverage highlighting the groups that benefit from judicial rulings displaces more sober legal coverage after the Court rules. See Johnston and Bartels (2010) and Zilis (2015).

Court to favor unpopular groups in society. To be sure, this perception may also form in response to a string of decisions – but, as the *Green* example and other cases in this manuscript will illustrate, controversial and high-profile decisions have the ability to affect opinion. Viewed in this light, the social group basis of political judgment is just as foundational as one's adherence to traditional norms of democracy. Of course, this is not to suggest that such values do not play a role – they do, and an important one at that – but rather that they represent only one ingredient in the complex mixture that constitutes institutional support.

From a theoretical perspective, the group antipathy and obdurate legitimacy models do, in fact, share some common ground. Both recognize limits to political awareness in the general public. Both suggest that citizens pay little attention to most Court decisions. Yet, the models diverge when it comes to how citizens "fill in the gaps" while constructing their opinions. One merit of the group antipathy model involves the extent to which it squares with other advancements in the study of public opinion. Zaller's (1992) influential receive-accept-sample (RAS) model, for instance, shows how instability in public opinion responses is a product of citizens' tendencies to rely on salient, or "top of the head," considerations. Group-based cues may operate in much the same way, making prominent the information that the Court tends to favor some segments over others. Citizens then integrate this information when assessing the institution. Once again, this does not forestall the possibility that they can integrate and weigh other information as well.

We can also consider the extent to which the group antipathy model enjoys empirical support, *even after* we have accounted for the effect of democratic norms on institutional support. In the chapters that follow, I present empirical models that examine the effects of group antipathy while controlling for democratic value support. This allows us to evaluate both models in light of one another. I also utilize experimental designs in which I isolate and manipulate group cues to consider their unique and specific influence.

The Relationship between Group-Based Support and Political Tolerance

As we evaluate the group antipathy model, we may not only be concerned about the effects of democratic values as a concept, but also the influence of political tolerance in particular. Scholars have examined tolerance and its relationship to institutional support and democratic society extensively (Gibson 1989, 1992; Peffley, Hutchinson, and Shamir 2015; Sullivan, Piereson, and Marcus 1993; Sullivan and Transue 1999). Importantly, evidence suggests a connection between tolerance and group affect (e.g., Bobo and Lacari 1989; Marcus et al. 1995), which is of considerable relevance for our purposes. A sensible objection to the group antipathy model may be that it captures the influence of political tolerance as opposed to group-specific dislike.

The Group Antipathy Model of Legitimacy

This objection has its limitations. First, from a conceptual perspective, we must distinguish tolerance, as classically understood, from group antipathy. The former concerns one's willingness to extend political rights to those with whom they have the strongest political disagreements. The latter, on the other hand, taps into affective attachments toward a wide variety of groups, including those to whom individuals feel warmly as well negatively disposed. This difference will allow us to test an implication of the group antipathy model that distinguishes it from the tolerance perspective – namely, that dislike toward *specific groups* can be directly linked toward *specific actions* taken by the Court and *specific perceptions* of the group that the institution favors. The group antipathy model anticipates that, even among those who are relatively tolerant, legitimacy should decline when they perceive the Court to favor a group they dislike. Again, this is not to dismiss the relationship between tolerance and group-based feelings. For members of the political majority, we would expect negative attitudes toward minorities to associate with lower levels of tolerance. But we should not conflate the *degree of dislike* with the *willingness to withhold political rights*.

I use three primary approaches to empirically distinguish between the effects of group antipathy and tolerance. First and most simply, I include a control variable to account for political tolerance in regression models, thereby demonstrating the unique influence of group antipathy even after we have accounted for the effects of tolerance. Second, I provide targeted tests that look at the influence of antipathy toward specific groups. If political tolerance were the only factor to shape legitimacy, we would not anticipate predictable patterns of group-specific responses. For example, we would not observe the effects of dislike toward immigrants, alone, to shape legitimacy after high-profile immigration rulings. But, in fact, we do. Third, I conduct experimental examinations in which I present subjects with decisions that extend political rights to a wide range of unpopular minority groups, a design which should induce tolerance to matter. In fact, I demonstrate the specific identities of the groups that benefit exert a primary influence on how citizens respond.

The Relationship between Group-Based Support and Ideological Support

Recent evidence indicates that citizens condition legitimacy on ideological disagreement with the Supreme Court (e.g., Bartels and Johnston 2013). Citizens also, however, evince predictable patterns of group antipathy based on ideological and partisan considerations (e.g., Brady and Sniderman 1985). Liberals tend to view certain groups, such as gays and immigrants, in more favorable terms than their conservative counterparts, and vice versa. Are the effects of group antipathy on legitimacy simply the product of ideological disagreement with the Court?

From a theoretical perspective, it is not clear that this is the case. Many models of political behavior emphasize that group-based considerations can *influence* ideological thinking (e.g., Conover and Feldman 1984). In Converse's early formulations (Converse 1964, 1970), citizens use the positions of strategic groups in order to refine their policy preferences. One implication, borne out by empirical evidence, is that citizens evince more stable issue positions on matters that involve high-profile groups, such as African Americans in the civil rights era. The work of Brady and Sniderman (1985) also calls into question the premise that ideology drives group-based thinking. They find that citizens understand the preferences of ideological groups by using group affect as a heuristic. In other words, it not the case that citizens formulate assessments of groups using policy-based deductions; rather, group affect provides "the means and motive to achieve a measure of coherence in their views" (Brady and Sniderman 1985, 1061). The understanding that many citizens pay limited attention to political affairs plays a key role in these models, an insight that squares with work in the Court literature (Gibson, Pereira, and Ziegler 2017).

Indeed, research on Supreme Court decision-making calls into question the premise that ideological deductions completely guide group-based thinking. Pioneering recent works demonstrate that judicial voting behavior varies depending upon the groups involved in a controversy. In an analysis of First Amendment rulings, Epstein, Parker, and Segal (2018) find that ideological commitments to the principle of free speech is undercut by justices' feelings toward the groups involved. This "in-group bias" means that justices are more likely to support free speech challenges made by parties with whom they closely identify – such as pro-life advocates for conservatives and whistleblowers for liberals. Baum (2017) goes further. Questioning common assumptions about judicial ideology and presenting decades worth of evidence, he argues not only that group affect impacts voting behavior independent of ideology, but also that affect underpins ideological behavior on the Court.

All of this is to suggest that, for the mass public as well as judicial elites, there exist complex linkages between group affect and ideology. Group affect is not, simply, a product of ideological deductions; it may in fact help generate the ideological affinities that citizens hold. From a theoretical perspective, the group antipathy account offers unique insights beyond those from ideological support models.

Moreover, the coming chapters make a series of empirical contributions that allow us to further unravel the linkages between group-based evaluations and ideological assessments. Empirical tests demonstrate the independent effect of group antipathy on legitimacy *even after controlling for ideological agreement with the Court*. This indicates that antipathy exerts a unique impact, beyond that for which existing studies account. I also conduct a series of "placebo" tests to further probe the influence of ideological considerations. I am able to show that citizens do not treat all groups similarly when evaluating the Court, but rather that they tend to leverage their feelings toward only those groups they perceive the institution to favor.

The Group Antipathy Model of Legitimacy

In Chapters 5 and 6, I probe the linkages between group antipathy and ideology even further. I demonstrate that group-based thinking underpins ideological perceptions. Specifically, I demonstrate that citizens assess "ideologically equivalent" rulings in different terms depending on the groups that benefit. For example, conservatives tend to support free speech rulings when they favor "conservative" groups but not "liberal" groups, and liberals tend to support religious freedom rulings when they favor "liberal" groups alone. Moreover, these group-based effects shape perceptions of institutional ideology. Rulings that favor liberal groups lead citizens to perceive the Court as liberal *irrespective of their legal or policy content*. The same pattern holds for conservative groups.

Finally, I demonstrate that the effect of group antipathy is more substantial than it commonly appears. It exerts a direct impact on judicial legitimacy: When citizens dislike a group the Court favors, they see the institution as less legitimate. But it also exerts an indirect effect at the same time: When citizens dislike a group the Court favors, they are also more apt to see the institution as an ideological adversary, which also harms their support for the institution. Both of these paths of influence operate at once, severely undercutting the Supreme Court's legitimacy.

The Relationship between Group-Based Support and Policy Support

One final consideration involves the extent to which group antipathy relates to support for the policies the Court endorses. In evaluating this perspective, it is first important to note that some models of legitimacy emphasize that policy disagreement with the institution – a form of specific (non)support – has a limited influence on diffuse support. As one study argues, "the legitimacy of the Supreme Court is not much dependent upon the Court making decisions that are pleasing to the American people" (Gibson and Nelson 2015, 173). To the extent that this is accurate and group antipathy ties into policy judgments, we should observe no empirical link between antipathy and legitimacy.

Second, a policy support model that excludes a role for group antipathy places tremendous cognitive demand on the public. Research emphasizes the limits of popular political awareness (Brady and Sniderman 1985; Converse 1964; Kinder and Kalmoe 2017; Lupia 1994). And, as discussed previously, it is altogether unclear the extent to which ideological thinking stands independent of group-based reasoning. It is even more difficult to conceive of a case in which large numbers of citizens could formulate policy positions without looking to the groups involved in a controversy. Rather, it is much more likely that issue positions depend, at least in part, on the groups implicated (see Lupia 1994).

To gain further empirical traction on this argument, I include a series of tests that enable us to examine the extent to which policy support exerts an independent influence on legitimacy. In most of these, the evidence suggests that group antipathy is a better predictor of diffuse support. Most powerfully, in

Chapter 5, I demonstrate that citizens evaluate otherwise identical policies differently depending upon the groups they affect.

Long-Term Implications and Contributions

The basic insight of the group antipathy model is that citizens penalize the Supreme Court when they perceive it to favor social groups that they dislike. This implies, in turn, that the Court may see its legitimacy decline when a large number of citizens believe it to favor relatively unpopular groups. This loss in support has considerable implications since the institution depends on legitimacy to ensure implementation of its decisions and protection of its independence.

What may precipitate a loss in support? At least two paths present themselves. First and most simply, high-profile rulings that protect the rights of unpopular segments can influence diffuse support. Following cases such as *Brown*, we would expect to observe negative evaluations of the Court increase among those who felt very averse to African Americans. Indeed, anecdotal evidence suggests that this occurred (Rosenberg 2008). Other rulings, as well, may give rise to similar doubts about the Court's institutional authority.

A second and perhaps more interesting path occurs when the Court acquires a reputation for favoring certain groups, *irrespective* of the decisions it issues. Citizens may acquire information about Court behavior through discussions within their social networks as well as signals sent from political elites (e.g., Franklin and Kosaki 1989). So, for instance, media coverage tends to present a systematically distinct portrait of the Supreme Court's ideological direction based on the cases it chooses to cover, which has consequences for how citizens' assess judicial policy preferences (Bartels and Johnston 2013). Coupled with the fact that Americans possess limited factual knowledge of the institution (Gibson and Caldeira 2009), this raises the possibility that some may perceive the Court to favor certain social groups *even if* its jurisprudence does nothing of the sort.

To offer an example, it is undoubtedly the case that some citizens continued to perceive the Court as a pro-black institution long after its rightward turn took place later in the twentieth century. As one study explains, "black attitudes toward the institution are not as negative as one might predict if attitudes were formed primarily by whether one is pleased or displeased by current judicial policies ... We can explain a portion of the reason why blacks 'oversupport' the Court as a residue of positive affect created largely during the era of the Warren Court" (Gibson and Caldeira 1992, 1140). In other words, institutional perceptions have some basis in the reality of its decision-making, but this is not the only factor in play.

As a result, political elites may attempt to undercut support for the Court by portraying the institution to favor unpopular groups in society (see Nelson and Gibson 2019 for a discussion of elite cues and the Supreme Court). For example, President Barack Obama contended that the Supreme Court has

The Group Antipathy Model of Legitimacy

"open[ed] the floodgates for special interests ... foreign corporations ... major corporations ... and America's most powerful interests" (Silverleib 2010). Some justices on the Court question the accuracy of the characterization, but to the extent that it influences public perceptions of the institution, it may have substantial consequences. Moreover, politicians may not be the only actors to use this tool. The justices themselves may. Justice Antonin Scalia, for example, made a number of accusations regarding the Court's improper favoritism toward certain parties during the course of his tenure. He contended that the institution had accepted the "so-called homosexual agenda" (*Lawrence v. Texas* [2003]) and that it enabled the "siege" of "illegal immigrants who invade [American] property, strain their social services, and place their lives in jeopardy" (*Arizona v. United States* [2012]). Scalia aimed, at least in part, to undercut support for rulings with which he disagreed. Yet, if such language can influence perceptions of the institution's favoritism toward disliked groups, it also has consequences for the health of the Court overall.

If anger at "Court favoritism" can damage legitimacy in the short term, what are the long-term implications? It is important to note, at the outset, that the group antipathy model does *not* imply that the reservoir of support will run completely dry over time. Group antipathy represents only one component of institutional support, albeit an important one. Other values and predispositions also influence legitimacy assessments (e.g., Bartels and Johnston 2013; Caldeira and Gibson 1992). Some work in the obdurate legitimacy vein suggests that the Court's support displays a stickiness over time due to the enduring nature of these predispositions. The symbols and trapping of judicial authority raise further the salience of legitimacy-reinforcing considerations, helping to safeguard institutional support (Gibson, Lodge, and Woodson 2014). It is not realistic to anticipate the Court's legitimacy to evaporate, absent a series of extraordinary and unforeseen events (Nelson and Tucker in press).

Even so, the group antipathy model has at least two serious long-term implications. To begin with, it raises the possibility that support for the Court will eventually polarize along group-based demarcations. As Caldeira and Gibson (1992) observe, "diffuse support for the Court is not a constant, and, however measured, it must ebb and flow even if relatively stable" (659). Some citizens will view the institution through long-term predispositions and values. But when the Court favors groups that they strongly dislike, others will evaluate the institution through this negative framework. A clear portion of its legitimacy will hinge on the extent to which citizens perceive it favor unpopular groups. This raises the possibility that its support will decline among those with negative attitudes toward minority groups – in fact, precisely what we observe in the empirical chapters to come – even as, just as surely, it is unlikely to dry up completely.

The second implication, and one that follows from above, concerns the behavior of the justices themselves. For strategic decision makers, whose authority depends on recognition of their institution's legitimacy, group-based legitimacy imposes a dilemma. Ruling in favor of unpopular groups can place it in peril. Justices that recognize these patterns may behave strategically when unpopular social groups seek rights-protections, helping to further inoculate the institution against politicized attacks. Scholars have surmised that *Korematsu*, for instance, represented such a form of strategic behavior (e.g., Edwards 1991), whereas other work demonstrates that the Court alters the language of its opinions when it anticipates public opposition (Black et al. 2016a, 2016b). This behavior makes plain the importance of the social group framework. If, to protect its legitimacy, the judiciary is forced to modify its decisions or even strategically rule against unpopular groups from time to time, it strikes a distorted balance between minority rights and majority will. This, then, represents the essence of the paradox: Since legitimacy plays a foundational role for the Court, the institution may be forced to abandon its protection of unpopular groups when doing so places its support in peril. Thus, the Court's ability to, in the words of Hamilton, "guard the Constitution and the rights of individuals from the effects of those ill humors ... and serious oppressions of the minor party in the community" is endangered by the fact that the institution is, according to Jefferson, "incontestably ... beyond comparison the weakest of the three departments of power." I test these insights in Chapter 7.

RESEARCH DESIGN STRATEGY

While Chapter 1 provides an overview of the book's outline, I pause here to detail the research design strategy that guides my examination of the group antipathy model. In the coming chapters, I explore its basic tenets using a variety of methodological approaches, groups, and applications. This is important because, as Linos and Twist (2016) demonstrate, distinct empirical methodologies may lead to different findings when it comes to public opinion about the Supreme Court. I design the book's empirical tests to complement one another, exploring results across several studies, measures, and approaches. In other words, I do not assume that any single approach offers a definitive test of the model, but rather that each has merits and drawbacks.

The chapters build on one another in a progressive fashion. Each piece of evidence speaks to a different piece of the puzzle, and each is designed to address the shortcomings of that which was presented prior. In this way, I am able to offer a diverse array of evidence, much of which is generally consistent with the predictions of the antipathy model.

The coming three chapters interrogate the central insight of the theory: that citizens penalize the Court when they receive a clear signal that it favors groups they strongly dislike (the Group Antipathy Hypothesis). I begin in Chapter 3 by using observational survey data in the wake of two recent and high-profile rights decisions. The chapter presents multiple complementary tests, using cross-sectional as well as dynamic panel analyses of institutional legitimacy. In so doing, I offer robust evidence consistent with the group antipathy account. I demonstrate that negative feelings toward gays and immigrants strongly shaped assessments of the Court in the wake of relevant rulings. Building on this insight, I examine the hypothesis from a distinct angle in Chapter 4. Since gays and immigrants can be considered "liberal" groups – self-identified liberals tend to rate them more favorably than do self-identified conservatives – I explore whether evidence when a conservative group is involved. I combine observational evidence and an original survey experiment to explore the effects of antipathy toward big business on assessments of the Court, leveraging the controversy surrounding *Citizens United*.

While observational analyses allow us to explore real-world implications, a primary drawback concerns their inability to isolate the precise causal influence of group antipathy, as disentangled from various other factors that may shape opinion. Therefore, in Chapter 5, I turn to a series of survey experiments to help address this shortcoming. The benefits of this approach are threefold. First, I am able to study a diverse array of political and social groups, representing a broad cross-section of American society. The experiments concern groups with distinct racial, ethnic, religious, socioeconomic, and ideological characteristics. Second, I vary the manipulations that are used to prime group considerations. This is important because citizens may receive information about the Court in variety of forms. I demonstrate that, irrespective of the cases described and information provided, citizens form perceptions of the groups that the Court favors and these have predictable effects on institutional support. Third, the experiments enable me to consider competing explanations, threats to inference, and the mechanics by which group antipathy operates.

Having amassed a wide variety of evidence that demonstrates the real-world and laboratory influence of group antipathy on institutional legitimacy, I turn in Chapter 6 to considering other implications. Put differently, this chapter moves beyond the primary theoretical insight of the antipathy model, explored in fine-grained detail in prior chapters, in order to explore a range of additional theoretical implications for the broader literature on institutional support. Finally, Chapter 7 extends the research design. In addition to discussing the substantive implications of the group antipathy model, I empirically evaluate some of the most important ones in this portion of the manuscript. Recognizing that its legitimacy rests on group considerations, the Court has some incentive to curtail minority rights protections. I show that it does so in a strategic fashion, a fact that has direct implications when it comes to understanding the degree to which the institution is a counter-majoritarian bulwark. To be sure, this chapter represents only a small step toward a full suite of empirical analyses concerning the implications of group antipathy for the Supreme Court and minority rights in the United States.

3

Under Siege

Gay Rights and Immigration at the Supreme Court

In 1788, Alexander Hamilton argued that judges served as the fundamental safeguard against "serious oppressions of the minor party in the community." After 225 years, questions over the extent to which judges would go to protect minority rights once again swirled around the Supreme Court. On the morning of June 26, 2013, the Court was slated to announce the final rulings of its term. Two blockbuster civil rights decisions loomed. In *United States v. Windsor* (2013), the Court faced a constitutional challenge to the federal Defense of Marriage Act (DOMA), under which the government interpreted marriage protections to apply only to opposite-sex unions. In *Hollingsworth v. Perry* (2013), the Court considered a challenge to a California referendum known as Proposition 8, which provided that only opposite-sex marriages would be recognized under state law.[1]

Opponents of same-sex marriage found little reassurance in the Court's rulings. Writing for the majority in *Windsor*, Justice Anthony Kennedy gutted DOMA. The law's principal effect, he argued, was "to identify a subset of state-sanctioned marriages and make them unequal" in violation of the Constitution. Kennedy did not stop there. He pointed out the basic violations of minority rights that stood at the heart of the law. "DOMA," he wrote, "contrives to deprive some couples married under the laws of their State, but not other couples, of both rights and responsibilities ... This places same-sex couples in an unstable position of being in a second-tier marriage. The differentiation demeans the couple, whose moral and sexual choices the Constitution protects." Despite their distinct reactions to the ruling, both supporters and opponents interpreted it as a clear (although, for some, unwarranted) victory for gay

---

[1] Analyses in this chapter are based on those originally published in Zilis (2018).

citizens. Plaintiff Edith Windsor, for example, beamed, "we won everything that we asked and hoped for" (Perlman, Hutchinson, and Warren 2013) while the National Organization of Marriage said the ruling aided "faux marriages" (Haven 2013).

This was far from the first accusation that the Court improperly favored certain groups in American society. One of the most aggressive of these came from Justice Antonin Scalia, who wrote that gay rights proponents would use the ruling to claim, "the traditional definition [of marriage] has 'the purpose and effect to disparage and to injure' the 'personhood and dignity' of same sex couples." Scalia's refrain was a common one. He had previously said the Supreme Court had given in to gay rights proponents and, more recently, had charged that the Court also favored illegal immigrants. Dissenting from the ruling in *Arizona v. United States* (2012), Scalia wrote that American citizens "feel themselves under siege by large number of illegal immigrants who invade their property, strain their social services, and place their lives in jeopardy." His opinion made explicit what he saw as a gulf between the Court's marble arches and the realities of Americans threatened by "unlawful and dangerous immigrants."

The modern Court is often involved in cases that directly implicate important social groups and political minorities in society. This is, of course, as the Framers and drafters of the Fourteenth Amendment envisioned. Moreover, the Court's involvement in these controversies means that citizens may perceive it to favor certain groups. This chapter considers whether recent high-profile rulings, specifically concerning gay rights and immigration in the United States, shaped perceptions of the institution and the willingness of Americans to support the Court. Applying group antipathy theory, I anticipate that these high-profile signals will negatively impact the Court's legitimacy among the specific subset of the population that dislikes gays and immigrants. In other words, the group-based attribution of legitimacy takes place as citizens perceive the Court to favor segments that they dislike.

I begin by discussing news coverage of the gay marriage and immigration rulings in detail. I demonstrate that the media interpreted these to protect the rights of important minority groups. In other words, although citizens were exposed to a variety of signals in the wake of the ruling, one concerned the link between the Supreme Court and specific social groups. With this in mind, I analyze survey data surrounding the *Windsor*, *Hollingsworth*, and *Arizona* holdings. Conducting both cross-sectional and dynamic analyses, I demonstrate predictable effects in opinion response based on how citizens felt toward immigrants and gays. Even after controlling for a variety of alternative explanations, the results demonstrate that negative affect toward these groups led to a decline in Court legitimacy, but only after the relevant rulings were released. I close the chapter by considering theoretical and normative implications.

SIGNALS FROM THE COURT

In order for the group-based attribution of legitimacy to take place, citizens must perceive a link between the Court and various social groups. Without this perception, there is little reason to expect that attitudes toward groups who have their day in Court will influence diffuse support. In addition to general trends in Court jurisprudence that involve the extension and protection of minority group rights, recent immigration and gay marriage cases raised further the salience of these issues, more strongly linking the Court and these social groups in popular perception. There are numerous indicators of the rulings' salience.

The 2013 gay marriage decisions – *Hollingsworth v. Perry* and *United States v. Windsor* – were both announced on the final day of the term, alongside a relatively obscure statutory interpretation case. The cases received front-page coverage in the *New York Times* and almost all other national news outlets. By most accounts, these cases were the most salient of the term (Clark et al. 2018). Though there were procedural issues involved in the cases, public discussions focused mainly on their implications for particular social groups. The beneficiaries of the decisions – gay Americans and same-sex couples, most proximately, and by extension their supporters – were clear.

To explore popular discussions of the rulings, I conducted a search of four leading national newspapers – the *New York Times*, *Washington Post*, *Los Angeles Times*, and *Chicago Tribune*. Given their high circulation as well as geographic and ideological diversity, these outlets represent an ideal mix for studying Supreme Court media coverage (see Collins and Cooper 2012, 2015).[2] I searched for coverage of social group indicators (*gay* or *same sex*) mentioned along with the Supreme Court in an article immediately following the ruling. This yielded some 130 stories, a substantial volume of coverage. The vast majority of these stories made clear a link between the Court and this segment of the population and, moreover, framed the rulings as "major victories [for] the gay rights movement." Even casual observers of coverage would likely have been exposed to this depiction. For example, the *Times*'s banner headline read, "Justices Extend Benefits to Gay Couples; Allow Same Sex Marriages in California." The *Washington Post* was similarly clear: "Victories for Gay Marriage."

---

[2] To be clear, this is not the only way in which Americans receive their news, but leading national newspapers play an important agenda setting role in shaping coverage of the Court so there is reason to expect similarities between the content found there and elsewhere. A search for internet news coverage, another prominent way in which citizens learn about the Supreme Court, demonstrates many of the same patterns in coverage. For example, day-of-decision coverage from the Huffington Post, a leading left-leaning website, described "same-sex couples whose eyes had glistened with tears" (Reilly and Siddiqui 2013) while the Drudge Report, a right-wing breaking news site, called it "Gay Day at the High Court" (Drudge Report 2013).

Turning to immigrants and the Court, the *Arizona* case similarly attracted considerable attention, though less than the Obamacare decision from the same term. The decision was announced on June 25, 2012, the second to last seating of the Court's term, meaning that it enjoyed three days in the national spotlight before the healthcare ruling was handed down. It similarly received front-page coverage in the *Times* and many other outlets. Applying the same search method used previously, major national news outlets published 105 stories that mentioned *immigrant* or *immigration* and the Supreme Court within three days of the ruling. In terms of the ruling's primary beneficiaries, some critics argued that it would allow the state of Arizona to continue to discriminate against Hispanics because it did not go far enough in invalidating its immigration enforcement law, whereas others situated it in a federalism context. However, many accounts portrayed the decision as a victory for Hispanic immigrants. This was driven by sustained media coverage of Scalia's dissent, in which he defines the beneficiaries of the ruling in great detail: "Arizona bears the brunt of the country's illegal immigration problem ... Thousands of Arizona's estimated 400,000 illegal immigrants – including not just children but men and women under 30 – are now assured immunity from enforcement, and will be able to compete openly with Arizona citizens for employment."

While these rulings demonstrated a Court that was potentially sympathetic to minority groups, other cases cut in a different direction. In particular, recent Court jurisprudence with respect to African Americans has shown the justices to be an uncertain ally of black civil rights leaders. Indeed, Gibson and Caldeira (1992) note that the Court's support has fallen sharply in the African American community due to the institution's increasingly conservative orientation, including on matters of racial justice. While rights-claims that involve African American interests have met with divergent success in the past few decades (such as with the Court's nuanced affirmative action rulings in 2003), recent terms have featured some clear setbacks for African Americans at the Court. The most dramatic manifestation of this was the decision in *Shelby County v. Holder* (2013).

Released one day before the same-sex marriage cases, *Shelby County* attracted widespread popular scrutiny and many observers saw the holding as a setback for African Americans. Evidence suggests that both the press and the public paid careful attention to the ruling. Leading national newspapers were saturated with front-page coverage. A *New York Times* story included a statement from President Obama that he was "deeply disappointed" with the outcome. Just as significantly, black media outlets scrutinized carefully the ruling. Nine leading black newspapers[3] published nearly 200 stories on the Voting Rights Act during June and July 2013. Almost all of these were critical

---

[3] The *Baltimore Afro American, Bay State Banner, Michigan Chronicle, Network Journal, New York Amsterdam News, New York Beacon, Sacramento Observer, Tri State Defender,* and *Washington Informer.*

of the Court and painted African Americans as harmed by the ruling. For instance, the National Association for the Advancement of Colored People called the decision an "outrage." Given the balance of this coverage, the substance of the ruling, and the close connection between the decision and black group interests in the eyes of many, there are strong reasons to expect that *Shelby County* was perceived as a setback for blacks. Given the predictions in Table 2.1, this is a case of rights limitation that we would expect to have little effect on legitimacy attitudes.

In order to fully account for the effects of group antipathy on opinion, I also consider that there are a large number of Supreme Court rulings that fail to capture public attention. A high degree of salience may contribute to the perception that the Court tends to favor a specific group, but absent this, we would not expect group antipathy to influence reactions to a case. Using data from the same time frame, we can explore this expectation using *Knox v. Service Employees International Union, Local 1000* (2012). In a 7-2 decision, released on June 21, 2012, the Court dealt a setback to the service union, ruling that it did not give the required notice to non-members when it charged an assessment fee. The case was overshadowed by other end-of-term rulings, including *Arizona*, and it received very modest media attention, putting it into the category of a weak signal that we would expect to have minimal influence on public opinion.

Applying the Group Antipathy Model

As rulings like *Windsor* and *Arizona* attracted considerable media coverage, it is likely that even moderately attentive citizens learned of the Supreme Court's willingness to protect the rights of prominent minority groups in society. To be clear, many citizens may not have understood the nuances of the rulings nor the balance of the legal issues involved. Yet, by learning of a link between the Court and prominent social groups, citizens nonetheless possessed a way in which to judge the institution. Most Americans have feelings toward various social groups, particularly when they, like gays and immigrants, are relatively visible. These attitudes supply the lens through which citizens can evaluate the Court.

To put things simply, the group antipathy model anticipates that when the Court is perceived to favor a specific social group, citizens will condition the legitimacy of the institution on their feelings toward the group in question. Perceived favoritism toward a disliked group may damage the institution. This leads to the expectation that, as dislike of gays increases, citizens will report lower levels of diffuse support for the Court after the *Hollingsworth* and *Windsor* rulings. Seeing as this case made salient the Court's willingness to protect gay rights, it should generate predictable opinion responses. By a similar logic, the *Arizona* case should have parallel effects when it comes to immigrants. As dislike of Hispanic immigrants increases, citizens will report lower levels of diffuse support for the Court after the *Arizona* ruling.

Study A: Landmark Court Decisions

On the other hand, the model also suggests that high-profile rulings against minority groups should have a minimal effect on legitimacy attitudes. This follows because citizens tend to place particular importance on feelings of threat raised by minority gains. The *Shelby County* setback should therefore lead to little reaction on the part of those that dislike African Americans, even as it represented a potential setback for black voting rights. The expectation is that, as dislike of African Americans increases, there should be no association with diffuse support for the Court after *Shelby County*. Similarly, given the low salience of the labor union dispute, we would expect that, as dislike of unions increases, there should be no association with diffuse support for the Court after the *Knox* ruling.

STUDY A: LANDMARK COURT DECISIONS

I draw on data from The American Panel Survey (TAPS), administered by the Weidenbaum Center at Washington University (Smith 2013). TAPS, a monthly online survey, recruits respondents as a national probability sample using an address-based sampling frame with replenishment. Further technical information is available at taps.wustl.edu. Importantly, TAPS includes valid indicators of legitimacy and other rule of law and Supreme Court-specific factors. I focus analysis on the subset of respondents who answered questions concerning all key covariates before and after these rulings, which means that the number of respondents included in the analysis is lower than it is in any single wave of the survey. This design choice is important for testing the group antipathy account in a rigorous fashion and it also allows us to observe the durability of effects over a long time span of more than a year.

In this chapter and the ones that follow, I rely on the following seven items to measure institutional legitimacy, following best practices in the recent literature (e.g., Gibson and Nelson 2015). The items are as follows, with factor loadings in parentheses.

- If the Court started making decisions that most people disagree with, it might be better to do away with the Court. (0.79)
- The right of the Supreme Court to decide certain types of controversial issues should be reduced. (0.80)
- The US Supreme Court gets too mixed up in politics. (0.61)
- Justices who consistently make decisions at odds with what a majority of the people want should be removed. (0.84)
- The US Supreme Court ought to be made less independent so that it listens a lot more to what the people want. (0.85)
- It is inevitable that the Court gets mixed up in politics; we ought to have a stronger means of controlling the Court. (0.86)
- Justices are just like other politicians; we cannot trust them to decide court cases in a way that is in the best interests of our country. (0.80)

Factor analysis of these items confirms their suitability as an index of diffuse support; the battery of these items administered in the July 2013 survey, after the immigration, gay marriage, and voting rights rulings, generates a single significant underlying factor with eigenvalue of 4.45 (the eigenvalue of the second extracted factor is 0.21). With their suitability confirmed, I follow common practice by creating an additive index of responses to these items, scaled 0–1, with higher *Legitimacy* values indicating a greater degree of loyalty to the Court. More information about the construction and properties of this variable and others described in the following sections is available in Appendix.

Measures

Recent Court decisions impacted both general and specific groups of individuals. Gay marriage decisions implicate attitudes toward lesbian, gay, bisexual, and transgender (LGBTQ) individuals, same-sex couples, and gay rights activists more specifically. Immigration rulings implicate attitudes toward Hispanics generally and immigrants in particular. Other rulings directly implicate African Americans and labor unions. I draw upon batteries of items to tap into affective attachments toward each of these social groups.

The *Gay antipathy* measure is composed of responses to two 11-point feeling thermometers (reverse coded), a common measure of group affect (e.g., Iyengar, Sood, and Lelkes 2012) regarding "gays" and "gay rights activists." Analysis of these items shows that they scale together (α = 0.76). I construct an additive index with higher values indicating increased antipathy to gays and gay rights proponents. The *Immigrant antipathy* measure is composed of six questions. These are a feeling thermometer to capture attitudes toward Hispanics as a group as well as more specific items that ask respondents about their level of concern regarding immigrant-caused crime, the burden placed on social institutions by immigrants, whether strict measures against illegal immigrants would lead to harassment of Hispanics, and whether these measures would exacerbate immigrant poverty and would go against the tradition of welcoming immigrants. Again, factor analysis suggests the unidimensional structure of these six items (the eigenvalue of the single significant factor is 2.20). I utilize a factor score for this measure. Finally, the *Black antipathy* and *Labor union antipathy* measures are composed of simple feeling thermometers to capture attitudes toward "African Americans" and "labor unions" as groups (reversed coded). When an item is administered at multiple time points, as some feeling thermometers are, I use the iteration prior to the final legitimacy battery. I scale all antipathy variables to range between 0 and 1, with higher values representing stronger dislike.

Other Covariates
To provide a difficult test of the theory, I evaluate whether the group-based attribution of legitimacy holds even after other explanations have been taken

Study A: Landmark Court Decisions

into account. I generate indicators to tap into fundamental political values that have been shown to influence legitimacy: support for the *Rule of law*, *Minority liberty*, and *Political tolerance*. I construct these scales using multi-item batteries and subject them to factor analysis to verify their underlying unidimensional structure. I then create additive indexes, scaled 0–1, for the three measures of democratic value support, with higher values indicating increased adherence to these values. They are described in Appendix.

TAPS also includes two items that enable us to measure ideological disagreement with the Supreme Court, a form of specific support. To create this measure, I draw on respondent's self-placement on a seven-point ideology scale and placement of the Supreme Court on a five-point ideology scale. *Ideological disagreement* is generated by taking the distance between Court's placement from one's self-placement; it is scaled from 0 to 1, with higher values indicating that respondents perceive the Court as ideologically distant from themselves.

Finally, I control for a variety of dispositional and demographic variables that may give shape to institutional legitimacy. I employ a 10-item battery to measure a respondent's level of political *Knowledge*. I include an indicator for self-reported *Republican* party identification and respondents' levels of *Income* and educational attainment (*Education*), with a four-category measure that ranges from less than high school to an undergraduate degree or higher. And I include variables for a respondent's gender (*Female*), race (*Black*), and ethnicity (*Hispanic*).

Analysis

By leveraging the developments surrounding the Court's high-profile group-rights decisions, I offer two primary tests of the group antipathy account. First, I conduct multivariate analyses to explore Court legitimacy both before and after the immigration and gay marriage rulings, with the expectation that dislike for these groups will shape legitimacy only after the relevant rulings. Finding these effects, I then conduct a dynamic analysis to explore individual-level changes in legitimacy during this time frame. Results show that dislike toward gays and immigrants associates with declines in an individual's support for the Court.

The Influence of Group Antipathy, Before and After the Rulings

Table 3.1 displays results from OLS regressions that predict diffuse support for the Supreme Court from dislike toward gays and Hispanic immigrants (two perceived beneficiaries of its recent jurisprudence), as well as a variety of other covariates. These models explore legitimacy among individuals who were queried both before and after its critical same-sex marriage and immigration rulings. Recall that the Group Antipathy Hypothesis anticipates that, in the wake of decisions that cause citizens to perceive the Court as sympathetic to gays and immigrants, greater dislike should diminish legitimacy.

TABLE 3.1 *Diffuse support at before and after minority rights rulings*

	(1) May 2012 Prior to all relevant rulings	(2) July 2012 After immigration ruling	(3) Jan. 2013 After immigration ruling	(4) July 2013 After immigration and marriage rulings
Gay antipathy	0.03	−0.03	−0.03	−0.07*
	(0.03)	(0.03)	(0.04)	(0.04)
Immigrant antipathy	−0.06	−0.14*	−0.11*	−0.12*
	(0.04)	(0.04)	(0.04)	(0.04)
Black antipathy	−0.01	0.00	−0.00	0.02
	(0.03)	(0.04)	(0.04)	(0.04)
Labor union antipathy	−0.03	0.01	−0.02	−0.01
	(0.03)	(0.03)	(0.03)	(0.03)
Political tolerance	0.10*	0.13*	0.13*	0.19*
	(0.03)	(0.03)	(0.03)	(0.03)
Minority liberty	0.25*	0.21*	0.27*	0.22*
	(0.04)	(0.04)	(0.05)	(0.05)
Rule of law	0.21*	0.28*	0.22*	0.22*
	(0.05)	(0.05)	(0.06)	(0.06)
Ideological distance	−0.18*	−0.14*	−0.19*	−0.20*
	(0.03)	(0.03)	(0.03)	(0.03)
Knowledge	0.21*	0.23*	0.21*	0.17*
	(0.04)	(0.04)	(0.04)	(0.05)
Republican	0.01	−0.04*	−0.04*	−0.05*
	(0.02)	(0.02)	(0.02)	(0.02)
Education	0.13*	0.18*	0.17*	0.12*
	(0.03)	(0.03)	(0.03)	(0.03)
Income	0.03	0.01	0.01	0.00
	(0.03)	(0.03)	(0.03)	(0.03)
Female	−0.02	0.00	−0.00	−0.01
	(0.01)	(0.02)	(0.02)	(0.02)
Black	0.04	0.08*	0.04	0.00
	(0.03)	(0.03)	(0.03)	(0.04)
Hispanic	0.05	0.03	0.02	0.00
	(0.03)	(0.03)	(0.03)	(0.03)
R^2	0.37	0.41	0.41	0.38
N	704	699	698	672

Note: Results are estimated OLS coefficients with standard errors in parentheses. *$p < 0.05$ (one-tailed). The expectation is a link between group dislike and legitimacy after relevant immigration/same-sex marriage rulings.

Analysis of the results from Table 3.1 provides support, from both a statistical perspective and a substantive one, for these expectations. In general, it shows that antipathy toward gays and immigrants decreases the legitimacy that the Court enjoys, but only after its rulings regarding these groups. These attitudes do not exert a meaningful effect on legitimacy prior to the same-sex marriage and immigration rulings.

On the other hand, there is no evidence available to reject the null hypothesis regarding dislike for African Americans and labor unions. In other words, there are no indications that respondents who feel negatively toward these groups evaluate the Court differently after its *Shelby County* and *Knox* holdings. There are a few potential explanations that could account for these null results. First, as shown in Table 2.1, I have hypothesized that low salience decisions such as *Knox*, as well as those in which the Court denies a group's claims, such as *Shelby County*, have negligible effects. The results are consistent with both hypotheses. Second, it may be the case that respondents were not aware of *either* of these decisions. Yet, this is not likely to have been the case for *Shelby County*, one of the most important rulings released by the Court in recent years. The low salience explanation is much more likely when it comes to the *Knox* case given the minimal level of media attention that the ruling garners. It thus makes sense that public opinion does not appear to have responded to the *Knox* holding, since much of the public was likely unaware it had been issued. Third, it is possible that the public may have reacted to *Shelby County* if not for the fact that it was overshadowed by *Windsor* and *Hollingsworth*. Again, note that the Court announced the same-sex marriage rulings just one day after *Shelby County*, potentially muting its effects. On the whole, the null effects may be consistent with the explanation that group antipathy does not operate across all cases, but rather in only high-profile disputes that clearly signal to the public the Court's sympathy to specific segments; however, more work is needed. I consider further the null effects in a second analysis presented in the coming pages.

A few other things to note: First, the table encompasses a large number of distinct tests of the group antipathy model and finds evidence that is consistent with it in each case. Negative feelings toward gays diminish legitimacy after the same-sex marriage holdings (model 4) and exert no comparable influence prior (models 1–3). Similarly, negative feelings toward immigrants diminish legitimacy after the *Arizona* ruling (models 2–4) but not prior. And despite the fact that the *Shelby County* ruling attracted a considerable amount of attention, attitudes toward blacks did *not* influence legitimacy prior to or after this holding (models 1–4), in line with the Rights Limitation Hypothesis. Neither did antipathy toward labor unions over the course of the study. In short, the consistency of these results is strong.

Another notable aspect is that the results have held even after we have controlled for the most powerful theoretical accounts of legitimacy in the existing literature. The statistically significant coefficients on *Ideological disagreement* suggest that perceptions of the Court's ideological location exert an influence on legitimacy. Furthermore, there is evidence of a fundamental link between democratic values and diffuse support (e.g., Caldeira and Gibson 1992; Gibson and Nelson 2015). Nonetheless, group antipathy continues to exert a meaningful and consistent effect even after other factors have been accounted for, indicating its explanatory power in a fully specified statistical model. To put this another way, we can better understand the scope of Supreme Court legitimacy by knowing the extent to which citizens feel negatively disposed to the social groups they perceive the institution to favor.

How large of an impact does group antipathy exert? In the post-ruling model (model 4), movement across the range of the gay antipathy variable leads to a predicted seven-point decline in legitimacy. Antipathy toward immigrants exerts a larger influence: a predicted 12-point drop in legitimacy. These effects are substantively meaningful, as they are each about one-half to two-thirds the magnitude of the effects of knowledge, historically one of the strongest and most consistent predictors of legitimacy.

In sum, an examination before and after relevant rulings provides clear evidence that social group attachments exert a direct influence on legitimacy. These results hold even though we have controlled for adherence to democratic values, partisan preferences, and specific support in the form of ideological disagreement with the Court. The subsequent section presents a dynamic analysis to explore individual-level changes in legitimacy, showing that dislike toward gays and immigrants associates with micro-level declines in diffuse support for the Court.

Dynamic Analysis Leveraging Micro-level Changes in Legitimacy over Time

To offer a more complete and rigorous examination of theoretical expectations, I employ a dynamic test that leverages the data to explore individual-level change in attitudes toward the Court from before to after its relevant rulings.[4] Given the Court's rulings during the time period under study, group antipathy theory anticipates that dislike for gays and immigrants should precipitate micro-declines in its legitimacy over time. To test this, I present in Table 3.2 a model with legitimacy change, from before to after the rulings in question, as the dependent variable. This enables us to discern whether group-based considerations lead to changes in the Court's diffuse support at the individual level over time. The model includes other control variables as specified above.

These results provide micro-level evidence that attitudes regarding the Court changed over the course of 2012–2013 as a result of group-based attachments. Even after we have controlled for a variety of other demographic and dispositional considerations, there is evidence that attitudes shifted along group-based

---

[4] To reiterate, the theoretical account that I specify does not require citizens to have been highly knowledgeable about particular rulings nor close followers of the Court to link their attitudes toward social groups with their support for the institution. There is likely not a one-to-one link between objective decision-making and perceptions of the Court's support for minority rights.

Study A: Landmark Court Decisions

TABLE 3.2 *The influence of group dislike on dynamics in legitimacy*

	(1) Pre-post
Gay antipathy	−0.10*
	(0.03)
Immigrant antipathy	−0.09*
	(0.04)
Black antipathy	0.02
	(0.03)
Labor union antipathy	0.02
	(0.03)
Political tolerance	0.10*
	(0.03)
Minority liberty	0.01
	(0.04)
Rule of law	0.01
	(0.05)
Ideological distance	−0.10*
	(0.03)
Knowledge	−0.03
	(0.04)
Republican	−0.04*
	(0.02)
Education	−0.03
	(0.03)
Income	−0.01
	(0.03)
Female	0.01
	(0.01)
Black	−0.02
	(0.03)
Hispanic	−0.05
	(0.03)
R^2	0.121
N	647

Note: Results are estimated OLS coefficients with standard errors in parentheses. *$p < 0.05$ (one-tailed). The expectation is a change in legitimacy after relevant immigration/same-sex marriage rulings.

demarcations.[5] Specifically, those who felt unfavorably toward gays became significantly less supportive of the judiciary over time and those who felt

[5] In addition to general ideological support, an alternative way to account for specific support would be to include policy attitudes in the model. The survey includes a pair of appropriate items,

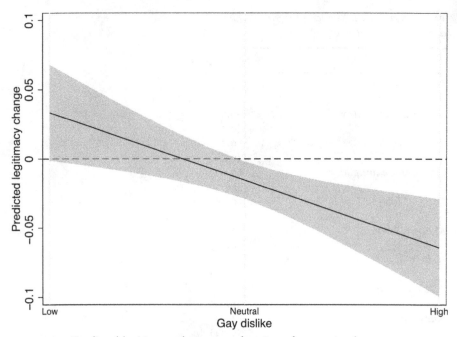

FIGURE 3.1 Predicted legitimacy change as a function of gay antipathy
Note: Predicted change in legitimacy and 95% confidence intervals, using the specification in Table 3.2. Substantively, the figure demonstrates that legitimacy declines after the rulings among respondents with high levels of dislike for gays.

unfavorably toward immigrants became significantly less supportive as well. This was not (only) an aggregate-level shift, but an individual- level one.

To interpret the main effects more fully, Figures 3.1 and 3.2 present predicted effects across various levels of group antipathy. The former shows that attitudes toward gays have a significant and substantively meaningful effect on the Court's shifting legitimacy. The Court's legitimacy is predicted to slightly increase, by about 0.03 units, for those with low levels of gay dislike, an insignificant effect. But its legitimacy decreases more substantially, by about 0.06 units, for those at the opposite end of the spectrum. This negative shift is roughly equivalent to a tercile difference in legitimacy change. The latter figure demonstrates a similar pattern when it comes to attitudes toward immigrants.

> administered at multiple time points, which ask respondents about their support for federal recognition of same-sex marriage and a federal plan to halt illegal immigration. When measured prior to or contemporaneous with group affect, these attitudes do little to diminish the effects of group-based attitudes. In later iterations involving same-sex marriage case alone, the policy attitude, measured immediately prior to the ruling, overwhelms the group attachment as measured months earlier. This raises the possibility that group affect shapes the later development of policy attitudes.

Study A: Landmark Court Decisions

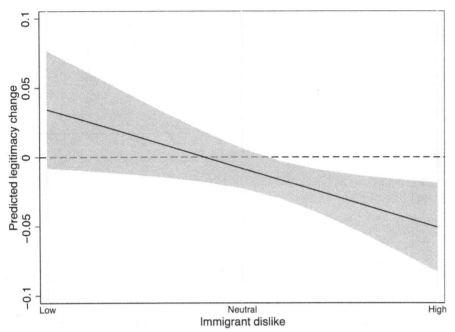

FIGURE 3.2 Predicted legitimacy change as a function of immigrant antipathy
Note: Predicted change in legitimacy and 95% confidence intervals, using the specification in Table 3.2. Substantively, the figure demonstrates that legitimacy declines after the rulings among respondents with high levels of dislike for gays.

Here, the difference between support for the Court at low levels and high levels of dislike is a non-significant change in the former case versus a significant decrease of about 0.05 units in the latter case. The asymmetry fits with a negativity bias that has been observed in other studies of the Court (e.g., Christenson and Glick 2019).

Additionally, it is important to consider that many citizens hold negative attitudes toward both groups simultaneously. To understand the cumulative effects of group antipathy, I simulate in Figure 3.3 changes in support among those with high levels of dislike for both groups and compare this to support among those with average levels of dislike for both. This demonstrates the combined effects of the Court's rulings amount to an approximate seven-point, or one quintile, difference in legitimacy assessments between respondents with high versus average levels of dislike for both groups.

A final way to evaluate the magnitude of these effects is to compare the coefficients that are estimated in Table 3.2, since variables are all placed on the same 0–1 scale.[6] In particular, quite a bit is known about the effects of political

---

[6] The patterns discussed in this paragraph are similar if we use standardized betas to compare.

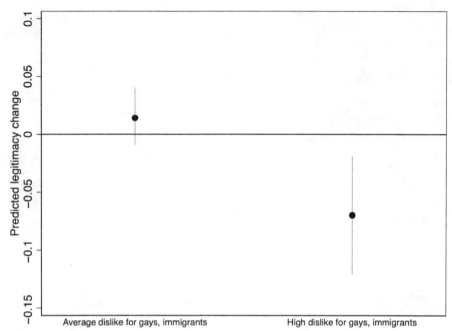

FIGURE 3.3 Cumulative changes in legitimacy, simulated
Note: Estimates and 95% confidence intervals simulated from the model presented in Table 3.2 using CLARIFY (King, Tomz, and Wittenberg 2000). Dislike variables vary between their means and 1 and all others held at their medians. Substantively, the figure demonstrates that the Court's legitimacy significantly declines when a respondent has high levels of disregard for both gays and immigrants, yet offers no evidence that legitimacy changes when a respondent has neutral feelings toward both groups.

knowledge, democratic values, and ideological disagreement on legitimacy, since these are some of the most extensively studied factors in the literature (e.g., Bartels and Johnston 2013; Gibson and Nelson 2015). The effects of group antipathy compare favorably to each. Movement across the range of the antipathy scale is predicted to damage legitimacy by a similar amount as does maximizing ideological disagreement with the Court and political (in)tolerance, a fundamental democratic value. The effects of group antipathy are also much larger than those from other democratic values, such as support for the rule of law, and from political knowledge, in the dynamic model. This suggests that group antipathy can alter Court legitimacy in the wake of high-profile rulings, even as knowledge and democratic values strongly correlate with it overall. Finally, group antipathy has larger effects than many other important political and demographic variables in the model. Taken together, these results imply that negative affect toward specific social groups is meaningfully depressing Court legitimacy.

DISCUSSION

The modern Supreme Court has not always been a friend to minorities, but on at least a few high-profile occasions, its actions have been unambiguous. Justice Kennedy's legal writings, for example, emphasize the importance of respect for the rights and dignity of gay Americans. This shares a spirit with Hamilton's view that the courts act as a bulwark against systematic oppression.

This chapter provides empirical evidence showing that protecting minority rights has direct consequences for the Court's public standing. The public often thinks in group-based terms when evaluating political affairs. Presented with strong signals about the Court's orientation toward important social groups in society, citizens leverage this information as a means to evaluate the Court. The patterns manifest themselves with respect to distinct minority groups following recent high-profile rulings. *Windsor* and *Hollingsworth* polarized legitimacy depending upon how citizens felt toward gay Americans, and *Arizona* did the same with respect to immigrants.

The findings not only emphasize the variable nature of judicial legitimacy, but also demonstrate that individual-level opinion change plays a prominent role. Citizens reacted to recent rulings by updating their views of the Court. Most notably, those with highly negative attitudes toward gays and immigrants became the most circumspect about the institution. Their concerns were not limited to a loss of confidence, but rather a rethinking of foundational loyalty. At the same time, we should not overstate the magnitude of these effects. While the Court suffered a meaningful decline in diffuse support, it continued to maintain a notable reservoir of goodwill in the aggregate.

How do these insights fit with existing understandings of diffuse support? Quite simply, there is a theoretical distinction between evaluations of the Court that are colored by abstract assessments like perceived ideological disagreement and those based on group considerations. While perceptions of ideology do not align neatly with the Court's ideological outputs (Bartels and Johnston 2013), we can often trace perceptions of support for specific groups to its high-profile jurisprudence. It should also be noted that specific support continues to influence generalized orientations to the judiciary, at least under certain conditions. For example, the models estimate a strong effect of ideological disagreement – itself a form of specific agreement – on legitimacy. Even after controlling for this factor, however, group-based considerations matter. Moreover, a group-based model of legitimacy imposes few strong assumptions on how citizens acquire and understand political information, which may be most valuable in controversies in which the press emphasizes group-based considerations, as well as those whose ideological implications are less clear. It remains an open question about the extent to which group-based judgments also imbue ideological assessments of the institution, which may heighten the impact of these considerations beyond what is demonstrated here. I consider this question more fully in Chapter 6.

Individual-level opinion change is only one route through which group-based considerations may influence legitimacy. Over the long term, as younger cohorts replace older ones, perceptions of the Court may also shift. For example, citizens coming of political age over the last decade have witnessed a Court place significant value on the equality of gay citizens. Older citizens may have distinct perceptions. After all, only a few decades ago, the Court allowed for the criminalization of same-sex sexual relationships. An implication is that perceptions of the institution's support for gay rights may evolve *even if specific individuals do not change their opinions*. Rather, any one citizen may consider a range of high-profile signals about the Court they have been exposed to and, as these signals change over time, perceptions of the "minority rights-focused" institution may differ by cohort. If accurate, the findings of this chapter represent a lower bound in the influence of group antipathy on legitimacy.

At the same time, it is reasonable to be cautious about the magnitude of effects uncovered here. *Windsor*, *Hollingsworth*, and *Arizona* received substantial popular attention. The larger number of low salience rulings is likely to have minimal influence on attitudes toward the institution, as the results for *Knox* demonstrate. Over the long term, it is possible that these effects may either magnify or dissipate. The long-term influence of minority rights rulings is also likely to depend on the salience and substance of other actions. For example, when the Court follows a high-profile ruling in favor of a controversial minority group with a number of similar decisions, this should strengthen the perception that the institution favors a particular segment, buttressing the influence of group-based attitudes. Gay rights rulings represent a clear example. Two years after *Windsor* and *Hollingsworth*, the Court struck down all limitations on same-sex marriage in *Obergefell v. Hodges* (2015). In other cases, where the Court eventually abandons or overturns a line of jurisprudence, this may rob group-based attitudes of their influence. So, for instance, the Supreme Court's shifting civil rights precedent in the latter half of the twentieth century altered the way in which African Americans evaluated the institution (Gibson and Caldeira 1992).

A final point of caution concerns the ideological patterns uncovered in this chapter. Both gays and immigrants may be considered "liberal" groups in the sense that self-identified liberals tend to rate these institutions more favorably than conservatives. Are the results simply the residual effect of liberalism? Chapter 4 seeks to answer this question by placing a conservative group into the spotlight. In the coming pages, I integrate observational and experimental evidence regarding the relationship between attitudes toward big business and the Supreme Court, particularly in the wake of the controversial *Citizens United* ruling.

4

Opening the Floodgates

Big Business, Citizens United, and Evaluations of the Court

The Constitution protects a diverse array of groups. The Framers viewed political and religious minorities as particularly worthy of safeguard, and later developments brought racial groups, women, and the poor into this fold. Yet, a separate strain in American political and jurisprudential thought has carved out a place for others, including those that inherently wield a measure of advantage. No less a constitutional thinker than James Madison emphasized the importance of protecting the rights of the wealthy. "The minority of the opulent," Madison argued, must be protected from majority domination (quoted in Matthews 2005, 54).

The Supreme Court has endorsed the view that the Constitution secures the fundamental rights of wealthy and powerful entities. Most prominently, in *Citizens United v. Federal Election Commission* (2010), the Court determined that the First Amendment's free speech clause prohibited Congress from restricting expenditures by corporations in candidate elections. The ruling prompted vigorous criticism. Justice Ruth Bader Ginsburg called it the worst decision the modern Court has produced. President Obama argued that the ruling "reversed a century of law" and "will open the floodgates for foreign interests." Chief Justice John Roberts worried about the impact of this criticism on Court legitimacy (Totenberg 2010). Surveys demonstrated that nearly 80% of Americans opposed the ruling, both in its immediate aftermath (Eggen 2010) and years later (Stohr 2015).

This chapter applies the group antipathy model to understand evaluations of the Supreme Court in the post–*Citizens United* era. This context is distinct from that of the previous chapter, which involved groups that Americans generally perceive as disadvantaged. Yet, the group antipathy model suggests that similar dynamics should guide attitudes toward the judiciary after *Citizens United*. Specifically, Americans should evaluate the Supreme Court in light of how they feel toward big business, the central group the ruling was perceived to benefit.

I provide evidence for this theoretical account with a multiple method approach, in three phases. First, I trace the volume and substance of media coverage before and after *Citizens United*. I show that the national media became significantly more likely to depict a link between the Supreme Court and corporate interests after the decision. Coverage of the link persisted for years. Second, using survey evidence, I show that the modern Court's legitimacy varies predictably as a function of affect toward business groups. In other words, when citizens view corporations in negative terms, they are less likely to see the Court as legitimate. Third, I use an experimental study in which I manipulate portrayals of the Court's orientation to big business. The results demonstrate that antipathy toward big business predictably shapes the Supreme Court's diffuse support.

These results speak to the power of rulings that benefit powerful, conservative segments to shape institutional legitimacy. I present some of the first systematic evidence as to how the Court's link with big business has damaged its diffuse support. More generally, this chapter offers complementary evidence consistent with the group antipathy model. Taken together with Chapter 3, it demonstrates that recent decisions in favor of both liberal *and* conservative segments have influenced attitudes toward the Supreme Court among citizens who view these groups negatively.

PERCEPTIONS OF A PRO-BUSINESS COURT

Most Americans do not read Court opinions, yet the media supplies significant information to the public about the most important developments at the Court. A handful of high importance rulings receive ample coverage (Zilis 2015), and media attention is often driven to cases that are expected to have a high political and legal impact (Strother 2017). In addition, the press is increasingly emphasizing a new "myth" of the Court that is focused on the justices' personal lives and personalities (Solberg and Waltenburg 2014). As Zaller (1992) notes, attitude formation has close ties to the information elites provide about political affairs. In other words, the flow of political information from important actors, including but not limited to political elites and the news media, plays a central role in structuring public opinion (see also Chong and Druckman 2007), and there is little reason to expect this to be different when it comes to the Court. Some of the literature on institutional legitimacy echoes these findings, suggesting that the press may help the Court safeguard its diffuse support. For instance, positivity theory (Gibson, Caldeira, and Spence 2003b; Gibson and Caldeira 2009; Gibson, Lodge, and Woodson 2014) draws a link between symbolic and descriptive portrayals of the judiciary, which often reinforce the message that courts are different, and supportive attitudes toward it. On the other hand, sensationalistic (Johnston and Bartels 2010) and politicized (Hitt and Searles 2018) coverage may lead citizens to view the courts through a political lens, potentially damaging support. In short, media coverage shapes

Perceptions of a Pro-business Court 53

not only the window through which citizens evaluate the political world, but also their attitudes about the Court.

Little systematic research has explored press portrayals of the Court in the wake of rulings such as *Citizens United* (see Davis 2014; Ura 2014 for more general discussions). But the previous chapter provides some clues. It demonstrates that media coverage may tend to zero in on group beneficiaries when describing high-profile rulings. Are similar dynamics in play with respect to big business and *Citizens United*? While there exist a number of avenues through which the media may have portrayed the Court after the decision, one important frame is the emphasis of a link between the institution and business interests.

To determine whether such a frame gained traction, I follow Collins and Cooper (2012), who develop an indicator of Supreme Court media coverage using a geographically and ideologically diverse set of major newspapers: the *New York Times*, *Washington Post*, *Los Angeles Times*, and *Chicago Tribune*. Employing these four papers, I conducted a keyword search for monthly mentions of the "Supreme Court" in the same paragraph as "corporate," "corporation," or "business." This provides a measure of how frequently coverage associated the judiciary with business interests and whether this has changed in recent terms.

Figure 4.1 plots a monthly time series of the number of stories mentioning the Court and business both by source and in the aggregate across all four papers. The announcement of *Citizens United*, in January 2010, demarcates the series into pre- and post-ruling coverage. The data demonstrate a significant and lasting increase in portrayals of the Court with corporations after the ruling. This is visible both across all news sources and in the total volume of coverage.

For example, it has long been understood that the *New York Times* offers the most robust coverage of the Court among the major national news outlets (Epstein and Segal 2000), and this pattern is observable in Figure 4.1, which offers a measure of face validity to the keyword search approach. In 2006, the *Times* published about eight stories per month that mentioned the Court and business groups together. This had fallen slightly by 2009, the year before *Citizens United* was decided. Then, coverage of the Court–business link doubled in the year of the ruling. In January 2010 alone, when the ruling was announced, the *Times* published 28 stories linking the Court with corporate interests. The other newspapers published 23 stories each, on average, that mentioned the link during this month. Furthermore, the shift in coverage sustained over time. In four of the five years after the ruling, the *Times* published more stories that mentioned the Court–business link than it did during *any* of the four years preceding the ruling. The patterns are similar in other papers.

The volume of coverage making the link between the Court and big business is substantial. On average, the four major newspapers published a total of over

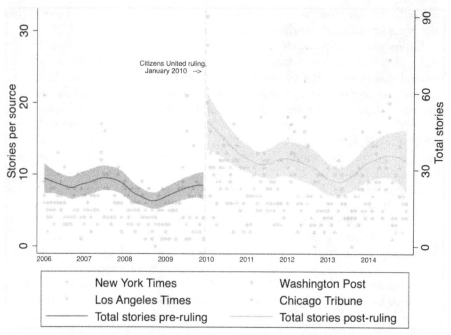

FIGURE 4.1 News coverage linking the Court with big business, by month
Note: Each dot represents the number of stories per month that mention the Supreme Court and corporations in proximity. Stories were selected using the Collins and Cooper (2012) method. Curves are lines of best fit, using a Kernel-weighted local polynomial smoothing, for total stories per month across all four sources. *Citizens United* was announced in January 2010, after which coverage of the Court–business link was significantly more prominent.

350 such stories in each of the five years after the ruling. This equates to about one story per day. Given what is known about the paucity of media coverage of the Court (e.g., Strickler 2014), this is considerable. It is likely that even mildly attentive observers of politics were exposed to discussions of the Court–business link, specifically in years immediately following *Citizens United*, and in all likelihood, this exposure took place repeatedly and on multiple occasions.

On the other hand, coverage did indeed fall a bit as the case receded from memory. It dipped to near its pre-decision levels three years after the ruling, in 2013, but then ticked back up in the periods that followed. Such coverage provides an informational basis – the Court's tie with big business – through which citizens can evaluate the institution.

Applying the Group Antipathy Hypothesis

For even moderately attentive observers of politics, a link between the Court and big business was likely visible in the years following *Citizens United*.

Study B: Survey Evidence

Additionally, many Americans express quite strong (and, as will be shown, oftentimes very negative) opinions about big business and corporate interests. They may readily draw on these opinions as a means to formulate assessments of political affairs involving the group. Indeed, these negative attitudes may help explain the decision's deep unpopularity itself since previous studies (e.g., Lupia 1994) show that citizens use group cues as a heuristic that allows them to make informed judgments about political actors and complex political affairs in other contexts.

In short, the post–*Citizens United* era features a highly visible link between business organizations and the Supreme Court. In assessing the institution, citizens have the ability to make this same attitudinal link, relying upon their feelings toward corporations when determining their level of diffuse support for the judiciary. This leads to the hypothesis that, as dislike of big business increases, citizens will report lower levels of Supreme Court legitimacy post–*Citizens United*.

STUDY B: SURVEY EVIDENCE

To test theoretical expectations, I again rely on data from The American Panel Survey (TAPS), administered by the Weidenbaum Center at Washington University (Smith 2013). The survey and key items are described fully in Chapter 3 and Appendix. The independent variable of theoretical interest in this study involves the degree to which a citizen feels unfavorable toward big business. I measure this with a simple feeling thermometer, a widely employed measure of affect (e.g., Iyengar, Sood, and Lelkes 2012), which respondents used to rate their degree of warmth toward "big business" on an 11-point scale. To create the *Business antipathy* measure, I reverse code responses to range from 0 to 1, with higher values indicating more negative feelings toward business groups. The mean level of disfavor on the *Business antipathy* measure, about 0.55, is somewhat high when compared to other groups like whites and African Americans, indicating that citizens generally view big business unfavorably, a fact that fits with anecdotal evidence about the negative response that many Americans had to *Citizens United*. I include control variables to account for other predictors of legitimacy, all of which are also described in Chapter 3. These include antipathy toward the other groups previously discussed, fundamental political values, and ideological disagreement, among other factors.

Analysis

Table 4.1 presents results from ordinary least squares (OLS) regressions that add business dislike to the main models from Chapter 3. This allows us to control for the existing ingredients that we know to shape legitimacy while exploring whether an additional group-based consideration exerts similar effects. The coefficient of interest is that on the *Business antipathy* variable,

TABLE 4.1 *Dislike for big business and Supreme Court legitimacy*

	(1) May 2012	(2) July 2012	(3) Jan 2013	(4) July 2013
Business antipathy	−0.08*	−0.07*	−0.06*	−0.05
	(0.03)	(0.03)	(0.03)	(0.04)
Gay antipathy	0.03	−0.03	−0.03	−0.07*
	(0.03)	(0.03)	(0.04)	(0.04)
Immigrant antipathy	−0.06	−0.15*	−0.11*	−0.12*
	(0.04)	(0.04)	(0.04)	(0.04)
Black antipathy	0.01	0.01	0.00	0.03
	(0.03)	(0.04)	(0.04)	(0.04)
Labor union antipathy	−0.04	0.01	−0.03	−0.02
	(0.03)	(0.03)	(0.03)	(0.03)
Political tolerance	0.09*	0.13*	0.12*	0.19*
	(0.03)	(0.03)	(0.03)	(0.03)
Minority liberty	0.25*	0.21*	0.27*	0.22*
	(0.04)	(0.04)	(0.05)	(0.05)
Rule of law	0.21*	0.29*	0.22*	0.21*
	(0.05)	(0.05)	(0.06)	(0.06)
Ideological distance	−0.18*	−0.13*	−0.18*	−0.19*
	(0.03)	(0.03)	(0.03)	(0.03)
Knowledge	0.21*	0.23*	0.22*	0.18*
	(0.04)	(0.04)	(0.04)	(0.05)
Republican	−0.00	−0.06*	−0.05*	−0.05*
	(0.02)	(0.02)	(0.02)	(0.02)
Education	0.12*	0.17*	0.18*	0.11*
	(0.03)	(0.03)	(0.03)	(0.04)
Income	0.03	0.01	−0.00	−0.00
	(0.03)	(0.03)	(0.03)	(0.03)
Female	−0.03	0.00	−0.01	−0.01
	(0.02)	(0.02)	(0.02)	(0.02)
Black	0.03	0.08*	0.03	−0.00
	(0.03)	(0.03)	(0.03)	(0.04)
Hispanic	0.04	0.01	0.01	−0.00
	(0.03)	(0.03)	(0.03)	(0.03)
R^2	0.368	0.405	0.400	0.370
N	685	683	679	655

Note: Results are estimated OLS coefficients with standard errors in parentheses. *$p < 0.05$ (one-tailed). The number of observations differs slightly from Chapter 3 due to missing data on covariates added to the models.

and it is statistically significant in three of the four models and in the direction of expectation across all four. This indicates that, in most instances, the Court enjoys less legitimacy when respondents view corporations in unfavorable terms. The effect is strong at first, about two years after *Citizens United*, but

Study B: Survey Evidence

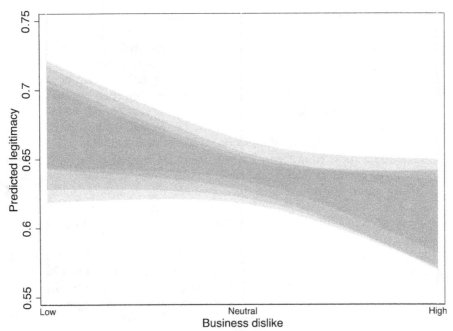

FIGURE 4.2 Variations in business affect and predicted legitimacy
Note: Figure displays confidence intervals for the effect of business dislike on predicted legitimacy for each of the four models. Lines of best fit are not included for simplicity of visualization, but the results are similar across all models. Substantively, the figure shows that business dislike has a highly consistent effect on legitimacy across multiple points in time post–*Citizens United*, although the effect falls just short of significance in model 4. On average, legitimacy is predicted to decline from approximately 0.67 to 0.61 as antipathy toward big business increases from low to high, a change between approximately the 61st and 50th percentiles in the dependent variable.

it becomes a bit more muted as we move into 2013. Finally, by July of 2013, the effect of business antipathy remains negative but falls just short of statistical significance, potentially indicating that its influence has weakened by this point. The pattern makes some sense, consistent with an interpretation that the ruling sharply influenced perceptions that the Court was pro-business, but this perception may have gradually died out as the case receded from memory and other rulings were issued.

On average across the models, movement from strongly positive to strongly negative feelings about business is predicted to shift Court legitimacy by about −0.06 points on the 0–1 scale. This is meaningful movement, an estimated effect of about one half the size of that for political tolerance, which has long been seen as one of the strongest predictors of diffuse support (e.g., Caldeira and Gibson 1992). Simply put, this effect suggests that citizens who view big business in negative terms often see the modern Supreme Court as more illegitimate than others.

Figure 4.2 visualizes this effect, plotting the predicted confidence intervals for legitimacy as business dislike varies over time. It is interesting to note the persistence of the negative effect. Not only does antipathy toward big business associate with Supreme Court illegitimacy, but its influence operates across multiple models over the course of 2012 and 2013, a period well after the Court's release of *Citizens United*. Of course, we must be cautious about attributing the effect to the ruling alone given the data available to us. At the same time, we know from Figure 4.1 that media coverage linking the Court to big business was prevalent years after the decision. Ultimately, we should guardedly interpret these results since they are not necessarily indicative of the effect of a single ruling alone, but rather what appears to be a more general perception, aided by the media, that tied the Roberts Court to big business groups.

It should also be mentioned that the influence of antipathy toward big business suggests that the results to this point are not a product of ideological considerations alone. While liberals are more likely to view corporations with disfavor, in turn negatively impacting their assessments of the Supreme Court, other groups like gays and immigrants tend to be held in lower esteem by conservatives. In other words, ideological preferences do not seem to have a consistent effect that could account for the combined patterns displayed across Chapters 3 and 4. Rather, it is the tie between the Court and groups of diverse ideological preferences that affects institutional legitimacy.

Turning briefly to the control variables in Table 4.1, we see predictable effects from considerations such as political knowledge, democratic values, and ideological distance from the Court. The former help safeguard the institution's diffuse support, whereas ideological distance has negative effects. Notably, we also see consistent effects from the key variables of theoretical interest that were originally identified in Chapter 3, indicating that negative views toward gays and immigrants continue to matter following relevant rulings even after accounting for anti-business affect. Overall, the survey results demonstrate that in order to understand the legitimacy of the modern institution, multiple considerations should be taken into account, and an important yet heretofore overlooked one involves popular antipathy toward the groups – both powerful and marginalized, right and left – found at the center of high-profile Supreme Court rulings.

STUDY C (BIG BUSINESS): EXPERIMENTAL EVIDENCE

While Study B shows an association between negative feelings about big business and negative assessments of the Court, it offers only limited leverage on the underpinnings of this relationship. Clearly, *Citizens United* represented an important and high salience signal, and our examination of media coverage is suggestive. But we cannot necessarily attribute the correlations found in Table 4.1 to any one action of the Court. A critical question thus becomes whether *specific* Supreme Court rulings concerning big business lead Americans to reconsider their diffuse support. Separating out these effects with greater precision requires a targeted research design. By leveraging the power of experimentation, we can isolate whether rulings concerning corporations have the ability to impact the institution's legitimacy.

Design

In the summer of 2018, I administered a large-scale survey experiment using a sample of respondents recruited by Survey Sampling International (SSI). SSI's participant pool is managed to allow the selection of samples to reflect the target population, in this case voting age US adults. SSI balanced respondents for this study by age, gender, ethnicity, and census region. Potential participants were contacted with notifications, including by email, and once within SSI's system, participants were matched with an available survey using multiple points of randomization. Respondents were replaced for straight-lining and speeding as well as the failure of two attention check questions, which could harm data quality. While the study was designed to test multiple implications of the group antipathy model (see Chapters 5 and 6), one particular goal was to isolate the effects that perceptions of a pro-business Court have on the institution's legitimacy. Therefore, for this portion of the analysis, I focus on 1,027 survey respondents who were randomly assigned to receive a campaign spending experiment focused on big business.[1]

In this portion of the experiment, the goal was to isolate the effects of group antipathy while holding other legal and policy considerations constant. There are a number of avenues for doing so, but perhaps the most demanding test is one that takes a single legal doctrine and manipulates whether big business (or some other group) stands to benefit. In other words, given identical rulings, do citizens evaluate the Court differently based only on whether they perceive benefits for a disliked group (such as big business) or some other segment?

To implement the experiment, respondents read a vignette modeled on actual news coverage of the Supreme Court's campaign finance jurisprudence. This helps to increase the mundane realism of the study and, coupled with the SSI sample, strengthens its external validity. A key feature of this coverage is its ability to allow for realistic manipulation of whether big business (or some other group) stood to benefit from the Court's rulings. Here, I focus on labor unions as the alternative group since these represent a natural counterpoint to big business organizations and tend to be viewed more favorably by liberals.

---

[1] A portion of the analyses presented in Studies C and D, which include multiple groups and are expanded upon in Chapters 5 and 6, is discussed in Zilis (in press).

TABLE 4.2 *Vignette for campaign finance experiment*

Supreme Court Further Expands Role of [Labor Union / Corporate] Money in Campaigns

Washington (AP) – In a ruling with profound implications for the role of money in American campaigns, the Supreme Court has punched an even bigger hole in the complex web of federal campaign finance regulations. The case concerned the ability for a [labor union / corporation] to support specific candidates for office. The Supreme Court's earlier decisions had permitted [union / corporate] spending on issue advertising, but the Court has now substantially extended the right to spend so that it includes candidate advertising. As a result, some [unions / companies] are vowing to take a much more aggressive approach in the upcoming elections.

Critics have warned that decision calls into question fundamental principles of equal access in American democracy. They fear that organizations will spend so much money they will be able to pick and choose who wins elections with little recourse from ordinary citizens. But the ruling has been cheered by those who said it returns the country to the core free speech precept that political speech should be protected, no matter who is speaking.

The Court argues it is returning to "ancient First Amendment principles." The stronger protections for [labor / corporate] influence in elections mean that a host of new legal issues may arise. In one recent case out of New York, a [union / corporate] board authorized spending over $20,000 to attack a judicial candidate as "unfit for office." The candidate, Melanie Taylor, sought an injunction, but a district court, applying the new Supreme Court standard, allowed the advertising campaign to go forward.

Now some [unions / corporations] are vowing an even more active role in politics. "The government may not suppress our right to speak on issues important to us," said John Davis, president of [National Labor, an activist trade union / National Investing, a wealth management firm]. "The ruling represents a shot in the arm for [workers / companies] whose voices had been suppressed."

Thus, all respondents read a campaign finance law vignette, but about half were randomly assigned to the big business condition and the others to the labor union condition. The full vignette is displayed in Table 4.2. Again, note that all information about the rulings is identical *except* the business/union manipulation.

The key dependent variable is *Legitimacy*, measured as before by utilizing the standard seven-item scale (Gibson and Nelson 2015). It includes questions about controlling the Supreme Court, making it less independent, removing judges, judges as politicians, doing away with the institution, removal of its jurisdiction, and the extent to which it is mixed up in politics. Responses to these items load strongly on a single underlying factor. I use a summative index ranging from 0 to 28 with higher values indicating stronger institutional loyalty.

To test the Group Antipathy Hypothesis, we need to explore the interaction between the randomly assigned treatment and whether a respondent is

Study C (Big Business): Experimental Evidence

predisposed to feel favorably toward big business. In this study and the experimental studies that follow, I leverage two considerations in order to create an overall index that proxies expected levels of group antipathy. First, the experiments I administer concern a wide variety of social groups, half of which the political right tends to view more favorably and half of which the political left does. This is clearly true with respect to big business (viewed more favorably by Republicans and conservatives and validated with pre-testing) versus labor unions (viewed more favorably by Democrats and liberals), and it is also true with respect to the other groups in the experimental studies described in the coming chapter. Second, the experimental treatments consist *only* of the randomly primed group, meaning that, with effective randomization, we can be confident that no other factors affect cross-condition variation in outcomes.

With these considerations in mind, I create a summary index of left–right political *Predispositions* to proxy the expected levels of group antipathy in the experiments. For example, the simple expectation in this module is that legitimacy should be lower among left-leaning respondents (who feel more negative toward big business) than right-wing respondents when exposed to the business treatment. I generate this index by summing responses to standard seven-point measures of party identification and ideology, although note that the results are substantively similar if we disaggregate the partisanship and ideology measures. The summative index ranges from 0 to 12, with the former representing self-identified very liberal, strong Democrats and the latter very conservative, strong Republicans.[2]

In addition to the measure of predispositions (combining party identification and ideology), I control for ethnicity (*Hispanic*), race (*Black*), gender (*Female*), and *Age*, measured with a categorical variable. I also use a three-item index to measure political *Knowledge*. See appendix for question wording.

I model the outcome of interest, *Legitimacy*, using a simple regression with key independent variables for predispositions and treatment assignment, as well as various controls. Our main interest concerns the interaction between group considerations and predispositions, which allows us to explore whether the identity politics surrounding big business influences diffuse support.

---

[2] Rather than use left–right predispositions to proxy dislike, another option is the feeling thermometer approach applied earlier. However, because many different groups are involved in the experimental tests, this would require a large battery of feeling thermometer questions. While not problematic on its face, this would slightly increase survey time and fatigue for respondents. A bigger cost is demand effects. By including a large battery of group thermometers, this would raise the possibility that respondents guess at the purposes of the experiment and alter their answers in response. This may also artificially raise the salience of groups in respondents' minds, making them more attentive to group considerations while reading the vignette and in turn decreasing verisimilitude. Ultimately, the proxy approach is a better option, buttressed by the fact that, in a separate survey, I show that group antipathy and left–right predispositions are strongly and predictably correlated.

Analysis

Table 4.3 and Figure 4.3 present the main results from the business experiment and they show strong support for the hypothesis that group considerations shape attitudes toward the Court. The coefficient on the interaction term *Group treatment* Predispositions* is of particular interest. This represents the effect of the treatment as attitudes toward the treated group become more negative. The negative coefficient here indicates a loss in legitimacy for the Court. In other words, the model shows that predispositions condition the effect of treatment: when a campaign finance ruling is framed such that labor unions benefit, conservatives react negatively. But *when the identical decision is framed to benefit big business, liberals react negatively.*

Figure 4.3 displays this effect graphically, showing how predicted legitimacy varies based on the treatment and predispositions. The left half of the figure displays effects among liberals and Democrats, who tend to be much less favorably disposed toward big business groups. As anticipated, these individuals rate the Supreme Court as less legitimate when its rulings benefit corporations as

TABLE 4.3 *Predicting institutional legitimacy, business experiment*

	(1) Campaign Spending Experiment
Group treatment	1.69*
	(0.65)
Predispositions	0.16*
	(0.07)
Group treatment	−0.20*
* Predispositions	(0.10)
Age	0.55*
	(0.11)
Female	0.12
	(0.36)
Black	−1.36*
	(0.56)
Hispanic	−0.91
	(0.57)
Knowledge	1.79*
	(0.19)
R^2	0.144
N	1027

Note: Results are estimated OLS coefficients with standard errors in parentheses. *$p < 0.05$ (one-tailed).

Study C (Big Business): Experimental Evidence

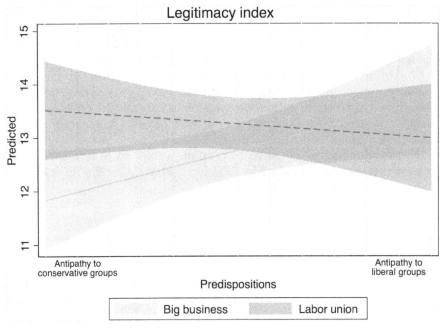

FIGURE 4.3 Experimental results
Note: Predicted effects and confidence intervals from the model in Table 4.3. Substantively, this shows how big business polarizes opinions about the legitimacy of the Supreme Court.

opposed to unions, with their predicted level of legitimacy falling from 13.70 to 11.83 among the strongest liberals, which represents roughly the difference between the 65th and 46th percentiles in support. Now, turning to the right half of the figure, we observe the inverse pattern for conservatives. When the Court rules in favor of unions, its legitimacy suffers a bit among the political right, although treatment is much less polarizing than is it for liberals.

This asymmetry is interesting in and of itself. It demonstrates that it is not only the far left that penalizes the Court for a pro-business ruling, but also left-leaners and even the political center. This comports with patterns in the survey data showing that a very large number of citizens possess high levels of antipathy toward big business. In this module, antipathy affects both liberals *and* moderates, with predictable negative effects on diffuse support. The result speaks to reactions in the wake of some of the Court's most notable rulings concerning corporations and *Citizens United* in particular. The decision was not only controversial but tremendously unpopular, in spite of the fact that the Court majority framed it as a simple extension of its First Amendment precedent. One reason for the negative reactions may be the high levels of antipathy that many Americans hold toward big business interests.

Moving on from the main results in the table, we can pause to consider a few other findings. The most predictable one helps to square this study with the existing literature on diffuse support: political knowledge is predicted to substantially heighten legitimacy. A few other subgroups show significant results as well. African Americans are, on average, a bit less supportive of the Court, perhaps comporting with Gibson and Caldeira's (1992) finding about the institution's rightward turn on civil rights matters. On the other hand, the significant coefficient on age shows an increase in support among older respondents.

What can we make of these patterns on the whole? To be sure, they do not offer direct evidence concerning *Citizens United*, although the campaign finance rulings that the experiment describes share important legal and political features with this case. They do, however, indicate how the Court's legitimacy suffers among Americans that are unfavorably disposed to the groups its campaign finance rulings benefit. Corporations are prominent among these. Of equal note is the fact that the rulings themselves, be they framed to benefit business or labor, are substantively identical. This is the power of experimental design, allowing us to isolate groups while holding law and policy constant. When we do this, we observe further evidence that the Court's entanglement with business interests has the capacity to undermine its legitimacy.

DISCUSSION

The results presented here further elucidate the importance of group-based considerations when it comes to popular evaluations of the Supreme Court. This chapter makes a few contributions. First, while finding evidence consistent with that presented in Chapter 3, it offers novel context. Given the right confluence of circumstances, rulings in favor of either liberal *or* conservative segments impact Court legitimacy. In addition, these results add nuance about the factors linking social group antipathy and evaluations of the judiciary. The media plays a key role. One of the reasons *Citizens United* may have influenced public opinion so potently has to do with its sustained coverage. Immediately after the Court ruled, the media made a habit of publishing stories that linked the judiciary with big business groups, and this persisted over a long period of time. Not all of this coverage necessarily portrayed the Court as a friend to corporations, but the vast majority did. Coupled with statements from political actors and even the justices themselves that depicted the institution as opening the door to corporate influence, this presented a clear portrait of a judiciary that favored big business. As with the same-sex marriage and immigration rulings, this coverage had direct consequences for how Americans perceived the institution. News coverage plays a critical role in tying the Supreme Court with groups in society.

Our brief examination of media coverage following *Citizens United* further hints at the persistence of group-based thinking about the Supreme Court. On

Discussion

average, the volume of reporting linking the Court and corporations remained higher even four and five years after the decision than it was immediately preceding the ruling. This durable Court–business link suggests that perceptions of a Court that is friendly to specific groups may remain long after a high-profile ruling is released. In this way, Chapter 4 complements evidence from Chapter 3, which found that group-based thinking about the Supreme Court persisted over one year following its immigration holding. At the same time, it is important to acknowledge the fact that such perceptions, while durable, may nonetheless wax and wane in response to multiple factors. The considerations emphasized by political elites and the news media play a prominent role in the shape of public opinion (Zaller 1992). Once these actors cease to highlight the Court's ties with a specific group, public perceptions may respond in kind. We may have witnessed this waning given the slightly diminishing effect of business dislike that we observed in the survey data.

Actions taken by the justices themselves may also have direct implications for public perceptions. Members of the Court's liberal wing rallied against *Citizens United* for years after the ruling was released, much as members of its conservative wing argued the Court acted as a pawn of the gay rights movement after rulings such as *Windsor*. Not all decisions, however, bring out such venom. This may help to dissipate the negative influence of group antipathy. The Court as an institution can take specific steps to further circumscribe these negative consequences. For example, it may choose not to grant certiorari to rulings that involve controversial groups or it may even issue rulings that go against a group's interest.

With the exception of the just-presented Study C, a major limitation to the findings presented thus far concerns the modest leverage they offer on the causal connection between group antipathy and Supreme Court legitimacy. To be clear, the evidence is *consistent* with the idea that when the public comes to perceive the Court as a friend to specific groups – following, say, a high-profile ruling – it has consequences for the institution's public support. But the manuscript has yet to demonstrate directly that this perception, alone, is the *critical factor* in structuring legitimacy. The best opportunity to examine the direct link between perceptions and support occurs in a carefully controlled setting. In the following chapter, I turn to this approach, presenting multiple experimental studies of the group antipathy account.

5

Experimental Tests of the Group Antipathy Model

On June 26, 2017, the Supreme Court stepped into a dispute with major political ramifications. The justices granted petitions for certiorari surrounding challenges to President Donald Trump's Executive Order 13780, Protecting the Nation from Foreign Terrorist Entry into the United States. The order had sparked controversy even before taking effect. While it ostensibly sought to "prevent infiltration by foreign terrorists," critics argued that it was "motivated principally by a desire to exclude Muslims from the United States" (*Trump v. International Refugee Assistance Project* [2017], 5). Some lower courts agreed. Thus, the Court's decision thrust it into the political spotlight involving a prominent religious minority in the United States.

In September 2017, just days before the Supreme Court was scheduled to hear full arguments in the case, the administration revised its executive order. The justices remanded the case with instructions to dismiss as moot, temporarily ending the controversy. Yet, whether the Court would find anti-Muslim bias at the core of future actions remained an open question. Ultimately, a related case reached the Court (*Trump v. Hawaii* [2018]).

The executive order saga illustrates how quickly controversies with group implications can engulf the judiciary. Within the span of 9 months, the order had been created, revised, reviewed by multiple lower courts, and placed on the Supreme Court's docket. The controversy also suggests that diverse groups have their day in Court. In the modern era, the institution has considered cases that have clear implications for not only immigrants, African Americans, and same-sex couples, but also Muslims, other religious minorities (*Employment Division v. Smith* [1990]), racial and ethnic categorizations (*Arizona v. United States* [2012]), and distinct sociodemographic segments (*Citizens United v. F.E.C.* [2010]), among others. It has ruled in favor of both conservative and liberal segments. How does the group antipathy model relate to the many other groups whose claims come before the Supreme Court?

Overview and Methodology 67

This chapter aims to accomplish three primary objectives. First and most basically, I examine the group antipathy model with the most diverse set of empirical evidence yet available. Using an experimental approach, I randomize exposure to information about rulings concerning an array of groups, evaluating the effects of the Court's support for various racial, ethnic, religious, social, and sociodemographic groups. Second, by manipulating, as opposed to measuring, group-based cues surrounding the Court, I offer rigorous tests of the group antipathy model. Finally, this chapter enables a fuller consideration of how the model fits with existing understandings of Supreme Court legitimacy. Rather than simply controlling for alternative accounts, I am able to unpack how group antipathy enriches our understanding of legitimacy. Belying the assumption that citizens evaluate the policy implications of rulings alone, I find that their interpretation depends, critically, on the groups that stand to benefit. I find that the same ruling, depending on who it benefits, leads to significant differences between the political left and the political right in their support for the Supreme Court.

In summary, this chapter provides the most diverse evidence yet available regarding the group antipathy model. The results indicate that negative feelings toward perceived beneficiaries lead to appreciable declines in Supreme Court legitimacy. This occurs even when the identical policy is at stake, as citizens evaluate even substantively equivalent rulings in distinct terms depending upon how they feel toward the groups involved.

OVERVIEW AND METHODOLOGY

By leveraging the power of experimental design, this chapter complements the evidence presented in Chapters 3 and 4 in a way that provides much greater clarity about the influence of group antipathy on institutional legitimacy. Specifically, I manipulate perceptions of the groups that the Court favors through the use of carefully controlled treatments administered by random assignment to respondents across four survey experiments. The internal validity of these studies is quite high, since I manipulate only a few key words (usually, the name of the group involved in a case) in each study. This leaves behind some of the messiness of the observational approaches, which involve decisions that have not only group-based implications but also legal and policy ramifications as well. In these studies, legal and policy ramifications are held constant.

Moreover, by using a diverse set of survey experiments, I show the influence that group antipathy has on legitimacy in multiple contexts and subject populations. I provide a summary in Table 5.1. The main experiment, Study C, offers perhaps the most demanding test of the antipathy model and is administered to a nationally reflective sample of the public. I use an "identical rulings" approach, which means that respondents are assigned to read about identical Court rulings but randomized based on which groups these decisions are

TABLE 5.1 *Summary of experimental evidence*

Study	Key description of Court action	Groups	Method
C	Identical rulings concerning oppositional groups	Prolife, prochoice, Muslims, Christian fundamentalists, labor unions, big business	Nationally reflective sample from Survey Sampling International (SSI)
D	Identical rulings concerning oppositional groups	Prolife, prochoice, Muslims, Christian fundamentalists	mTurk sample
E	Multiple rulings concerning a single group	Immigrants, African Americans, Muslims, big business	mTurk sample
F	Pending case	Muslims	mTurk sample

framed to benefit. Chapter 4 presented initial evidence from this study, showing how citizens assess the Court in starkly different terms depending on whether they perceive its campaign finance jurisprudence to benefit business or labor, but I present broader evidence in this chapter, spanning four other groups and two other areas of law. Study D is a second study that uses this same design, showing similar effects in a convenience sample of the population.

Next, Study E, involves a "multiple rulings" manipulation. I assign subjects to read about the Court's jurisprudence with respect to one of four groups (immigrants, African Americans, Muslims, or big business), randomly varying whether they learn that the Court has consistently ruled in favor of or against the group. This serves as a complement to Studies C and D, which focus on one high-profile ruling at a time. In Study E, I show that perceptions of Court favoritism toward specific groups can also come about in response to a larger number of non-landmark decisions, with predictable implications for legitimacy. Finally, Study F uses a "pending case" design to explore how granting certiorari to a group-rights case can have implications for legitimacy, even if the Supreme Court has not yet issued a ruling.

STUDY C (ALL GROUPS): IDENTICAL DECISIONS AND GROUP ANTIPATHY

To this point, we have amassed an array of evidence suggesting that both specific rulings as well as general perceptions of Court favoritism toward groups shape legitimacy assessments. Perhaps, the most demanding test that we can supply of the model, however, is one that explores whether substantively *identical* rulings have a variant impact on legitimacy when framed to favor distinct groups in society. This allows us to examine a critical *but for*

Study C (All Groups): Identical Decisions and Group Antipathy

proposition: *But for the groups its rulings concern, the Court could expect a consistent stream of support from citizens.*

Consider the First Amendment, which establishes fundamental free speech protections, irrespective of a speaker's identity. This implies that courts must evaluate identical acts of speech or protest using the same framework, no matter the speaker. What happens when we put the proposition of public support to the test under this framework?

According to conventional wisdom, citizens will not distinguish between otherwise identical rulings that involve distinct groups. Citizens may interpret strong free speech protections, for example, to indicate the Court is "liberal" and committed to protecting civil liberties. Thus, the story goes, liberals will view the institution in positive terms, regardless of whether speech protections are applied to the National Rifle Association or the American Civil Liberties Union.

The group antipathy model sees things differently. Because Americans possess strong feelings toward groups like the National Rifle Association (NRA) and American Civil Liberties Union (ACLU), the model anticipates that they will leverage their feelings as a means to assess the situation. In other words, there are reasons to expect that antipathy toward the groups plays a key role in shaping attitudes. Most simply, we can extend the Group Antipathy Hypothesis to suggest that Court rulings benefitting conservative groups (such as the NRA) should cause liberals to judge the institution as less legitimate, even when these rulings are substantively identical to ones that favor more liberal segments (such as the ACLU).

Design

I present the full version of the experiment first introduced in Chapter 4 here. To review, this is based on a survey administered to a sample of respondents recruited by Survey Sampling International (SSI), managed to reflect the population of voting age US adults. All told, 3,117 respondents completed the survey. Appendix describes respondent demographic information and other sample attributes in more detail.

The survey included an embedded manipulation to isolate the effects of group considerations on legitimacy. Respondents were randomly assigned to read a vignette describing recent rulings of the Supreme Court concerning various groups in American society. The vignettes were designed to emphasize external validity, modeled based on actual news items and concerning high-profile groups that have had cases come before the Court.[1] The business/union vignette, presented in Chapter 4, represented one of multiple conditions. In addition to big business and union groups, these included other segments that conservatives tend

---

[1] I address fully the steps taken to maximize external validity in the Appendix.

to view more positively than liberals (prolife groups, Christian fundamentalists) and their counterparts that liberals tend to rate more favorably (prochoice groups, Muslims). A key feature of the design involves its ability to isolate group-specific effects while holding law and policy constant. Table 5.2 presents the full experimental stimuli to illustrate. As it shows, rulings are described in *identical terms, so that the only factor that differs is the groups that benefit*. This is critical to getting at the idea that identity politics, and not sincere legal or policy disagreements, shape diffuse support.

For *Legitimacy*, I utilize our usual seven-item scale, scaled from 0 to 28, with higher values indicating stronger institutional loyalty. Full question wordings are presented in Appendix. The key independent variable is a respondent's political preferences, which are expected to interact with group-based considerations to shape legitimacy attitudes. For example, strong conservatives should find their support for the Court weakened when liberal groups benefit. I measure these preferences with an index of left–right *Predispositions*, which I generate by summing responses to standard seven-point measures of party identification and ideology. This is advisable because partisanship and ideology correlate strongly ($r = 0.63$, $p < 0.001$) and should jointly shape group-based feelings, although again note that the results are substantively similar if we disaggregate the measures. The summative index ranges from 0 (the political left) to 12 (the political right). I also include control variables as described in the previous chapter. In each of the models, our main interest concerns the interaction between group considerations and predispositions.

Analysis

Does the legitimacy of the Supreme Court vary based on group considerations, even after we hold the legal and political principles involved in a case constant? I explore this with a set of models in Table 5.3 and graphical interpretations, beginning in Figure 5.1. The main model focuses on the key interaction between the treatment and predispositions, while the fully interactive model explores how political knowledge conditions these effects.

To briefly summarize the main results, they show that the legitimacy of the Supreme Court varies meaningfully and predictably as a function of group-based considerations. This is represented by the significant coefficient on the interactive term in the main model, and it is visualized more fully in Figure 5.1, a few aspects of which are notable. First, the predicted levels of legitimacy take on the same cross-cutting pattern that we initially observed in the experimental analysis in Chapter 4. This means that liberals ascribe the Court significantly less institutional support when its rulings benefit groups like prolife activists, Christian fundamentalists, and corporations, whereas conservatives give it lower levels of support after it rules in favor of prochoice groups, Muslims, and labor unions. These differences occur despite the substantive equivalence of the rulings themselves. For very liberal Democrats, the predicted difference in

Study C (All Groups): Identical Decisions and Group Antipathy

TABLE 5.2 *Full experimental stimuli*

[Note: Free expression condition]

Supreme Court Allows [Pro-Choice/Pro-Life] Groups Leeway for Aggressive Protest

Washington (AP) – In response to recent developments at the Supreme Court, some [pro-choice/pro-life] groups are vowing to use strong new protest tactics to exercise their First Amendment rights. In the past 5 years, the Court has issued two rulings that substantially broaden the ability of [pro-choice/pro-life] groups to stage aggressive demonstrations near clinics, churches, and other public spaces. The rulings are based on the premise that the constitution protects even the most offensive language when it is under the guise of political protest.

In one landmark ruling, the Court held that even language that may "inflict great pain" is entitled to strong First Amendment protections. The lone dissenter in the case wrote that the Court was protecting "outrageous conduct" that would "allow the brutalization of innocent victims" targeted by aggressive protestors. In a second case, the Court invalidated "buffer zone" areas that had been implemented to protect ordinary citizens from harassment from aggressive protestors. All nine justices agreed that these protections violated the First Amendment.

Taken together, the decisions offer greater legal protection for [pro-choice/pro-life] groups who engage in aggressive protest. In one recent case out of Massachusetts, a small group of [pro-choice/pro-life] protestors blocked a sidewalk while shouting obscenities at counter-demonstrators. Three members of the group were arrested for breaching the peace, but a district court, applying recent Supreme Court standards, threw out the case.

As some [pro-choice/pro-life] groups consider new organizing strategies and aim to grow their bases of support, the Court's rulings have provided them a powerful tool. According to John James, the president of Americans for [**Choice/Life**], a [pro-choice/pro-life] lobbying group, "We now have the legal protection necessary to make sure the message of [choice/life] is heard, loud and clear."

[Note: Religious freedom condition]

Supreme Court Offers Legal Exemptions for [**Muslim/Christian Fundamentalist**] **Groups**

Washington (AP) – Recent developments at the Supreme Court have exempted [**Muslim/Christian fundamentalist**] organizations from federal law when compliance would raise a religious objection. In the past 10 years, the Court, under its religious freedom doctrine, has issued rulings that substantially broaden the ability of religious groups to ignore federal mandates. In response, some [**Muslim/Christian fundamentalist**] groups are vowing to seek exemptions from a wide variety of regulations.

In one landmark decision, issued in 2014, the Court ruled that even the most powerful religious organizations may object to federal law, including mandates to protect employee rights and prevent discrimination. These objections would then pave the way for exemptions so that the organizations do not have to comply with the law. The dissenting justices in the case argued that exemptions will allow religious groups with powerful lobbying organizations to gain special treatment. In an earlier case, a unanimous Court offered additional exemptions for religious groups.

Taken together, the decisions offer greater legal protection for [**Muslim/Christian fundamentalist**] organizations to flex their political muscle while enjoying immunity from some aspects of federal law. In one recent case out of Colorado, the owner of [an Islamic/a Christian] bookstore refused to answer questions posed by federal agents who were investigating child labor violations. After the owner cited a religious objection, a district court, applying recent Supreme Court standards, excused him from testifying.

As [Muslim/Christian fundamentalist] groups consider strategies to wield political influence, the Court's rulings have provided them a powerful tool. According to Jonathan Sharan, the head of [an Islamic/a fundamentalist] lobbying organization in Dallas, the rulings are "a shot in the arm for the often-overlooked rights of devout [Muslims / Christians]."

[Note: Campaign spending condition]
Supreme Court Further Expands Role of [Labor Union/Corporate] Money in Campaigns

Washington (AP) – In a ruling with profound implications for the role of money in American campaigns, the Supreme Court has punched an even bigger hole in the complex web of federal campaign finance regulations. The case concerned the ability for a [labor union/corporation] to support specific candidates for office. The Supreme Court's earlier decisions had permitted [union/corporate] spending on issue advertising, but the Court has now substantially extended the right to spend so that it includes candidate advertising. As a result, some [unions/companies] are vowing to take a much more aggressive approach in the upcoming elections.

Critics have warned that decision calls into question fundamental principles of equal access in American democracy. They fear that organizations will spend so much money they will be able to pick and choose who wins elections with little recourse from ordinary citizens. But the ruling has been cheered by those who said it returns the country to the core free speech precept that political speech should be protected, no matter who is speaking.

The Court argues it is returning to "ancient First Amendment principles." The stronger protections for [labor/corporate] influence in elections mean that a host of new legal issues may arise. In one recent case out of New York, a [union/corporate] board authorized spending over $20,000 to attack a judicial candidate as "unfit for office." The candidate, Melanie Taylor, sought an injunction, but a district court, applying the new Supreme Court standard, allowed the advertising campaign to go forward.

Now, some [unions/corporations] are vowing an even more active role in politics. "The government may not suppress our right to speak on issues important to us," said John Davis, president of [National Labor, an activist trade union/National Investing, a wealth management firm]. "The ruling represents a shot in the arm for [workers/companies] whose voices had been suppressed."

Note: A subject was randomly assigned to read one story, focused on a single policy and group.

legitimacy across treatment conditions varies between the 47th and 53rd percentiles, whereas for very conservative Republicans, it varies more substantially between the 53rd and 64th percentiles. This is interesting in and of itself, because it suggests that the political right responds a bit more aggressively to social group cues than the political left.

TABLE 5.3 *Predicting institutional legitimacy, identical decision experiment*

	(1) Main	(2) Interactive
Group treatment	1.16*	0.41
	(0.39)	(0.68)
Predispositions	0.15*	-0.00
	(0.04)	(0.07)
Group treatment * Predispositions	-0.20*	-0.04
	(0.06)	(0.10)
Age	0.65*	0.65*
	(0.07)	(0.07)
Female	0.14	0.13
	(0.21)	(0.21)
Black	-1.46*	-1.46*
	(0.34)	(0.34)
Hispanic	-0.50	-0.52
	(0.35)	(0.35)
Knowledge	1.61*	1.03*
	(0.11)	(0.29)
Group treatment * Knowledge	–	0.55
		(0.41)
Predispositions * Knowledge	–	0.11*
		(0.04)
Group treatment * Predispositions * Knowledge	–	-0.11
		(0.06)
R^2	0.129	0.131
N	3,117	3,117

Note: Results are estimated ordinary least squares (OLS) coefficients with standard errors in parentheses. *p < 0.05 (one-tailed).

On a related note, if we look at the slope of the two curves in the figure, we see that the effects of the conservative group treatments are more powerful than those from the liberal group treatments, leading to a steeper slope. There are two ways to potentially account for this asymmetry. First, it may be the case that the conservative treatments were a bit more "surprising" on average to respondents, leading to stronger effects. This would occur if respondents had *a priori* expectations that the Court would favor liberal groups but were then exposed to the opposite information. However, there is not much empirical support for this expectation. In Chapter 6, I analyze respondents' ideological perceptions of the Supreme Court from this study and I find that, on average, respondents perceive the institution as slightly right of center, or between the "moderate" and "slightly conservative" categories. There is therefore little reason to expect that the conservative group treatments to have been particularly surprising. A second and potentially better way to account for the asymmetry is to consider the possibility that antipathy is more keenly felt toward the conservative groups, versus the

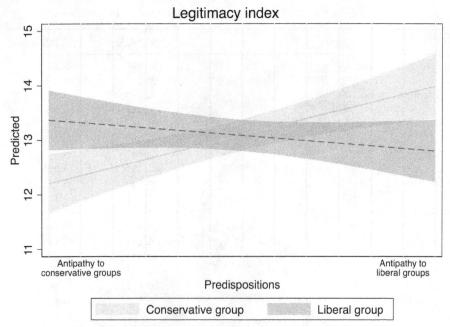

FIGURE 5.1 The effect of group attitudes on institutional legitimacy
Note: Predicted values and 95% confidence intervals from the main model in Table 5.1. Substantively, this shows how social groups polarize opinions about the legitimacy of the Supreme Court.

liberal groups, primed in the experiment. In other words, it is possible that citizens have powerful affective associations when it comes to groups like big business, but a bit more muted attitudes concerning, say, labor unions. This would lead to the steeper slope on the conservative treatment predictions in Figure 5.1.

In the main model, we also see other effects consistent with the findings from Chapter 4. Namely, African Americans display lower levels of diffuse support, whereas older respondents and the politically knowledgeable have high levels, squaring with the well-known idea that to know the Court is to love it. The relative size of group antipathy's effects is a bit more complex to interpret given the interactive specification, but one way we can do so involves looking at the distinct levels of legitimacy at the extremes of the left–right scale. For example, as we move from Democrats to Republicans, legitimacy is predicted to be nearly two points higher when a conservative group benefits from a ruling. The predicted two-point change is greater than the effect from racial identification and it is more substantial than the effect from a one-point increase in political knowledge, albeit less than the effect from movement across the range of the knowledge scale.

Given the critical role that knowledge plays in our theories of diffuse support, as well as the broader literature on heuristics and cue-taking, we would do well to explore whether knowledge also conditions the effects of

Study C (All Groups): Identical Decisions and Group Antipathy

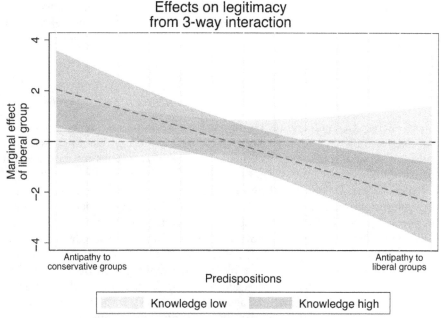

FIGURE 5.2 The interaction between groups and knowledge vis-à-vis legitimacy
Note: The figure displays marginal effects and 95% confidence intervals from the experimental treatment when interacted with knowledge and predispositions using the secondary legitimacy model from Table 5.3. Substantively, this shows that increased levels of political knowledge strengthen the effects of group considerations on Supreme Court legitimacy.

treatment. For this purpose, I present a second model featuring a three-way interaction and display a marginal effects plot in Figure 5.2.

The figure is interesting because it shows that the effects of the group treatment are concentrated among those with higher levels of political knowledge. Specifically, about 77% of the sample answered one or more political knowledge items correctly, and the model estimates a significant effect of treatment among individuals in this category. For example, for high-knowledge liberals, exposure to a liberal group treatment has the marginal effect of buttressing support for the Court by about 2 points on the legitimacy scale. But for knowledgeable conservatives, exposure to a liberal group treatment has the marginal effect of depressing it by more than 2 points. However, the treatment does not have a significant influence on legitimacy for the remaining 23% (very low knowledge) portion of the sample.

This result suggests how integrating social group thinking into our models of diffuse support modifies conventional wisdom. To know the Court is to love it, but in some cases, only conditionally. In fact, in certain contexts, knowledge can actually prove detrimental to the Court, polarizing its legitimacy along group-based demarcations. Those with higher degrees of knowledge place significant weight on whether rulings benefit groups that they feel warmly toward. When they do not, loyalty to the Court suffers.[2] I explore a series of additional results below.

Disaggregated Legitimacy

Next, Table 5.4 and Figure 5.3 unpack the results disaggregated by each specific legitimacy item. One reason that this is important has to do with the substantive significance. For example, some legitimacy items tap into general perceptions of the Court – e.g., whether it is "too mixed up in politics" – whereas others deal with making fundamental changes to, or even abolishing, the institution (see Bartels and Johnston 2020). While the former are certainly important, and all of these shed light on the concept of diffuse support more broadly (Gibson, Caldeira, and Spence 2003a), one may worry less about the harmfulness of group antipathy if its effects are limited to politicization perceptions. However, they are not. The table indicates that the coefficients on the key interactions are consistently significant for the legitimacy items when modeled separately. This even includes the aggressive "do away with" the Court item.

The figure displaying predicted effects shows some interesting patterns. While the antipathy interaction has similar substantive effects across the seven items, the mean level of predicted support for the Court varies substantially by item. The item-specific mean is at its highest for the "do away with Court" item (the bottom left panel), indicating that many respondents are supportive of the institution when this item is asked. This makes sense. Getting rid of the institution is perhaps the most dramatic step that could be taken to threaten the rule of law, so citizens will likely oppose it in all but the most extreme cases. Nonetheless, group antipathy has effects on opinion even when it comes to this item; liberals are more willing to abolish the institution when the Court favors groups they dislike, and vice versa. These patterns echo in the other items as well, although the average level of support for the institution is a bit lower. For example, respondents express a relatively high desire for stronger control of the Court and elimination of its independence.

Finally, it is interesting to note that while liberal and conservative response patterns are generally inverse and symmetrical across all seven items, the "remove justices" item shows something a bit different. Conservatives are, on average, a bit less willing to endorse the removal of justices, and they are *very* unlikely to do so when the law seems to benefit conservative groups. This pattern may be attributable to the political context from the time at which the survey was administered. In the late summer of 2018, the Supreme Court

---

[2] In the Appendix, I conduct a similar analysis using the knowledge interaction for Studies A and B and find the same type of effects in an observational setting.

TABLE 5.4 *Predicting institutional legitimacy, disaggregated*

	Legit item 1	Legit item 2	Legit item 3	Legit item 4	Legit item 5	Legit item 6	Legit item 7
Group treatment	0.15*	0.24*	0.11	0.20*	0.15	0.15*	0.17*
	(0.07)	(0.08)	(0.08)	(0.07)	(0.08)	(0.07)	(0.07)
Predispositions	0.02*	0.02*	0.04*	0.03*	0.01	0.01	0.01
	(0.01)	(0.01)	(0.01)	(0.01)	(0.01)	(0.01)	(0.01)
Group treatment *	−0.02*	−0.04*	−0.03*	−0.03*	−0.02*	−0.02*	−0.03*
Predispositions	(0.01)	(0.01)	(0.01)	(0.01)	(0.01)	(0.01)	(0.01)
Age	0.11*	0.09*	0.09*	0.07*	0.16*	0.01	0.12*
	(0.01)	(0.01)	(0.01)	(0.01)	(0.01)	(0.01)	(0.01)
Female	0.08*	−0.15*	−0.00	0.07	0.07	0.04	0.01
	(0.04)	(0.04)	(0.04)	(0.04)	(0.04)	(0.04)	(0.04)
Black	−0.22*	−0.18*	−0.18*	−0.26*	−0.37*	−0.02	−0.22*
	(0.06)	(0.07)	(0.07)	(0.06)	(0.07)	(0.06)	(0.06)
Hispanic	−0.04	−0.08	−0.00	−0.05	−0.18*	−0.02	−0.13
	(0.06)	(0.07)	(0.07)	(0.06)	(0.07)	(0.06)	(0.07)
Knowledge	0.18*	0.29*	0.27*	0.19*	0.30*	0.11*	0.26*
	(0.02)	(0.02)	(0.02)	(0.02)	(0.02)	(0.02)	(0.02)
R^2	0.073	0.100	0.090	0.061	0.139	0.013	0.107
N	3,117	3,117	3,117	3,117	3,117	3,117	3,117

Note: Results are estimated OLS coefficients with standard errors in parentheses. *p < 0.05 (one-tailed).

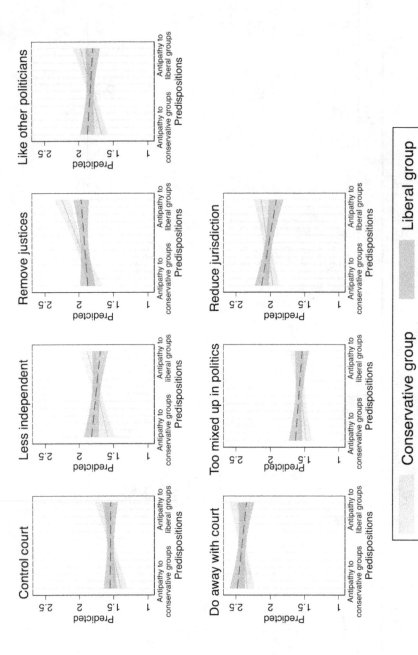

FIGURE 5.3 The effect of group attitudes on institutional legitimacy, disaggregated
Note: Predicted values and 95% confidence intervals for each legitimacy item using the models from Table 5.4.

had a vacant seat, for which President Trump had nominated Brett Kavanaugh, a fairly conservative circuit court judge, to fill. It is quite possible that, given the salience of the ongoing nomination battle, conservatives saw value in protecting the makeup of the bench, which would soon include a strong Republican-appointed majority, and thus expressed lower levels of support for justice removal overall.

Group-Specific Effects

We can also explore the Court's legitimacy by disaggregating the group-specific results from the experiment. Table 5.5 and Figure 5.4 present these results. Again, we find largely consistent patterns that show how group considerations condition legitimacy attitudes, although it is important to note that while the specific results for the Muslim/Christian comparison are in the direction of expectation, they fall short of conventional levels of statistical significance. This may be a function of the reduced statistical power in the disaggregated analysis combined with high levels of stickiness when it comes to institutional

TABLE 5.5 *Predicting institutional legitimacy, disaggregated by group*

	(1) Free expression (Prochoice/Prolife)	(2) Religious freedom (Muslim/Christian)	(3) Campaign spending (Union/Business)
Group treatment	1.44*	0.35	1.69*
	(0.70)	(0.67)	(0.65)
Predispositions	0.22*	0.05	0.16*
	(0.07)	(0.07)	(0.07)
Group treatment * Predispositions	−0.28*	−0.10	−0.20*
	(0.10)	(0.10)	(0.10)
Age	0.62*	0.76*	0.55*
	(0.12)	(0.11)	(0.11)
Female	0.44	−0.22	0.12
	(0.37)	(0.36)	(0.36)
Black	−1.71*	−1.34*	−1.36*
	(0.59)	(0.60)	(0.56)
Hispanic	−0.24	−0.35	−0.91
	(0.66)	(0.61)	(0.57)
Knowledge	1.66*	1.41*	1.79*
	(0.20)	(0.20)	(0.19)
R^2	0.128	0.127	0.144
N	1,042	1,048	1,027

Note: Results are estimated OLS coefficients with standard errors in parentheses. *p < 0.05 (one-tailed).

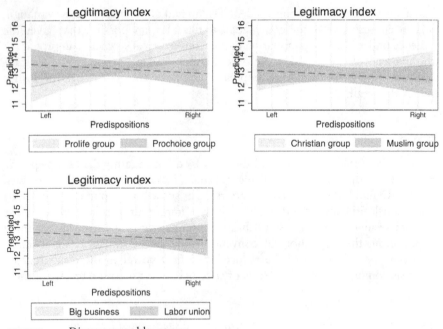

FIGURE 5.4 Disaggregated by group
Note: Predicted legitimacy and 95% confidence intervals from Table 5.5.

legitimacy, but it is nonetheless worth considering alternative explanations. For one, it may be the case that liberals and conservatives do not strongly polarize in their levels of antipathy toward these specific religious groups. For another, it may be the case that feelings toward both groups are quite negative, leading to something of a "floor effect" on how much legitimacy may tumble across conditions. There is some evidence consistent with this. Specifically, notice that the predicted levels of legitimacy are much lower on average in the religious freedom condition than in the others, a result that could arise from respondents who have strong negative feelings toward *both* Muslims and Christians.

A third explanation is that the null effects for these groups were the product of chance alone, and there is also some evidence to support this. In a second experiment, I utilize an identical treatment, varying Muslim/Christian fundamentalists groups involved in a case (as well as others). Below, I discuss this experiment, Study D, and its results fully. I note here, however, that the patterns for the religious groups are statistically significant and in the appropriate direction in Study D. This provides some supportive evidence that there may be nothing anomalous about the influence of religious groups on legitimacy attitudes, but rather that the modest results here are a function of limited statistical power.

Still, it is important to acknowledge that not every social group has the capacity to influence diffuse support. Group-based considerations are most powerful when groups are highly salient, citizens feel strongly toward them, and they have clear political resonance. Many judicial controversies involve these very groups – not only political protestors, labor unions, and religious organizations, but also other prominent minorities and pressure groups. At the same time, controversies involving less well-known groups may not have as strong an influence on support.

Additional Institutional Perceptions: Politicization

As a final implication of the group-based model, I evaluate here whether group antipathy influences whether respondents see Supreme Court justices as guided by politics (as opposed to the law). This is important because research demonstrates that perceptions of politicization can undermine support for the institution (Christenson and Glick 2015). To measure this, I included an item that required respondents to rate their agreement with whether "Supreme Court justices primarily base their decisions on non-legal factors, such as personal beliefs and political preferences." Responses are used as the dependent variable in the analysis presented in Table 5.6, coded such that higher values represent perceptions of a legalistic (e.g., apolitical) Court.

Group-based considerations shape the fundamental perception of the political vs. legalistic nature of the Supreme Court. The "inverse support" patterns

TABLE 5.6 *Predicting perceptions of the Supreme Court as a legal institution*

	(1) Legal perceptions
Group treatment	0.10
	(0.07)
Predispositions	0.02*
	(0.01)
*Group treatment * Predispositions*	−0.02*
	(0.01)
Age	0.09*
	(0.01)
Female	0.09*
	(0.04)
Black	−0.13*
	(0.06)
Hispanic	−0.06
	(0.07)
Knowledge	0.13*
	(0.02)
R^2	0.044
N	3,117

Note: Results are estimated OLS coefficients with standard errors in parentheses.
*$p < 0.05$ (one-tailed).

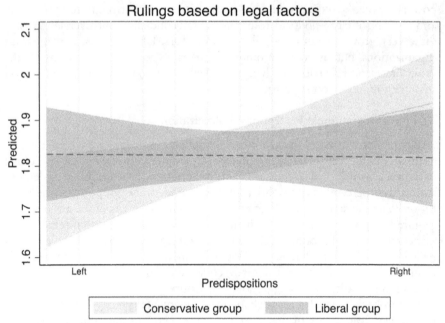

FIGURE 5.5 The effect of group attitudes on legal perceptions
Note: Predicted legal perceptions and 95% confidence intervals from Table 5.6.

in Figure 5.5 strongly echo those for the legitimacy items, indicating another way in which social groups can polarize Court support. They also show, once again, that decisions in favor of conservative, as opposed to liberal, groups have stronger substantive effects on perceptions, a fact that can be seen from the more dramatic slope of the light curve.

Interestingly, the results indicate that legalistic perceptions may serve as a potential mechanism that links group considerations with legitimacy. In other words, citizens may evaluate whether the justices are motivated by political considerations *on the basis* of whether their decisions tend to benefit disliked groups. If they do, this provides citizens an incentive to see the Court as politicized, since it is using the law to protect groups that they strongly dislike. With these perceptions of politicization in place, a logical next step is to question its legitimacy more generally, leading to the negative influences that we observed earlier in Study C.

STUDY D: ADDITIONAL IDENTICAL DECISION STUDY

To provide added evidence, I repeated Study C using a survey experiment administered to respondents recruited through Amazon's Mechanical Turk (mTurk) in the summer of 2017. Not only is research using mTurk becoming

Study D: Additional Identical Decision Study

increasingly common in political science (e.g., Arceneaux 2012; Crawford and Pilanski 2012) and judicial politics (e.g., Christenson and Glick 2015), but mTurk's subject pool has desirable properties when compared with traditional subject pools (Berinsky, Huber, and Lenz 2012; Buhrmester, Kwang, and Gosling 2011; Hansford, Intawan, and Nicholson 2018). I carefully monitored the quality of the subject pool, restricting participation in the study to only US citizens aged 18 years and older who had a track record of high-quality participation on mTurk. All subjects had participated in previous Human Intelligence Tasks (or HITs, as they are called) with a greater than 95% approval rate for their participation. Respondents were eligible for participation after being screened based on their age (18 or older), location (US only), and history of high-quality prior work (95% or greater approval rate) in order to participate, and they were checked for attentiveness throughout the survey.

Respondents were randomly assigned to one of four treatment conditions following those from Study C, focusing on prochoice, prolife, Muslim, or Christian fundamentalist groups. Full experimental stimuli are presented in the first two rows of Table 5.2, which use the same vignettes.[3] As before, I focus on *Legitimacy* as the dependent variable (DV) of interest. Responses to these items all load, at levels between 0.61 and 0.80, on a single significant latent "legitimacy" factor (eigenvalue = 4.00). I use an additive index to measure the dependent variable (mean = 24.67, observed range 0–42), with higher values indicating increased loyalty to the Court.[4]

The key independent variables of interest are the assigned treatment and a respondent's left–right *Predispositions*, measured here as in Study C. I also captured variables for *Female*, *Black*, *Hispanic*, and *Age*. In addition, the political knowledge battery measured subjects' ability to correctly answer questions about political affairs. These include five items about which branch has the last say when it comes to constitutional interpretation, federal spending, the identity of the Chief Justice of the United States, identification of the filibuster provision, and the requirements to override a presidential veto.

The sample differs a bit from the SSI sample, allowing us to test the theory in two distinct populations. It is common for mTurk workers to be a bit younger and more liberal than the general population, although not to the degree that is typically seen in studies of college undergraduates (Buhrmester, Kwang, and Gosling 2011). These patterns hold. The Study D sample is a bit younger, more knowledgeable, more liberal, and less diverse than the nationally reflective sample from SSI.

---

[3] In a slight variation from Study 1, some respondents were randomly assigned to see a relevant visual image with their vignette (e.g., a picture depicting the group involved). This had no effect on results, which are pooled here.
[4] The scale range differs from Study C to Study D because the former supplied respondents with five response options, whereas the latter offered seven (including "Somewhat agree" and "Somewhat disagree" for each statement).

Analysis

As in Study C, there is a strong conditioning effect from group considerations. Table 5.7 presents the main results and Figure 5.6 a graphical interpretation. Again, the model estimates a significant coefficient on the key interaction term. Focusing on the predicted effects plot shows precisely how groups shape legitimacy, beginning with within-party variation. Among liberal Democrats, depicted on the left-side of the x-axis, legitimacy is significantly higher when a liberal group benefits. This difference is significant at p = 0.020 at the farthest left point of the scale. On the other hand, among more conservative respondents (depicted on the right-side of the x-axis), the patterns of legitimacy invert. Support for the Court is significantly higher when conservative groups benefit. This difference in legitimacy is significant at p = 0.026 among the most right-leaning respondents. In terms of across-party effects, when presented with liberal group, predicted legitimacy is 27.12 on the far left but only 21.40 on the far right (the mean for all subjects is 24.67). This is approximately the difference between the 39th and 61st percentiles in diffuse support. In short, this shows that legitimacy is sticky but nonetheless conditional on group cues.

TABLE 5.7 *Predicting institutional legitimacy, additional identical decision experiment*

	(1) Study D
Group treatment	2.35*
	(1.01)
Predispositions	−0.04
	(0.12)
Group treatment * Predispositions	−0.44*
	(0.16)
Age	0.05
	(0.02)
Female	−1.40
	(0.65)
Black	−1.41
	(1.26)
Hispanic	−0.69
	(1.15)
Knowledge	2.10*
	(0.27)
R^2	0.131
N	798

Note: Results are estimated OLS coefficients with standard errors in parentheses.
*p < 0.05 (one-tailed).

Study D: Additional Identical Decision Study

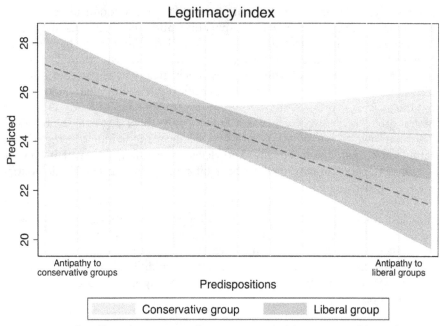

FIGURE 5.6 The effect of group attitudes on institutional legitimacy, additional model
Note: Predicted values and 95% confidence intervals from the legitimacy model in Table 5.7.

To contextualize effect sizes, we can again compare the impact of treatment to that from the well-known variable of political knowledge. In looking at Figure 5.6, notice that movement across the predispositions scale is predicted to decrease legitimacy by about 6 points when a liberal group benefits. This dwarfs the estimated effect that comes about from a one-point increase in political knowledge. On the other hand, Figure 5.6 also demonstrates an asymmetry, since legitimacy changes very little across political predispositions when a conservative group benefits. The effect in this case is much smaller than that from knowledge. However, recall that Study D is administered at a distinct time. One potential reason for the asymmetry we observe may be due to the fact that many respondents already saw the Court as somewhat conservative in the wake of the high-profile confirmation of Justice Neil Gorsuch, so they did not react as dramatically to additional information that the Court favored conservative groups.

Substantively, this shows how social groups polarize opinions about legitimacy.

Another interesting distinction between Studies C and D is that, while antipathy matters in both, it leads to more powerful effects for liberal groups here, whereas it had strongest effects concerning conservative groups in the prior analysis. To get to the bottom of this difference, I conducted a series of additional analyses (presented in Appendix) and one result stands out as instructive. This is the fact that political knowledge appears to have slightly different conditioning effects on legitimacy across the two studies. In short, the marginal influence of knowledge is much greater when it comes to the liberal group treatment in Study D. Specifically, the marginal influence of treatment is to depress legitimacy by more than 5 points in Study D when a liberal group is involved, whereas it falls by only about 2 points in Study C.[5] This may owe to the fact that most knowledgeable individuals in the mTurk sample are quite high on the knowledge dimension, given that mTurk respondent pools already tend to be a bit more sophisticated about politics than the general population.

Overall, the main findings from this second study closely mirror those from the main analysis. This is notable given the fact that Studies C and D were administered more than a year apart from one another and drew on very different samples, providing a measure of confidence in the major findings. In the Appendix, I include a full battery of additional and disaggregated analysis of the type displayed previously for Study C, and these also show consistent results.

STUDY E: MULTIPLE DECISIONS

The influence of group antipathy depends on citizens perceiving the Supreme Court to favor specific disliked groups in American society. While high-profile cases shape these perceptions (see Studies A, C, and D), group-based perceptions may not only be the result of high-profile rulings. Other forms of information may also influence perceptions of the Court. For example, political elites may frame the Court as an ally of certain segments. This occurs when media outlets detail the frequency with which the justices rule in favor of specific organizations, portrayals which may shape perceptions of the institution even in the absence of high-profile rulings. A more concerning example occurs when savvy political actors frame the Court as an ally of unpopular groups *irrespective* of the decisions it renders. For example, some critics of the institution have recently charged that its affirmative action decisions "perpetuate a regime that weighs the color of a student's skin more heavily than the contents of her report card" (National Review 2016) even as the Court made explicit that academic criteria had the largest impact on admissions decisions (*Fisher v. University of Texas* [2016], 8–9).

Therefore, an important aim of Study E is to explore whether legitimacy shifts as a result of frames that emphasize that the Court generally favors

---

[5] These differences are not quite as great as they appear at first glance; the legitimacy scale ranges from 0 to 28 in Study C, but 0 to 42 in Study D. Nonetheless, even accounting for these differences, the marginal effect is greater in the latter.

Study E: Multiple Decisions 87

certain groups, without pointing to a particular ruling as evidence. Put differently, we now have evidence that specific decisions shape group-based assessments; do communications about the Court's general orientation toward social groups also have such an effect?

Design

In May 2016, I recruited subjects through Amazon's mTurk. Again, I took careful steps to monitor the quality of the respondent pool, restricting participation in the study to only US citizens aged 18 years and older who had a track record of high-quality participation on mTurk. All respondents had participated in previous tasks with a greater than 95% approval rate for their participation.

In the study, subjects were tasked with answering a short survey about their political attitudes. Within this survey, I embedded the experimental treatment, using a between-subjects design. Respondents were randomly assigned to read about the Court's orientation to one of multiple social groups, which were chosen with a variety of purposes in mind. First, to give the study a measure of mundane realism, I focused on well-known groups who have been the subject of high-profile legal challenges in recent years. This approach increases the believability and ultimate effectiveness of the treatments (Aronson et al. 1990, 215). Second, I again chose groups that vary in their ideological nature – some traditionally rated more favorably by liberals and some by conservatives. And third, I chose groups with a variety of defining characteristics – some racial and ethnic in character, others with certain social or economic characteristics. These choices help to maximize external validity (Druckman et al. 2011), ensuring that results are generalizable beyond only one or two specific groups.

More specifically, subjects were randomly assigned to a treatment focused on the success of claims brought to the Court by big business, immigrants, Muslims, or African Americans. Respondents were then randomly assigned to receive either a group favoritism or group opposition treatment. The favoritism vignette described an academic study that found that the Court was strongly supportive of the group's claims, ruling in its favor in about 80% of cases. The opposition version of this vignette explained that the Court was anti-group, rejecting its claims in 80% of cases.[6] The vignettes are reproduced in Appendix.

---

[6] The manipulations in the African American group condition were unsuccessful, as subjects did not perceive a difference in the Court's support for African Americans regardless of whether they were assigned to the favoritism or opposition treatment ($p = 0.18$, two-tailed). The reason for this is because mTurk subjects already saw the Court as very sympathetic to black interests, which appears to have caused a ceiling effect, whereby the favoritism treatment failed to produce the intended bump in perceived support beyond already high baseline levels. Further buttressing evidence in favor of this explanation, the results of an internal analysis, using the results of the

From the perspective of external validity, these vignettes echo many news and opinion pieces that have been published in recent years. For example, the *New York Times* published a prominent 2013 story entitled "Corporations Find a Friend in the Supreme Court." The story offered scholarly evidence that the Roberts Court was "far friendlier to business" than any Court since World War II and described recent increases in the probability that Justices Scalia, Thomas, and Kennedy voted for business interests (Liptak 2013). In another instance, major news organizations like *New York Times* and the *Economist* presented evidence that certain justices ruled in favor of conservative groups, such as religious organizations, over 60% of the time when they brought free speech claims before the Court (Liptak 2014; "Playing Favourites" 2014). From a different angle, publications sometimes emphasize that the institution treats with skepticism a group's claims; one opinion piece argued "the last forty years of conservative hegemony on the Court has yielded racially regressive results pretty much across the board" (Miller 2010). In other words, it is common for news organizations to frame the Court as favoring certain groups. This design also retains a high measure of internal validity, since only a few key words in the vignettes differ across conditions.

Legitimacy is measured as before. The eigenvalue of the single significant extracted factor is 5.46. The variable is scaled from 0 to 42, with higher values indicating increased support for the Court as an institution.

I anticipate that the group favoritism treatment will affect Court legitimacy, moderated by a respondent's predispositions regarding the treated group. I measure this moderating factor by capturing ideological predispositions, as in Study D. However, I make an adjustment here to ensure that this measure is scaled in the correct direction by reversing its direction for respondents in the conservative group conditions. In other words, the predispositions measure will always indicate higher levels of opposition to the treated group, meaning that it is higher for conservatives in the immigration and Muslim conditions and for liberals in the big business condition. It is scaled from 0 to 6. I present models that also control for a variety of demographic and dispositional factors as above.

Analysis

We turn now to the analysis of Study E results. The randomization was generally successful. There are no significant differences in the population across conditions by gender, race, or degree of political knowledge. I present results from a fully specified model in Table 5.8.

---

manipulation check as a proxy for the treatment (Aronson et al. 1990), suggest that a more effective manipulation of Court sympathy to African Americans may have had the intended effects. I therefore exclude the analysis of these subjects from subsequent results, concluding instead that support for the Court can only be influenced when there is a change in whether the institution is perceived as supportive of a group.

TABLE 5.8 *Legitimacy as a function of group favoritism*

	(1) **Study E**
Group treatment	1.71
	(1.13)
Predispositions	−0.06
	(0.23)
Group treatment * Predispositions	−0.59*
	(0.34)
Age	−0.01
	(0.03)
Female	−0.07
	(0.66)
Black	−3.52*
	(1.28)
Hispanic	−0.75
	(1.26)
Knowledge	2.67*
	(0.23)
R^2	0.172
N	759

Note: Results are estimated OLS coefficients with standard errors in parentheses.
*$p < 0.05$ (one-tailed).

Again the key quantity of interest is the estimated coefficient on the *Group treatment * Predispositions* term. The coefficient is in the expected direction and significant at $p = 0.05$ (one-tailed). In substantive terms, this indicates that when respondents are presented with information that the Court favors a group, its legitimacy declines, but only among those with negative attitudes toward the group. To fully understand the substantive impact of group dislike, Figure 5.7 presents an effects plot to visualize the statistically significant interactive effect.

The two lines depict the contrasting behavior of respondents depending upon the treatment they were assigned. The light curve depicts those who received the group opposition frame. Support for the Court, among these respondents, is not linked with attitudes toward the group, which can be seen by the fact that the predicted legitimacy is close to flat (slope = 0) across the range of the dislike scale. In other words, legitimacy persists at an "average" level, irrespective of a respondent's feelings about various social groups, when the Court rules against them.[7] However, once the Court is framed as

---

[7] Specifically, this "average" level is predicted as a legitimacy score of approximately 23 points on the 42-point scale, indicating a very small lean toward "slight disagreement" on statements that oppose Court legitimacy.

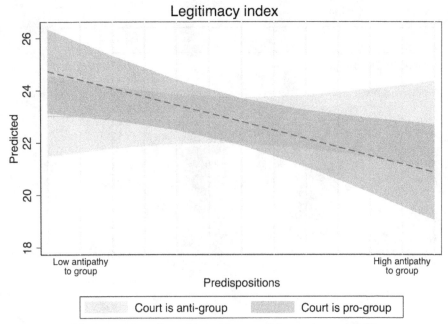

FIGURE 5.7 The interactive effect of favoritism condition and group dislike
Note: The figure depicts predicted levels of legitimacy across experimental conditions.

supporting these groups, attitudes toward the institution polarize depending upon respondents' feelings. This can be seen by the solid dark line, which depicts predicted legitimacy among respondents in the group favoritism condition. The line has a strong, negative slope, showing how antipathy damages legitimacy.

The comparison between respondents who display low and high levels of dislike in this condition is instructive. Among those with low levels of dislike, who can be seen in the left half of the figure, the Court enjoys a robust degree of support – in fact, even higher than it does among corresponding respondents in the opposition condition. The magnitude of support is estimated to be around 23.77. This is above the mean level of expressed support, which sits at 22.91. On the other hand, support for the Court plunges among those with highly negative group attitudes, who are depicted in the right half of the figure. The magnitude of support for these individuals is estimated to be around 21.13. The difference between these sets of respondents (those low versus high in group dislike) corresponds to a difference of 10 percentage points on the legitimacy distribution, or roughly the difference between the 57th and 47th percentiles in support.

The contrasting slopes of the two curves are also notable. When we see a strong negative slope on the pro-group curve, this is indicating yet another measure of support for our basic Group Antipathy Hypothesis. In substantive terms: when the Court rules in favor of a disliked group, its legitimacy suffers. But we also see a slope of nearly zero on the anti-group curve, representing the case when the Court rules *against* a group. In this instance, legitimacy does not respond. This is consistent with the Rights Limitation Hypothesis, or the idea that the Court does not receive a "bonus" in diffuse support when it denies a group's claims.[8] This offers further support for the asymmetric predictions of the group antipathy model, showing how negative antipathy is particularly powerful. I unpack further additional implications from Study E in Appendix.

STUDY F: A PENDING CASE CONCERNING THE "MUSLIM BAN"

The beginning of this chapter introduced the controversy of President Trump's "Muslim ban," which he originally proposed in the midst of his presidential campaign. As a final way to interrogate the group antipathy model, we can consider whether group evaluations prospectively shape the legitimacy of the Supreme Court, even before the Court has chosen to rule on a controversial minority rights issue like the ban. Study F explores whether negative affect toward Muslims influenced Americans' assessments of the Supreme Court once they were aware it would grant certiorari to a case reviewing President Trump's executive order (but prior to ruling on the case).

To explore the effect of the Supreme Court's decision to review a minority-targeted policy, I administered another experiment through mTurk during the fall of 2016. After recruitment to the study, subjects answered a brief series of questions about political affairs, embedded within which was the experimental treatment. Respondents were randomly assigned to either a control condition, in which no mention of the Muslim ban was made, or a treatment condition in which they learned that the Supreme Court was likely to review the constitutionality of the ban and rule in a fashion opposite to their preferences. Specifically, the experimental treatment consisted of a question informing respondents that Trump had "previously proposed banning all Muslims from entering the United States" but "if implemented, an immigration ban is likely to be reviewed by the Supreme Court." All participants were then asked to respond to a series of items regarding their support for the Court.

There are a few noteworthy facets of this design. First, by priming a high-profile policy proposal and presenting Trump's actual language, this helped to increase mundane realism. Additionally, it is important to note that the Court had yet to issue a decision in the case (in fact, at the time the experiment was

---

[8] This is also consistent with patterns in the aftermath of *Shelby County* that were discussed in Chapter 3. After the Court struck down civil rights protections in the case, it did not garner increased loyalty from citizens with high levels of anti-black affect.

administered, Trump had yet to assume the presidency). However, respondents varied markedly in whether they had *a priori* expectations about the Court's sympathy toward Muslims. To measure this, I included a Likert item for *Supreme Court Muslim support*, in which respondents rated their level of agreement that the Court is "generally supportive of the interests of Muslims." This is important because these perceptions should condition expectations about how the Court would rule in the case should it grant certiorari.

Analysis of key demographic and dispositional indicators suggests that randomization was successful. A Kolmogorov–Smirnov test indicates that there are no discernible differences between respondents assigned the treatment and control protocols on the basis of age, gender, race, partisan identification, ideology, and perceptions of the Court. Overall, there is no evidence to reject the null hypothesis that the treatment and control groups are balanced.

Analysis

With balance across conditions, we can now explore the effects of the experimental manipulation on attitudes toward the Court. The dependent variable of interest is institutional legitimacy, measured as before.[9] To explore treatment effects, I use regression analysis, the results from which are presented in Table 5.9. As with earlier studies, we are interested in the interaction between the treatment – which consists of priming subjects with information that the Court will review the Muslim ban – and their predispositions about this group, proxied using political ideology. However, Study F introduces a wrinkle in that the Court had not yet ruled in the Muslim rights case. This means that subjects' *expectations* about a ruling have a key role to play. If anti-Muslim animus shapes institutional legitimacy, this means that the Court should enjoy even lower levels of diffuse support among those subjects in the treatment group that expect a pro-Muslim ruling. This calls for a three-way interaction between the treatment, predispositions, and expectations about the Court's ultimate ruling. Model estimates are presented in Table 5.9, but given the complexity of interpreting three-way interactions from coefficient estimates, I focus subsequent discussion on a marginal effects plot, displayed in Figure 5.8.

The plot displays the marginal effect of the treatment, that the Supreme Court will take the Muslim ban case, as conditions by predispositions and perceptions of the Court as a "pro-Muslim" institution. It shows how, even in a pending case, group considerations loom large. Notice, first, in focusing on the left-hand side of the figure, that the treatment has no significant effect among those with liberal predispositions. This may be attributable to a few factors, including the

---

[9] Here, respondents were given seven response options after each of the seven legitimacy items. Therefore, the theoretical range of the legitimacy measure in Study F is from 0 to 42, with higher values representing strong diffuse support.

Study F: A Pending Case concerning the "Muslim Ban"

TABLE 5.9 *Legitimacy and exposure to minority-targeted policies*

	(1) **Study F**
Group treatment	−0.52
	(3.78)
Predispositions	−0.46
	(0.89)
SC Muslim support	1.09
	(0.77)
Group treatment * Predispositions	1.96
	(1.25)
Group treatment * SC Muslim support	0.43
	(1.03)
Predispositions * SC Muslim support	−0.15
	(0.23)
Group treatment * Predispositions * SC Muslim support	−0.64*
	(0.33)
Age	0.04
	(0.03)
Female	−0.33
	(0.70)
Black	−5.53*
	(1.41)
Republican	−0.90
	(0.68)
Knowledge	2.67*
	(0.28)
R^2	0.254
N	666

Note: Results are estimated OLS coefficients with standard errors in parentheses. *$p < 0.05$ (one-tailed).

fact that liberals have stronger *a priori* expectations that the Court will review the case. There is a bit of evidence to support this explanation. Respondents in the control group were asked to assess the constitutionality of the Muslim ban, a question that gives insight into how they think the Court may ultimately rule in the case. There is a strong negative correlation between perceptions of constitutionality and liberalism, a fact that indicates that liberals largely believed the law to be unconstitutional, raising the likelihood that the Court would review, and thus muting the effects of treatment among this group.

However, in turning to the right half of Figure 5.8, which represents conservatives, we can see the conditioning effect of group considerations in full force. Among these individuals, the treatment is predicted to decrease the Court's legitimacy, but only when respondents view the Court as a pro-Muslim institution. When they see the Court as anti-Muslim, the opposite pattern emerges.

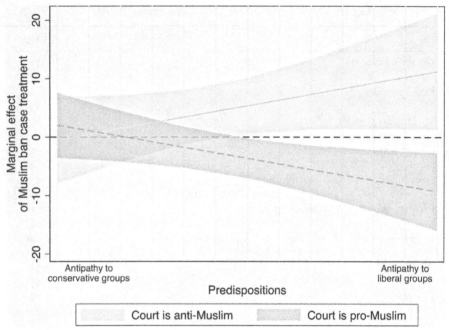

FIGURE 5.8 The heterogeneous effect of antipathy and expectations
Note: Figure plots the average marginal effect of treatment using the model specified in Table 5.9. This indicates that individuals with strong anti-Muslim sentiment rate the Court as less legitimate when they view the Court as a pro-Muslim institution *and* when it is likely to review the constitutionality of the travel ban.

The effect of treatment is to diminish legitimacy by about 9.30 points on the scale, or a little less than one standard deviation (10.17).

To summarize what is happening here: conservatives have high levels of antipathy toward Muslims but are *a priori* unsure whether the Court will review Trump's immigration ban. When treated with information that the Court is very likely to review, conservatives then begin considering whether the Court is sympathetic to Muslim interests. If they perceive the Court as "pro-Muslim," group antipathy takes over. The Court's legitimacy suffers.

In short, perceptions of pro-Muslim Court appear to lay the groundwork for the institution to lose support when subjects expect it to review the ban. Part of this effect may be attributed to an anticipatory response: the belief among some that the decision to review is the decision to strike down. But it should be noted that the Court's legitimacy is shaped by a series of other factors in the experiment. The negative and significant coefficient on *Race* further indicates diminished loyalty to the Court among African Americans. In terms of political predispositions, there is no evidence that party identification shapes diffuse support, but the politically knowledgeable display higher levels of support, squaring with a large body of other evidence to this effect.

Summary and Discussion

SUMMARY AND DISCUSSION

Controversy surrounding the Supreme Court and religious bias arose very quickly after the adoption of President Trump's travel ban. This chapter suggests substantial ramifications should similar controversies come about again. When it comes to the Court's protection of Muslim rights, multiple experimental studies demonstrate negative influences on institutional legitimacy. This makes plain the paradox of protecting minority rights. When protecting vulnerable religious groups can imperil the authority of the Supreme Court itself, the justices may think twice about doing so. In fact, some observers suggested that the Court was eager to wash its hands of the contentious case (e.g., Sherman 2017) and this squares with other evidence surrounding the institution's willingness to duck controversy with its certiorari decisions (Harvey 2013; Harvey and Friedman 2009).

At this point, I pause to summarize the evidence across Chapters 3–5. There are consistent indications of the influence of group antipathy on legitimacy. These chapters employ both observational and experimental data, implementing a series of empirical tests with each. Across the three chapters, empirical evidence concerns conservative groups and liberal groups as well as those with divergent political, social, racial, ethnic, and sociodemographic characteristics, and the vast majority of this evidence is consistent with the antipathy model. To summarize briefly the evidence to this point:

- In recent years, a number of high-profile rulings have preceded declines in Supreme Court legitimacy, specifically among citizens with high levels of antipathy toward the groups involved. Survey evidence shows lower levels of institutional legitimacy among citizens who possess negative feelings toward gays, immigrants, and big business.
- Additionally, negative feelings toward social groups, as opposed to positive ones, are particularly powerful in shaping legitimacy.
- The negative pattern of opinion response has implications for the Court's aggregate level of legitimacy, but it is a change that we can observe at the individual level as well.
- These effects tend to persist over a period of time, as much as a year or longer in some instances. It is reasonable to expect that their influence may weaken or strengthen over time. Perceptions tend to vary based on media depictions of the Court and its subsequent actions.
- Similar effects appear time and again in carefully controlled experimental settings. Evidence suggests that legitimacy varies predictably following signals concerning the extent to which the Supreme Court favors certain groups in society.
- Most notably, the Court's legitimacy varies depending upon social group attitudes even when holding constant the law and policy impact of a single ruling.
- Various groups in society precipitate these effects, including conservative and liberal as well as multiple political and social segments. All told, multiple

experiments in this chapter demonstrate a significant negative influence from group antipathy on legitimacy.
- This does not mean, however, that all rulings, or even all rulings related to social groups, affect Court legitimacy. Rather, much the opposite is the case. Low salience rulings and decisions in which the Court denies a group's rights-claims have little to no effect on legitimacy. These represent the vast majority of cases.

All told, the perception that the Supreme Court favors disliked groups has clear implications for institutional legitimacy. This perception usually forms in response to very notable cases or multiple rulings. Its normative importance is worthy of attention. In many of the cases discussed, the Court argued that its rulings protected basic constitutional rights, yet negative reactions followed, a fact that makes plain a conflict between the institution's fundamental responsibilities and the resource it requires to function effectively.

Thinking more broadly about institutional legitimacy, other considerations also contribute to support for the Court and these may help safeguard it from the most negative effects, including precipitous and severe declines in support. Democratic values play such a role, as does political knowledge. But we also know that ideological considerations have implications for support, and these are worthy of further attention, particularly because they may interact with the group considerations we have observed to this point. In the following chapter, I unpack the complicated relationship between group rights, ideological perceptions of the Supreme Court, and institutional legitimacy in further detail.

6

How Citizens Use Groups to Evaluate Judicial Preferences

A tense scene transpired outside the 1984 Republican National Convention. To protest the policies of the Reagan administration, members of the Communist Revolutionary Youth Brigade vandalized buildings and staged "die-ins." The protest culminated as one member set the American flag on fire while others chanted "we spit on you." Charged with a crime for his actions, Gregory Lee Johnson fought all the way to the Supreme Court. In *Texas v. Johnson* (1989), the justices found that the First Amendment protected his actions, sparking a firestorm of controversy. While criticism came from all quarters, conservatives were particularly incensed, spearheading a congressional push for a constitutional amendment to protect the American flag (Clark and McGuire 1996). As with earlier controversies, such as the Pentagon Papers case, the ruling seemed to illustrate the proposition that strong First Amendment protections were the product of a liberal Supreme Court.

This, of course, changed with *Citizens United* (2010), when the Court found itself under siege from the left. Why did the patterns of ideological support suddenly shift?

To be sure, many differences characterize these cases. Yet from the perspective of average Americans, perhaps the most notable ones included the actions and parties involved. In one, the Court ruled in favor of aggressive leftist protestors desecrating a powerful American symbol. In another, the institution favored major moneyed interests with the ability to dilute the political power of ordinary Americans. Free speech similarities aside, these cases signaled to ordinary Americans that the Rehnquist and Roberts Courts had very different ideological priorities.

The above observation squares with at least three pieces of recent evidence. Epstein, Parker, and Segal (2018) argue that Supreme Court decisions in First Amendment cases evince in-group bias, meaning that, in addition to legal considerations, ideological compatibility with the groups involved influences justices' votes. Indeed, "shared ideological values with the speaker's message (expression) may be equally if not more important in explaining the justices' decisions than their attitudes towards the First Amendment" (2). Broadening this perspective, Baum (2017) finds that a wide range of Supreme Court jurisprudence reflects a similar in-group logic. As he writes, "justices' attitudes towards political and social groups can affect their votes and opinions in specific ways that are not systematically affected by ideology" (24). If the behavior of judicial elites is susceptible to group-based thinking, it is not much of a stretch to think that the perceptions of ordinary citizens may follow such a pattern. Indeed, Kinder and Kalmoe (2017) demonstrate the persistence of group-based thinking with the ability to shape ideological assessments in American public opinion.

Should we care whether Americans use group cues to infer the Supreme Court's ideological preferences? Put differently, what differences does it make if opinions on First Amendment policy respond to the groups involved? As Bartels and Johnston (2013) show, an important component of judicial legitimacy derives from citizens' ideological compatibility with the institution, meaning that ideological perceptions have a fundamental role to play. Their work also shows that Americans have a wide range of subjective perceptions when it comes to the Court's preferences, raising questions about how these originate.

To understand the comprehensive influence of group cues on perceptions of the US Supreme Court, it is therefore imperative to explore their implications when it comes not only to institutional legitimacy but also ideological perceptions. This chapter takes up that charge. Using two survey experiments introduced in the prior chapter, I explore how group cues shape perceptions of Supreme Court ideology. Then, I utilize a conjoint experiment to isolate the effects on ideological perceptions of group cues from other signals. Across all three studies, I find consistent evidence that citizens perceive rulings benefitting liberal groups as indicative of a liberal Court and those benefitting conservative groups as indicative of a conservative Court, *even when the rulings themselves are substantively equivalent*.

Moreover, I show that these effects have substantial implications for institutional legitimacy. By re-specifying the models presented in the previous chapter in a way that allows me to account for ideological perceptions of the institution, I demonstrate that group-rights decisions have a compound influence on diffuse support. First, there is an unmediated effect: rulings have a direct impact on legitimacy among citizens who dislike the groups that benefit. But, also, a mediated effect implies that these rulings affect perceptions of Supreme Court ideology, itself an antecedent of legitimacy.

STUDIES C AND D: THE IDENTICAL DECISION
STUDIES REVISITED

We return first to the identical decision studies that were described in Chapter 5. Recall that in these studies, subjects read about a variety of First

Studies C and D: The Identical Decision Studies Revisited

Amendment rulings but were randomly assigned to a condition that framed either a liberal group (such as unions, Muslims, or prochoicers) or a conservative group (such as big business, Christian fundamentalists, or prolifers) as the beneficiary. Rather than analyzing legitimacy, as we did in the prior chapter, I focus here on the effects when it comes to perceptions of the Supreme Court's ideological preferences. This allows us to test whether varying the groups that benefit from a decision influences the way in which Americans perceive the Court's ideological direction.

I measure ideological perceptions of the Court using an item that asks respondents to rate its location on a seven-point ideology scale, from extremely liberal (lower values) to extremely conservative (higher values). I expect that the liberal group treatments will decrease conservative perceptions, and vice versa. In the models discussed in the Analysis section, I also control for a variety of other predispositional and demographic factors described in the prior chapter.

Analysis

Table 6.1 presents the results concerning ideological perceptions from the Survey Sampling International (SSI) and mTurk studies. In both, subjects perceive the institution as slightly right-of-center overall. The average value of the dependent variable (DV) is 3.68 in Study C and 3.54 in Study D, where

TABLE 6.1 *Ideological perceptions of the Supreme Court*

	(1) Study C	(2) Study D
Group treatment (liberal)	−0.08*	−0.19*
	(0.05)	(0.08)
Predispositions	−0.09*	−0.07*
	(0.01)	(0.01)
Age	0.004	0.003
	(0.01)	(0.003)
Female	−0.12*	−0.12
	(0.05)	(0.09)
Black	0.07	0.28*
	(0.08)	(0.17)
Hispanic	0.04	0.13
	(0.08)	(0.15)
Knowledge	0.07*	0.05
	(0.03)	(0.03)
R^2	0.060	0.068
N	3,117	798

Note: Results are estimated ordinary least squares (OLS) coefficients with standard errors in parentheses. DV is perceived Court conservatism. *$p < 0.05$ (one-tailed).

three indicates a moderate and four a slightly conservative institution. This is not surprising given that the studies were administered around the time that high-profile Trump nominees took the bench. Yet, the average obscures significant variation in perceptions, a fact which squares with the Bartels and Johnston (2013) perspective. For example, in Study C, a plurality of respondents (27.65%) rate the Court as "conservative," but another 17.16% see it as liberal, slightly liberal, or even very liberal. From where does this heterogeneity originate?

The coefficient of theoretical interest is the one on the *Group treatment* variable and it is statistically significant and in the direction of expectation across both models. This represents the effect of the liberal group treatment – in other words, exposure to information that First Amendment rulings benefitted liberal groups at the expense of conservative ones. In Study C, the coefficient is estimated to be −0.08. On the one hand, the effect is somewhat modest, representing only about one-tenth of a standard deviation in perceptions of judicial ideology. On the other, it is one of only a handful of factors that appears to influence ideological perceptions, and none of the others is dramatically larger from a substantive perspective. It is also worth noting that these results imply that ideological perceptions shift from just a single area of jurisprudence and its application to one group. In short, a preliminary analysis of the results from Study C shows that ruling in favor of a liberal group leads to a modest increase in perceptions that the Court is liberal, even when this ruling is *substantively identical* to one in favor of a conservative group.

Turning to Study D, we find consistent results. Once again, by manipulating the group that First Amendment ruling benefits, we can observe predictable effects on perceptions of Supreme Court ideology. Here, the effect is of greater magnitude, which may have something to do with multiple factors, including the relatively high knowledge of the mTurk sample. From a substantive perspective, the liberal group frame decreases perceptions of Court conservatism by about one-sixth of one standard deviation.

It is also interesting to note that the experimental treatment is one of only two factors that has the same effect on ideological perceptions across the two studies. In addition, subjects' self-reported ideological preferences also seem to matter, as the estimated coefficient on conservatism shows. This suggests that subjects tend to perceive the Court as ideologically distant on average; conservatives rate the institution as more liberal, and liberals see it as more conservative. This result is worth unpacking further in future work, given the important implications of ideological perceptions when it comes to institutional support. One possible underpinning is that conservatives and liberals have a tendency to look to different sets of trusted elites to learn about the Court, and both sets of elites have reason to highlight ideologically divergent decisions. Relatedly, these elites may have an incentive to emphasize rulings that benefit disliked groups. In short, Studies C and D demonstrate that the rulings benefitting liberal groups decrease the perception that the Supreme Court is conservative.

STUDY G: CONJOINT ANALYSIS

In addition to the vignette experiments described above, I administered an additional experimental study that utilizes a conjoint experimental design to explore perceptions of Supreme Court ideology. The design has been used increasingly in the political science literature in order to isolate the effects of specific attributes in the presence of a large number of other factors (Hainmuller, Hopkins, and Yamamoto 2014; Sen 2017). This is advantageous in the context of Supreme Court perceptions because any one decision of the institution has the ability to send multiple signals – not only the groups involved but the size and ideological makeup of the majority coalition, the treatment of precedent, the use of judicial review, and others. It is certainly possible that some of these influence perceptions of Court ideology, meaning we want to isolate the unique impact of each. To enable this, conjoint analysis operates by presenting respondents with randomized, distinct profiles in which multiple core attributes vary.

In 2018, I recruited subjects through mTurk, again observing best practices to ensure data quality. Subjects were tasked with learning about prominent First Amendment rulings from the US Supreme Court over the past five decades. As the instructions described, "these rulings occurred at different points in time, meaning that they were issued by different groups of justices." For each ruling, the information presented to respondents included six sets of attributes, values for which were randomly assigned. The key attribute was the *group that benefitted from a ruling*, which included many of the same liberal and conservative segments referenced in prior chapters. Specifically, the listed groups included immigrant advocacy organizations, Islamic organizations, and labor unions (on the left) and Christian fundamentalists, big business, and prolife demonstrators (on the right). Other attributes also varied: the *ideology of the majority opinion author*, whether a ruling *struck down legislation*, how it related to *prior precedent*, the *vote outcome in the case*, and the *legal area*. Table 6.2 displays the full set of attributes and traits included in the experiment, and Table 6.3 shows one possible pair of case comparisons that a respondent may have seen. Each respondent was presented with seven sets of comparisons total.

There are a few things to emphasize about this design. First, because we vary multiple attributes simultaneously, we are able to isolate the effect of any one attribute independent of the others. This is known as the average marginal component-specific effect (AMCE). So, for example, we can isolate the influence of a social group *independent* of the ideology of the opinion author. Additionally, the design retains a measure of verisimilitude by focusing on a few of the most important attributes that receive media coverage. This acknowledges the fact that most citizens pay only limited attention to rulings, receiving a few bits of information following high-profile cases.

To evaluate perceptions of Supreme Court ideology, I followed up each case-pair by asking respondents to assess the institution: "Which Court do you

TABLE 6.2 *Possible ruling profiles presented to respondents*

Attribute	Potential traits
Most prominent beneficiaries	Christian fundamentalists groups, Big business organizations, Prolife demonstrators, Immigrant advocacy organizations, Islamic organizations, Labor unions
Did the ruling strike down legislation?	Yes, No
Ideology of opinion author	Conservative, Moderate, Liberal
Legal area	Campaign contributions, Membership exclusions, Political speech
Prior precedent related to the ruling	Prior decisions were largely consistent with ruling, Prior decisions were largely inconsistent with ruling
Vote outcome in case	9–0, 7–2, 5–4

TABLE 6.3 *Example pair of rulings presented to respondents*

	Ruling A	Ruling B
Most prominent beneficiaries	Christian fundamentalist groups	Labor unions
Did the ruling strike down legislation?	No	No
Ideology of opinion author	Moderate	Liberal
Legal area	Campaign contributions	Political speech
Prior precedent related to the ruling	Prior decisions were largely consistent with ruling	Prior decisions were largely inconsistent with ruling
Vote outcome in case	9–0	5–4

believe to be more liberal? The Court that issued Ruling A *or* the Court that issued Ruling B?" Because the dependent variable is dichotomous, I use a logistic specification and cluster standard errors by respondent, which accounts for each subject seeing multiple judge profiles (Hainmuller, Hopkins, and Yamamoto 2014).

Analysis

In Figure 6.1, I present the results in graphical form by depicting a set of AMCEs for each case attribute. There is a dashed vertical reference line at x = 0, and when confidence intervals do not overlap this line that demonstrates that the trait has a systematic effect relative to the reference category. Of course,

Study G: Conjoint Analysis

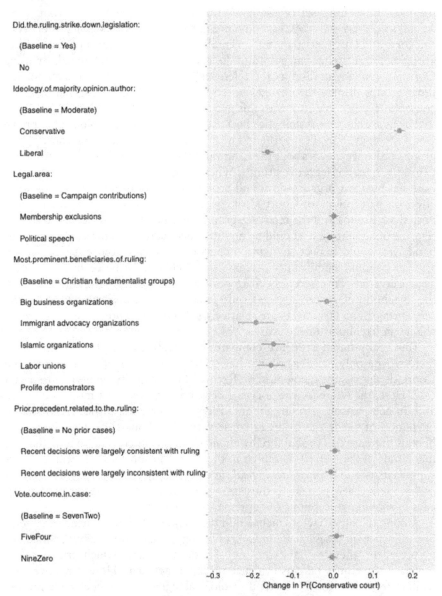

FIGURE 6.1 Conjoint analysis of social groups and Supreme Court ideology
Note: Figure shows the effects of the randomly assigned ruling attributes on the probability of perceiving the Supreme Court as conservative, analyzed using the cjoint package. The effects of a trait are significant, relative to the reference group, where confidence intervals do not overlap the dashed line (representing the reference group). Of note from a substantive perspective is the fact that rulings in favor of liberal groups decrease the propensity to view the Court as conservative, compared with those in favor of conservative groups. The other factor to have a similar effect is the ideology of the majority opinion author.

the most interesting set of estimates for our purposes concern group cues. Again, to display the AMCEs, conjoint analysis requires specifying a reference category, and I use Christian fundamentalists here, but we can choose any other group as the reference category and the results would be unchanged. By using Christian fundamentalists as the reference group, the point estimates for the other groups display the changes in the likelihood of perceiving the Court as conservative, as compared with this group.

The figure shows a systematic effect of group cues on perceptions of Supreme Court ideology. Specifically, there is a clear division between how conservative groups influence views about the Court and the effect that liberal groups have. Consider, first, conservative groups. When compared with the reference group, both big business organizations and prolife demonstrators have no significant effect on perceptions of Court ideology. This fact is entirely sensible because both these groups and the reference group are generally perceived as conservative, meaning that there should be no differences across the three. On the other hand, we would expect that, in comparison to the reference group, liberal segments should significantly decrease the likelihood of perceiving the Court as conservative. This is exactly what we observe. For each of the liberal groups, the likelihood of perceiving the Court as conservative declines relative to the reference group. The effects are relatively substantial, representing a 15–20% change in likelihood in each case.

This group-based influence compares favorably to the effects from other factors. The only other attribute that clearly shapes perceptions of Supreme Court ideology is the ideological preference of the majority opinion author in a case. Here, the reference category is a decision authored by a moderate justice and, in comparison, a ruling authored by a conservative justice increases the likelihood of seeing the Court as conservative by about 16%. Decisions from liberals decrease this probability by about 16%. It is interesting to note that the magnitude of these effects is similar to those from group cues. The author traits supply citizens an *explicit ideological signal* while the group traits offer only an *indirect one*. Their potency is thus strong evidence of the importance of group cues in shaping perceptions of Supreme Court ideology.

Among the other factors included in the conjoint design, none has a systematic influence on assessments of Court ideology. This is notable when it comes to precedent alteration and the use of judicial review, which critics of the judiciary sometimes take as evidence of liberal activism. However, after controlling for other, more powerful ideological signals, these cues have no discernible effect in Study G.

THE COMPOUND INFLUENCE OF GROUP CUES ON INSTITUTIONAL LEGITIMACY

While we know from Chapters 3–5 that group antipathy has a direct influence on Supreme Court legitimacy, the analyses presented above suggest an additional implication: group cues also shape perceptions of Supreme Court ideology. This indicates that group cues may have a compound effect on legitimacy – both unmediated and direct as well as mediated through ideological perceptions – potentially increasing their impact beyond what we have been able to detect thus far. Put differently, it is possible that, in controlling for ideological perceptions of the Court in models of legitimacy, we are artificially muting the true effect of group cues, for these cues also imbue ideological assessments of the institution.

To gain some empirical traction on this question, I return once more to our identical decision studies and re-specify the institutional legitimacy models that were initially presented in Chapter 5 so that they include a control for ideological disagreement with the Court. This is measured as the distance between a respondent's self-placement and her placement of the Court on an ideological scale following the treatment. To be clear, by including ideological disagreement as a control variable, this model suffers from post-treatment bias, meaning that it *underestimates* the effect of group cues on institutional legitimacy. Nonetheless, the treatment continues to exert a statistically significant, direct influence on legitimacy, *even after* we have controlled for the effects of ideological disagreement in the same model.

Considering the results from Chapter 5 (from models without the ideological disagreement control) and Table 6.4 (from models with the control added) in tandem, we can say that group-based thinking has a compound effect on institutional legitimacy. Framing a Court-made policy to benefit a disliked group has a *direct effect* by diminishing the institution's legitimacy. But it also has an *indirect effect* by leading to the perception that the Court is an ideological adversary, which in and of itself diminishes the reservoir of diffuse support. This is visualized in Figure 6.2, which combines the results of the Study C ideological perceptions and legitimacy models that are presented in this chapter. As this figure shows, the randomly assigned group treatment not only interacts with antipathy to significantly diminish Supreme Court legitimacy, but it also informs ideological perceptions of the Court, which is important because ideological disagreement further weakens diffuse support.

DISCUSSION

When it comes to public attitudes toward the judiciary, a key ingredient concerns ideological perceptions. These matter not only from the perspective of institutional legitimacy, but they also have consequences for strategic behavior. The Supreme Court is an insulated institution that is nonetheless responsive to public opinion in a number of ways. Whether the public tends to think the Court is a bit too liberal or conservative, then, has serious implications for both behavioral and institutional studies.

Unfortunately, institutional perceptions are poorly understood, a point that Bartels and Johnston (2013) make in their seminal study. Research on public

TABLE 6.4 *Alternative specification controlling for ideological disagreement*

	(1) Study C	(2) Study D
Group treatment	1.14*	2.28*
	(0.39)	(1.00)
Predispositions	0.11*	−0.16
	(0.04)	(0.12)
Group treatment * Predispositions	−0.19*	−0.43*
	(0.06)	(0.16)
Age	0.67*	0.05*
	(0.07)	(0.02)
Female	0.17	−1.07
	(0.21)	(0.65)
Black	−1.49*	−1.64
	(0.34)	(1.25)
Hispanic	−0.54	−0.63
	(0.34)	(1.14)
Knowledge	1.65*	2.23*
	(0.11)	(0.26)
Ideological disagreement (post-treatment)	−0.23*	−0.89*
	(0.07)	(0.22)
R^2	0.132	0.16
N	3,117	705

Note: Results are estimated OLS coefficients with standard errors in parentheses. *p < 0.05 (one-tailed).

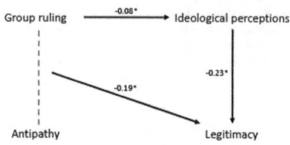

FIGURE 6.2 The compound influence of social group cues on legitimacy
Note: Figure displays the combined influence of social group cues on legitimacy by showing coefficient estimates from the analysis of SSI data across two models. The significant coefficient running from group treatments to ideological perceptions is estimated in Table 6.1. The significant coefficients running from the interaction and from ideological perceptions to legitimacy are estimated in Table 6.4.

Discussion

opinion suggests that citizens cue from simple and easy-to-understand heuristics to assess the political world, and this insight provides leverage when it comes to an institution that the public follows only occasionally. Lacking a detailed understanding of the Court, Americans are apt to rely on prominent signals such as high-profile decisions, elite communications, and group cues. Therefore, one important contribution of this chapter, and the group antipathy account more generally, is to show the importance of group cues when it comes to ideological assessments of the Supreme Court. When we isolate the effects of group cues, it compares favorably to many other factors and even comes close to equaling the influence of explicit indications of judicial ideology (such as the ideological preferences of a majority opinion author). Simply put, Americans perceive the Court's preferences through a group-based lens.

For our purposes, ideological perceptions are worthy of attention specifically due to their implications for institutional legitimacy. Because group cues directly affect legitimacy but also have an influence on ideological perceptions, their effect is potentially much more substantial than it appears at times. To illustrate, consider again the evidence from Chapter 3, which demonstrates how the Court's recent gay rights rulings damaged its legitimacy among a subset of the population even after controlling for post-decision ideological disagreement with the institution. It is quite possible that this approach may underestimate the cumulative influence of *Hollingsworth* and *Windsor*. By signaling support for gay Americans, the Court may have caused some citizens to update their perceptions of its ideological direction. Whether or not they were careful students of the Equal Protection Clause, Americans likely interpreted a decision celebrated by gay rights activists as indicative of judicial liberalism, a fact which undoubtedly increased ideological dissatisfaction with the Court among conservatives. By controlling for this factor, we may have obscured some of the ultimate impact that occurs when the institution protects minority rights.

Across the preceding four chapters, a substantial body of evidence suggests the multifaceted ways in which group cues and group antipathy shape the legitimacy of the modern Supreme Court. This not only squares with anecdotal observations regarding public opposition to high-profile rulings, but it also has significant normative implications when it comes to the Court's place in our democratic system. Because of this, it is interesting to consider whether the institution responds in a strategic fashion. In the following chapter, I shift the focus to examining a set of implications from the group antipathy model when it comes to judicial behavior. A simple question motivates this analysis: If the minority rights rulings have the capacity to harm the legitimacy of the Supreme Court, does the institution adjust its behavior to combat these negative effects?

7

Group Antipathy and Strategic Behavior on the Supreme Court

The central insight of the group antipathy model is that Americans assess the Supreme Court based on their feelings toward the social groups involved in a controversy. When citizens perceive the judiciary to favor a disliked group, this weakens their loyalty toward the institution. As this occurs, support for Court curbing rises. More citizens venture that the Court should be placed under popular control. They believe it should lose jurisdiction over controversial matters. A small number, even, endorse doing away with the Court altogether. Returning to Alexander Bickel's famous formulation, these attitudes bring into stark relief the counter-majoritarian dilemma. Justices of the modern Court risk their authority if they protect unpopular segments in society too vigorously.

When group antipathy controls evaluations of the judiciary, a number of significant implications result. One involves how the Supreme Court chooses to respond. Might the justices alter their behavior to preserve legitimacy? A few paths are possible. For one, the Court may double down on protecting unpopular groups. In this *guardian* role, the Court places such a high importance on fundamental rights that it is willing to accept the negative consequences associated with its unpopular actions. In the short term, this helps minorities secure basic rights and liberties, but over the long term, it may have negative ramifications for the institution and the rule of law in the United States. If the Court finds its reservoir of diffuse support run dry, it may lose the political authority necessary to operate as an independent body. A second path available to the Court involves the use of strategic behavior. Recognizing the negative consequences that can result from minority rights rulings, the justices might strategically moderate their behavior. In this *responsive* role, they will forgo taking action to protect unpopular groups when they find their legitimacy in peril.

Here, the Court strikes the opposite bargain: maintain political authority, but forgo its counter-majoritarian responsibility.[1]

Two pieces of evidence provide a clue as to how the Court balances these competing roles. The first is that the Court appears to place some value on protecting fundamental rights. In spite of its majoritarian tendencies, it has at times issued decisions that risk public backlash. *Brown v. Board of Education* (1954) represents the quintessential example, as the Court recognized the resistance that the ruling would spark (Tushnet and Lezin 1991), but more recent rulings also demonstrate a willingness to safeguard rights. At the same time, a wealth of evidence suggests that the institution engages in strategic decision-making (Epstein and Knight 1997). The Court exhibits majoritarian tendencies, adjusting its actions so as to not move too far out of step with public opinion (Black et al. 2016a; Hall 2014; McGuire and Stimson 2004; Mishler and Sheehan 1993).

In a *strategic guardian* role, the Court balances the tendencies against one another. The institution must weigh carefully the consequences of unpopular rulings, which may spark backlash, face implementation difficulties, and imperil diffuse support. Issue too many of these, and the Court risks its political authority. Even so, the institution has incentives to protect unpopular segments from time to time. First, scholars increasingly recognize that "law matters" when it comes to judicial decision-making, a perspective that indicates that legal constraints help to structure Court-produced policy outcomes (Bailey and Maltzman 2008; Bartels 2009; Bartels and O'Geen 2015; Epstein and Knight 1996; Richards and Kritzer 2002). Put differently, policy preferences and strategic considerations play a role in shaping rulings, but so too do the legal rules of the game, which serve as a form of constraint.[2] Applying this framework to minority rights jurisprudence, we can infer that strong legal constraints observed by the judiciary – such as the emphasis on equal protection considerations that developed in the wake of *United States v. Carolene Products* (1938) – may increase the institution's propensity to issue counter-majoritarian decisions. Second, because attitudinal preferences influence decision-making on the Court (Segal and Spaeth 2002), some justices may weigh specific rights protections more heavily than other considerations, leading to unpopular rulings on occasions. Indeed, many recent rulings have failed to achieve the *Brown* model of unanimity. Third, it may be the case that, over the long term, the public *prefers* a modest degree of counter-majoritarian decision-making from the Court, even if specific rulings bring about short-term displeasure. If

---

[1] See Epstein et al. (2005) for an extended and complimentary discussion regarding competing models of Supreme Court behavior during wartime.

[2] Within this literature, there is considerable debate about the specific manner in which legal constraints influence justices' decision-making. One influential model, jurisprudential regime theory, posits that decisions proceed in a stable fashion until influential precedent punctures the old legal regime, leading to rapid changes in the law (Richards and Kritzer 2002).

issued on select occasions, counter-majoritarian rulings may help to emphasize that the Court cares enough about the rule of law to check the power of the other branches – if citizens find this desirable.

These discussions raise questions upon which this chapter will shed preliminary light. Does the Court's jurisprudence indicate that it follows the strategic guardian model of decision-making, issuing unpopular minority-rights rulings, but only from time to time? How frequently has the modern Court ruled in favor of unpopular groups? And under what conditions is the Court more or less likely to do so? To be clear, these questions are not simply about the counter-majoritarian nature of the Supreme Court, at least insofar as much of the existing literature conceptualizes it. It is a common for scholars to conceive of counter-majoritarian behavior to consist of decision-making that is out-of-step with the public's ideological priorities (e.g., Hall 2014; Mishler and Sheehan 1993). And this is, indeed, one way in which the Court can contradict the public. But our interest here centers on a specific type of counter-majoritarian decision-making: protection of the rights of unpopular segments in society. Depending upon the group involved, these actions may repel either liberals or conservatives (and sometimes both), yet their importance rests in the fact that they have negative implications for Supreme Court legitimacy. As such, it is imperative to understand the extent to which they remain a feature of modern Court jurisprudence.

TYPES OF STRATEGIC ADJUSTMENT

The Supreme Court is a reactive institution. It depends upon cases being brought before it before it can weigh in on a political controversy, and it is required to respond only to the legal issues brought before it. The Court also exercises almost total discretion over its docket, meaning that it can choose to avoid or duck controversy as it sees fit.

Given that the Court places value on maintaining its legitimacy, and its potential awareness that going too far in the protection of minority rights can imperil this goal, we can conceptualize the strategic options available to the Court in three stages. First, at the *selection stage*, the Court may select the cases to which it grants certiorari in part based upon the group-based legitimacy implications that may result. Put differently, the Court may find it advantageous to docket only a small number of controversial rights cases in any given term, and it might also choose to grant certiorari to an even smaller number when it believes its popular support is in peril. Second, at the *voting stage*, the Court may strategically adjust the direction of its decisions in order to forestall public outcry. For example, in the wake of *Green v. New Kent County*, the Court observed public outcry over busing and other forms of proactive integration and backtracked on this line of jurisprudence (Stancil 2018). Finally, in terms of *strategic bargaining*, the Court may make other adjustments to safeguard its legitimacy once a case outcome has been decided. For example,

Testing the Argument

evidence suggests that the Court majority is attentive to opinion language in order to maximize public support and compliance with controversial decisions (Black et al. 2016a, 2016b; Owens, Wedeking, and Wohlfarth 2013), implying the following group-rights rulings, the justices may try to emphasize less controversial aspects of their rulings. In addition, the Court may strive to generate the largest possible majority coalition in order to strengthen the popular authority of a ruling, as it did in the case of *Brown*.

TESTING THE ARGUMENT

In order to explore the Court's behavior in cases that involve social groups, we must start with a systematic way to categorize these cases. As the previous chapters indicate, prominent group rights cases span a variety of legal issues (e.g., those involving the 1st and 14th Amendments), involve a range of policies, and implicate a variety of segments in society. The Supreme Court Database (SCDB; Spaeth et al. 2017) remains the most valuable source for data on Court rulings. But given the diversity of cases mentioned in this section, its use presents some challenges. For example, the Court may expect some First Amendment cases to trigger discussions of their group-based implications (e.g., *Citizens United*), but other First Amendment cases may have little discernible group component (such as those dealing with potentially obscene material distributed by private parties).

Cognizant of these challenges, I develop multiple separate indicators, spanning from broad to narrow, of group-rights rulings. In other words, these indicators combine various aspects of the SCDB to either permissively or restrictively define whether a case has features that make it one concerning social group interests. This allows us to place "upper" and "lower" bounds on the range of such cases that may occur in a given term.

To begin with the most broad, one way to identify group-based claims concerns the legal matters they involve. The *Broad* indicator categorizes cases as relevant to a social group when they concern legal issues that commonly (but not always) involve group claims. In particular, these are cases that involve any claims surrounding the First Amendment as well as the Civil War Amendments (which establish equal protection provisions). So, for instance, the indicator encompasses diverse rulings such as *Citizens United* and *Lawrence v. Texas*. Of course, the broad measure means that we may sometimes generate "false positives" by capturing additional cases in the data. Next and more restrictively, the *Intermediate* indicator captures only those cases that involve an equal protection matter before the Court. This overlooks those First Amendment cases and thus represents a more restrictive definition than the *Broad* measure. The benefit, however, is that the *Intermediate* measure does not encompass as many "false positives," or cases that do not necessarily implicate group interests (e.g., obscenity cases). Finally, to eliminate as many false positives as possible, I create a *Narrow* measure of group cases. These cases involve the legal provisions from the First Amendment as well as the Civil War Amendments, but they are further restricted to include only those disputes in which a named party represented a prominent social grouping (e.g., a "racial or ethnic minority," as categorized by the SCDB). In other words, this indicator requires that both the party *and* the legal issue relate to prominent social groupings in order for a case to be identified. Table 7.1 summarizes the various measures.

Taken together, these measures have some notable merits. Relying on the SCDB's comprehensive and validated indicators, they provide an efficient and replicable way to catalog a large number of cases based on their group-focused implications. This means that we are easily able to categorize decades worth of decisions to determine whether they implicate social group interests and, in turn, are likely to generate some measure of public response. Indeed, the measures show face validity, doing a fairly good job of capturing both recent and past cases that implicate group rights. For example, all three indicators capture *Brown v. Board* (1954) as well as *Fisher v. Texas* (2016), a high-profile affirmative action case. That being said, not all cases are perfectly categorized by these measures. For instance, *Arizona v. United States* (2012) presents a challenge because the federalism dispute between levels of government does not appear, from a legal perspective, to implicate group interests. It is only because of the political substance of immigration, the issue involved, that group interests become prominent in popular discussions of the case.

Exceptions not withstanding, there is empirical evidence that the measures are valid indicators of prominent social group cases. To more rigorously assess validity, I begin with the observation that group-based cases tend to attract popular attention and generate controversy on the bench (Baum 2017). This implies that media may be more likely to cover heavily cases and justices to dissent in cases that involve prominent social groupings. Additionally, as these controversial cases occur, and division on the bench increases, the Court's opinions themselves may become more caustic.

We can therefore empirically examine these expectations to see whether the above factors correlate with our measures of group-based rulings. Table 7.2 displays the correlations between the three measures of group-rights cases with salience, division, and opinion negativity. The measures correlate strongly with indicators of case salience, a fact that attests to a basic form of face validity: controversial group cases tend to attract media attention. In terms of division on the bench and opinion content, the face validity of the measures is not as strong. The one exception, however, concerns the broad legal issue measure. Using this, we see strong evidence that the justices are more divided among themselves and willing to write more negative opinions in group cases. Given the strong validity of this measure, I focus subsequent discussions on it, although I also include the other indicators of group-rights rulings for context.

TABLE 7.1 *Measures of group-rights rulings at the Supreme Court*

Measure	Explanation	Construction
Broad (legal issue)	Cases that involve a legal issue that commonly impacts social group rights	Uses the Legal Provision Supplement Indicator (lawSupp) from the SCDB to capture cases specific to the 1st and 13th–15th Amendments (codes 200–204 and 226–234).
Intermediate (equal protection issue)	Cases that involve Equal Protection claims only	Uses the Legal Provision Supplement Indicator (lawSupp) from the SCDB to capture cases specific to 14th Amendment equal protection claims (codes 227–232).
Narrow (combined issue and party measure)	Prominent cases that involve a legal issue that commonly impacts social group rights *and* have a prominent social group as a named party	Uses the Legal Provision Supplement Indicator (lawSupp) from the SCDB to capture cases specific to the 1st and 13th–15th Amendments. Refines these to only constitutional issues using the lawType variable. Then, refines using petitioner and respondent codes, depending upon whether a prominent social group is a named party, such as "racial or ethnic minority," "religious organization," or "lesbian, gay, bisexual, transsexual person or organization."*

Broader ← → Narrower

Note: *Specifically, the parties include minority governmental employee or job applicant; minority female governmental employee or job applicant; business, corporation; religious organization, institution; lesbian, gay, bisexual, transexual person or organization; Indian, including Indian tribe or nation; racial or ethnic minority employee or job applicant; minority female employee or job applicant; racial or ethnic minority; person or organization protesting racial or ethnic segregation or discrimination; racial or ethnic minority student or applicant for admission to an educational institution; union member; union, labor organization, or official of (codes 10, 11, 122, 130, 162, 182, 183, 222, 223, 224, 247, 249).

113

TABLE 7.2 *Validating group-rights cases with division, salience, and content*

Measure	Salience		Division on the bench		Opinion content
	New York Times front page	Political	Majority votes	Unanimous ruling	Negativity
Broad	0.19*	0.20*	−0.06*	−0.07*	0.04*
Intermediate	0.12*	0.10*	−0.01	−0.02	−0.06*
Narrow	0.09*	0.11*	−0.02	−0.02	0.02

Note: Cell entries are correlation coefficients, *p < 0.05. Group case measures are described in Table 7.1. The *New York Times* front page indicator is from Epstein and Segal (2000) and the political salience measure is based on early coverage from the *New York Times*, *Washington Post*, and *Los Angeles Times* (Clark, Lax, and Rice 2015). Division on the bench is measured using voting outcomes from the SCDB. Finally, opinion negativity measures the degree of negative rhetoric in majority opinions using Wedeking and Zilis (2018).

UNDERSTANDING PATTERNS IN GROUP-RIGHTS RULINGS

We begin with a look at some descriptive trends involving group-rights rulings in the modern era. This is valuable because, even as much is known about many of the Court's behavioral patterns, such as the frequency with which it issues liberal decisions or strikes down legislation (e.g., Clark 2009; McGuire and Stimson 2004), very few systematic analyses focus on cases with implications for important social groups (but see Baum 2017; Epstein, Parker, and Segal 2018). Figure 7.1 displays the proportion of rulings in a given year that fits into this category, using our three distinct measures. Additionally, Table 7.3 provides a similar proportional breakdown, this time highlighting distinct eras based on the Chief Justice of the United States.

There are some interesting patterns that shed light on the selection stage. Beginning with Figure 7.1, observe that the broad measure captures a much higher proportion of group rulings than the other measures. In some years, the broad measure shows that over 20% of rulings concern group-related issues, whereas the narrower measures rarely break the 10% threshold. Again, this variation supplies upper and lower bounds on the range of rulings that the public may interpret to involve social groups; examining patterns across multiple indicators allows us to generate more robust inferences. Also notable is the fact that these frequencies ebb and flow over time. All three measures suggest that the Court devoted the highest proportion of its docket to cases implicating social groups between the early-1960s and mid-1970s. The percentage declined most clearly during the early years of the Rehnquist Court in the mid-1980s and early-1990s, and it has remained at relatively low levels since. Most recently, with this shrinking percentage alongside the Court's contracting docket, the Roberts Court has heard only a handful of cases with any social group

Understanding Patterns in Group-Rights Rulings

TABLE 7.3 *Proportion of Supreme Court social group rulings, by Chief Justice*

	Broad measure (% of rulings)	Intermediate measure (%)	Narrow measure (%)
Vinson Court (1946–1953)	10	2	3
Warren Court (1953–1969)	12	5	4
Burger Court (1969–1986)	18	5	4
Rehnquist Court (1986–2005)	13	2	2
Roberts Court (2005–2017)	9	2	2

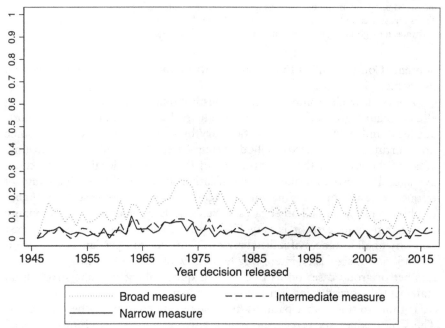

FIGURE 7.1 Proportion of Supreme Court rulings that concern social groups over time
Note: Data from the SCDB, with construction of three measures described above.

implications in recent years. Nonetheless, some of these have proven quite controversial.

Table 7.3 provides additional evidence of the marked decline in such cases during the Roberts Court. Using the broad measure, the Roberts Court has devoted about 9% of its docket to group-rights cases, which equates to about seven or eight such rulings in a year. Using a more restrictive measure identifies only about two cases per year having such implications. Either way, these are sharp declines from the Warren, Burger, and even Rehnquist eras. It is not yet clear what underlies this drop. Overall, the evidence suggests that the modern

TABLE 7.4 *Descriptive patterns*

	Most common issue area	Judicial review (%)	Precedent alteration (%)	Unanimous decisions (%)	Liberal decision (%)	Salient cases (%)
Group-rights cases (broad)	First Amendment	29	3	31	57	28
Other cases	Criminal procedure	4	2	41	50	10

Note: Cells display the proportion of cases with a specific characteristic. Group-rights cases are measured using the broad indicator. Salient cases are measured using the front-page *New York Times* measure from Epstein and Segal (2000). Other data are from the SCDB. Substantively, this illustrates how group-rights cases differ systematically from others.

Supreme Court is willing to put only a small number of group-rights cases on its agenda.

Besides their clear implications for institutional legitimacy, does anything else distinguish group-rights cases from others? Table 7.4 explores how important legal and political characteristics vary by case type. It makes clear some noteworthy differences. Not only do group-based cases tend to cover distinct areas of the law, but they are arguably of much greater legal significance on average. The justices strike down legislation at any extremely high rate of frequency (29% of the time on average) in group-rights cases; this figure tumbles to just 4% of all other cases. Given a declaration of unconstitutionality in a group-rights case, it is very likely that it concerned state laws: a vast majority of all instances of judicial review. Coupled with the data on precedent alteration, this signals an interesting tension: while the Court only puts a small number of group cases on its docket, it is quite willing to make strong legal statements by overturning legislation with them.

Turning to some other patterns, the role of case controversy becomes clear. The Court issues six percentage points fewer unanimous decisions in social group cases compared with others; it also issues five to four rulings at a much higher frequency in these instances. Such controversy associates with attention to a case. The media, serving as a key link between case outcomes and the public, covers group cases much more readily than other rulings. Although we noted this pattern earlier, the findings in Table 7.4 further suggest that the public has reason to view the judiciary through a group lens. Cases that involve social groups tend to attract significant attention.

One final, curious pattern emerges: the tendency of group-rights cases to result in liberal decisions. In well over half of group-rights disputes (57%), the Court decides in a liberal direction, whereas its decision-making is much more balanced in other cases. This is also evident in Table 7.5, which displays the frequency of liberal rulings by case type across chief justices. Since the 1950s,

Study H: Judicial Strategy and Group-Rights Rulings

TABLE 7.5 *Frequency of liberal decisions*

	Group-rights cases (broad measure) (%)	Other cases (%)	Difference (percentage points more liberal)
Vinson Court (1946–1953)	50	49	+1
Warren Court (1953–1969)	79	66	+13
Burger Court (1969–1986)	51	44	+7
Rehnquist Court (1986–2005)	51	43	+8
Roberts Court (2005–2017)	51	48	+3

the Court has consistently issued a higher percentage of liberal rulings in group-rights cases, with the difference peaking at 13 percentage points during the Warren Court. In fact, though the Warren Court was quite left-leaning overall (nearly two-thirds of its "other case" rulings went in this direction), it made the strongest liberal imprint in social group disputes. The pattern fits with rulings that loom large in the popular imagination of the Warren era, such as *Brown v. Board of Education*, a fact suggests how much of a Court's reputation can result from a few high-profile controversies (see Hetherington and Smith 2007).

STUDY H: JUDICIAL STRATEGY AND GROUP-RIGHTS RULINGS

We began with a simple question about the elements of Supreme Court strategy when group-rights claims are involved. Observing that the public conditions legitimacy on its views about social groups involved in high-profile cases, the Court has an incentive to adjust its behavior. It may do so at both the certiorari and merits stages. The previous section sheds some light on the former, suggesting that the justices are willing to take only a small number of cases with serious social group implications each term. Limiting the prevalence of these cases may allow the Court to minimize popular controversy over its actions. To be sure, these patterns are only suggestive and we should be cautious about their interpretation at this point. Nonetheless, docketing decisions remain a fruitful area for future study.

When it comes to the merits stage, we can conduct a fuller examination. This is because the strategic Court model offers a simple hypothesis: rulings should be particularly influenced by concerns about popular legitimacy in group-rights cases. In other words, as the public becomes more liberal, the Court should be more likely to issue liberal rulings, but in group-rights cases especially. The hypothesis thus takes a simple finding from the responsiveness literature – that the Court tends to follow public opinion when it rules (e.g., Hall 2014; McGuire and Stimson 2004; Mishler and Sheehan 1993) – and marries it with a specific mechanism – legitimacy maintenance. This points to the fact that the Court should be likely to follow the public in a specific subset of cases.

To test this hypothesis, I model the probability of a liberal decision, measured using the SCDB's decision direction variable, using a logistic regression. The covariates of interest are group case measure (using the *Broad*, *Intermediate*, and *Narrow* variables) as well as the public's policy mood. To capture the latter, I use Stimson's aggregate policy mood data, which captures public liberalism across a range of indicators over time (Stimson 2018). This reliable measure is the one most commonly applied in work on Supreme Court responsiveness (Black et al. 2016a, 2016b; McGuire and Stimson 2004; Mishler and Sheehan 1993).

I also include a variety of control variables. One factor that should strongly influence decision direction is the ideological preference of the median justice in the Court's majority coalition (Carrubba et al. 2012). To account for this, I use the Martin and Quinn (2002) score of ideological preferences for each justice on the Court, taking the value of the majority coalition median's preference in a given case. Using the SCDB, I include an additional control for the lower court disposition of a case, based on the idea that the Supreme Court is more likely to grant certiorari to a case when it wishes to overturn a lower court ruling. In the coming paragraphs, I also discuss why we may want to account for the justice's expectations about whether a decision will be politically salient to the public. Clark, Lax, and Rice (2015) supply an appropriate measure of *Salience* by capturing latent political salience that takes into account the pre-ruling period in the *New York Times*, *Washington Post*, and *Los Angeles Times*. Finally, in all of the models, I control for legal issue area and natural court using fixed effects. Table 7.6 presents results across six models.

We begin with Models 1–3, which allow us to explore whether the Supreme Court responds to public preferences in social group cases. Is the Court more likely to issue a liberal decision in group cases, as opposed to all others, when it knows that the public prefers liberal rulings? To test this, the models include an interaction between the *Group case measure* and *Public mood*.

Based on the estimates from Models 1 to 3, there is no evidence consistent with the idea that the Court strategically adjusts the direction of its social group rulings to account for the public's ideological preferences. Not only are the coefficients on the *Group case measure*, *Public mood*, and interactions terms statistically indistinguishable from 0, but upon plotting out their marginal effects (Brambor, Clark, and Golder 2005), it becomes clear that there is no conditioning effect (these results are not shown). The null finding is consistent irrespective of whether we use a broad, intermediate, or narrow indicator of group cases.

Turning briefly to other results from Models 1 to 3, they are intuitive. Liberal decisions become significantly less likely when the median justice in the Court's majority coalition has conservative preferences and also when a lower court has ruled in a liberal direction, indicating that the justices prefer to reverse when they take a case on appeal. These, and not the ones concerning responsiveness, are the only significant results from Models 1 to 3.

	Models without salience			Models with salience		
	(1)	(2)	(3)	(4)	(5)	(6)
Group case measure						
Broad	−0.21			0.12		
	(1.31)			(1.35)		
Intermediate		0.91			1.77	
		(2.42)			(2.57)	
Narrow			−1.19			0.02
			(2.85)			(3.03)
Public mood	0.002	0.004	0.003	0.0001	0.002	0.002
	(0.01)	(0.02)	(0.02)	(0.02)	(0.02)	(0.02)
*Group case measure * Public mood*	0.01	−0.01	0.02	0.0003	−0.02	0.001
	(0.02)	(0.04)	(0.05)	(0.02)	(0.04)	(0.05)
Salience	~	~	~	1.29	0.74	0.77
				(1.00)	(0.88)	(0.87)
*Group case measure * Salience*	~	~	~	−3.06	−4.16	−4.82
				(1.95)	(3.40)	(3.76)
*Public mood * Salience*	~	~	~	−0.02	−0.01	−0.01
				(0.02)	(0.01)	(0.01)
*Group case measure * Public mood * Salience*	~	~	~	0.05	0.06	0.08
				(0.03)	(0.05)	(0.06)
Conservative majority (median)	−2.62**	−2.62**	−2.62**	−2.62**	−2.62**	−2.62**
	(0.09)	(0.09)	(0.09)	(0.09)	(0.09)	(0.09)
Lower court disposition – liberal direction	−1.19**	−1.19**	−1.20**	−1.19**	−1.19**	−1.19**
	(0.07)	(0.07)	(0.07)	(0.07)	(0.07)	(0.07)
Lower court disposition – unspecified direction	−1.61	−1.62	−1.62	−1.62	−1.61	−1.61
	(0.92)	(0.92)	(0.92)	(0.92)	(0.92)	(0.92)
Issue area fixed effects?	Yes	Yes	Yes	Yes	Yes	Yes
Natural court fixed effects?	Yes	Yes	Yes	Yes	Yes	Yes
Pseudo-R²	0.324	0.324	0.324	0.325	0.325	0.324
N	5,320	5,320	5,320	5,320	5,320	5,320

Note: Entries are coefficient estimates from a logistic regression predicting the likelihood of a liberal ruling with standard errors in parentheses. For the group case

The findings provide reason to question whether the Supreme Court is particularly "responsive" in group-rights cases. Perhaps, the Court places a higher importance on its "guardian" function? However, we may also interrogate these results a bit further by adding nuance to our theoretical expectations. Recent work on responsiveness suggests that the justices' expectations about public attention can shape their behavior (Casillas, Enns, and Wohlfarth 2011; Giles, Blackstone, and Vining 2008). Although there is some division as to the precise way in which case salience may matter, one sensible expectation is that justices tend to be more responsive in cases where they expect the public is paying closer attention. Because public attention to the Court is sporadic, there is limited incentive for responsive justices to worry about upsetting citizens in all but the most well-known, controversial cases. Indeed, these are the very types of controversies reviewed earlier in the manuscript.

The above discussion suggests the potential for an interaction between responsiveness and case salience. Simply put, if the Supreme Court is concerned about its legitimacy when it resolves social group controversies, it is much more likely to adjust when it knows the public is paying attention ahead of time. To capture this possibility, I include a three-way interaction in Models 4–6 of Table 7.6. By examining interaction effects, we can see whether the Supreme Court is responsive in some cases more than others.

Models 4–6 present coefficient estimates but, again, to explore the interactive effects of interest, we need to plot out predicted probabilities. These are displayed in Figures 7.2–7.4. Each of the figures displays the discrete marginal effect of a group case on the probability of a liberal ruling based on the three-way interaction. In other words, these figures show how responsiveness varies across salient and non-salient group cases.

To briefly summarize the differences between Figures 7.2 and 7.4, each displays the results based on an empirical model using, respectively, the broad, intermediate, and narrow indicators of group-based cases. Across all three indicators, the results are substantively consistent. They indicate that social group cases condition the probability of a liberal decision; the discrete marginal effect of case type is generally only significant when the case is salient and as the public becomes more liberal. Put differently, the justices display a heightened level of responsiveness in salient group cases.

To make this finding concrete, we can consider the results from Figure 7.2 in more detail. This displays marginal effects using the *Broad* group case measure. When the public's policy mood is at its most conservative (mood $\approx$ 53, the lowest observed value in the data), the discrete marginal effect of a group case on decision direction is statistically indistinguishable from 0, irrespective of whether the case is salient or non-salient. However, as the public becomes more liberal, liberal rulings become more likely in social cases but only if they are politically salient. For example, when the public is very liberal (mood $\approx$ 72), the discrete marginal effect of a salient group-based case is to increase the probability of a liberal ruling by about 0.43 points. When this same case is non-salient, the effect remains

Study H: Judicial Strategy and Group-Rights Rulings

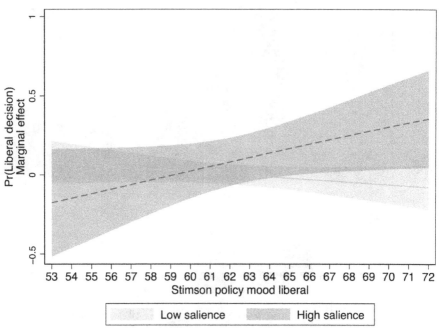

FIGURE 7.2 Effect on decision direction of group-rights cases (broad measure)
Note: Figure displays, using the broad measure model, the discrete marginal effect of a group-rights case on the likelihood of a liberal ruling as salience and the public's policy mood vary across their observed ranges. This effect differs significantly for salient versus non-salient cases across the range of the mood scale. Substantively, this indicates that the Court is more likely to rule in line with the public in salient cases concerning group rights.

statistically indistinguishable from 0. We see a very similar substantive result using the *Narrow* measure. Finally, when we turn to the *Intermediate* measure, the results are a bit more nuanced. The discrete marginal effect falls short of significance for salient cases when the public mood is liberal. But there is a significant effect of the salience–case type interaction across the range of the mood scale.

What might we make of the slightly distinct results from Models 4 to 6? In all three models, as public liberalism increases, there exists a significant interaction between expected case salience and group-rights cases – irrespective of how this latter factor is measured. At the same time, the relationship takes on slightly different forms depending upon the group-rights measure that we employ. The outlier is the *Intermediate* measure, for which responsiveness appears more muted. Why might this be the case? Consider that the *Intermediate* measure is distinct in that it deals *only* with Equal Protection claims, whereas the others also include First Amendment cases (the *Broad* indicator) or are limited by the parties involved in a case (the *Narrow* measure). Keeping these differences in mind, it is entirely possible that the justices display

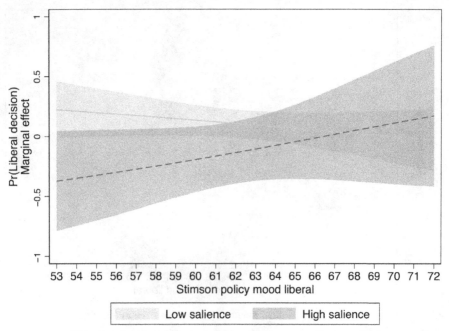

FIGURE 7.3 Effect on decision direction of group-rights cases (intermediate measure)
Note: Figure displays, using the intermediate measure model, the discrete marginal effect of a group-rights case on the likelihood of a liberal ruling as salience and the public's policy mood vary across their observed ranges. This effect differs significantly for salient versus non-salient cases across the range of the mood scale. Substantively, this indicates that the Court is more likely to rule in line with the public in salient cases concerning group rights.

a bit less responsiveness in Equal Protection disputes, perhaps because the Court's standard of review for dealing with "suspect classifications" is well-established and longstanding. This potentially limits the interpretive leeway available to the justices. In contrast, standards such as the First Amendment's speech doctrines have shifted quite a bit over time.

Summarizing the results from Models 1 to 6, we see some evidence that the Supreme Court is responsive to public opinion when cases involve group rights, but only for a subset. The Court is particularly concerned with straying from public mood when it knows its actions will be politically salient. Yet, in non-salient disputes, the Court is no more responsive in group-rights cases than it is involving others on its docket.

DISCUSSION AND FUTURE DIRECTIONS

We began this chapter with an observation and a question. Observing that the Court values its legitimacy but social group cases can place this peril, we asked

Discussion and Future Directions

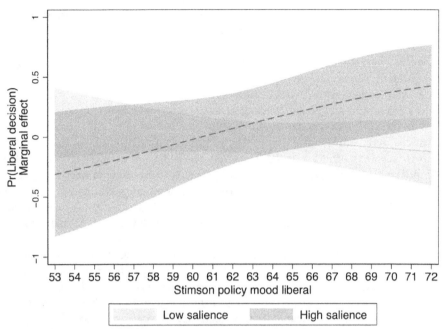

FIGURE 7.4 Effect on decision direction of group-rights cases (narrow measure)
Note: Figure displays, using the narrow measure model, the discrete marginal effect of a group-rights case on the likelihood of a liberal ruling as salience and the public's policy mood vary across their observed ranges. This effect differs significantly for salient versus non-salient cases across the range of the mood scale. Substantively, this indicates that the Court is more likely to rule in line with the public in salient cases concerning group rights.

whether this has implications for judicial behavior. More specifically, this chapter advances a new conceptualization of legitimacy's effects. Prior work tends to emphasize the idea that the Supreme Court reacts to the public's preferences for more liberal or conservative policy. It does, in no small part because of an indirect accountability mechanism – the president, chosen by popular election, has the ability to place members on the Court when a vacancy arises (Dahl 1957). Yet, it is well known that the Supreme Court cares deeply about its legitimacy, which it requires to function as an effective and authoritative institution. Responsiveness research makes claims about how the link between case output and legitimacy can influence judicial behavior, but few studies have directly linked specific insights from the legitimacy literature with an analysis of Court behavior.

The mechanism of legitimacy-maintenance becomes a more pressing concern when we see it through the theoretical lens of group rights. There is ample evidence that the public conditions its assessments of the institution on how they feel about the social groups involved in high-profile cases. By implication, the Court has reason to strategically defer in this subset of cases. It is this perspective for which this chapter provides empirical evidence.

Going forward, scholars would do well to consider more fully why courts may prove responsive in some cases but not others (e.g., Casillas, Enns, and Wohlfarth 2013). One area of attention is the assumption that "the Court" acts as a collective, with all justices behaving similarly. In actuality, justices have distinct personalities (Black et al. 2020) and differ in the importance they place on various considerations as they rule (Mark and Zilis 2019). Some justices may be quite attentive to the shape of public opinion on equal rights cases, whereas others may be less likely to display responsiveness. It is also important to recognize that more work needs to be done concerning social group cases in particular. This chapter provides an initial framework for studying the influence of legitimacy concerns when group-rights are involved, but much more work remains to be done. A few avenues may prove particularly fruitful.

First, case salience plays a prominent role, conditioning the willingness of the justices to strategically adjust their decision-making. This remains a fruitful area for future attention. However, when it comes to social group cases, scholars should pay careful attention to how salience can change over time. The justices may be aware of how their actions can influence the public's attentiveness. Therefore, they may have reason to adjust opinion language and other aspects of a decision beyond its simple ideological direction. For example, it would be useful to examine whether a Court majority tends to emphasize the non-controversial aspects of a ruling that protects the rights of an unpopular social group by, perhaps, speaking in more anodyne or non-specific terms. These adjustments also raise an interesting possibility about the strategic interplay on the Court, since dissenting justices may have reason to overemphasize the negative group-based aspects of the same ruling.[3] Recent work has suggested that the justices themselves tend to think in group-based terms when resolving controversies (Baum 2017). The justices, it is argued, rarely make "deductive" ideological judgments, but instead develop a set of consistent "ideological" patterns based upon how they feel about social groups involved in legal controversies.

As scholars continue to explore case law and responsiveness, they cannot neglect issues of selection. This chapter suggests that one way for the Supreme Court to avoid social group controversies is to simply limit the number of such controversies it puts on its docket. And, indeed, the Court only accepts a handful of social group cases each term. But why grant certiorari to any? Might the Court be better off if it entirely avoids these hot button issues?

These questions are not simple ones to answer. Even as the Court values its legitimacy, even as it considers the public, it also values other things as well. We

---

[3] Consider Scalia's dissent in *Arizona v. United States* (2012).

know that justices care about their own policy preferences (Segal and Spaeth 2002), which may make them willing to suffer a modest loss in legitimacy if it can lead to a more preferable policy outcome. It may also be the case that the Court takes seriously its guardian role. That is, the justices may place some value on protecting basic constitutional rights, even when these actions are highly unpopular. Ultimately, when we bring group antipathy into the mix, a nuanced portrait of Court decision-making emerges.

8

Conclusion

Consider the language of the law. On what principles do landmark rights cases hinge? In *Brown*: "It is doubtful that any child may reasonably be expected to succeed in life if he is reasonably denied the opportunity of an education. Such an opportunity, where the state has undertaken to provide it, is a right that must be made available to all on equal terms." Six decades later, in *United States v. Windsor*: "The power the Constitution grants it also restrains. And although Congress has great authority to design laws to fit its own conception of sound national policy, it cannot deny the liberty protected by the Due Process Clause of the Fifth Amendment." The principles and justifications driving these decisions, the Court argues, apply universally.

Now, consider the language undergirding popular perception. As Southerners raged over race-mixing, political elites gave voice to their sentiments. "These are not bad people," President Eisenhower told Chief Justice Earl Warren. "All they are concerned about is to see that their sweet little girls are not required to sit in school alongside some big black bucks" (O'Donnell 2018). Decades later, acceptable language conventions have evolved but discussions of landmark rulings still hinge on group-based considerations. Success of the "so-called homosexual agenda" (Justice Scalia's terminology in *Lawrence v. Texas*) eventually led to what one prominent internet site described as "Gay Day at the High Court" (Drudge Report 2013). To be sure, many Americans rejoiced over *Brown*, *Green*, and *Windsor*. The cases represented, in the Court majority's view, the value of counter-majoritarianism when it comes to protecting foundational rights. But it does suggest that many citizens – supporters and critics – tend to see certain cases in terms of winners, losers, and the groups involved. Doing so represents a simple approach to understanding what may appear to be a complex legal or political calculus made by the Court.

The main argument of this manuscript – that group-based thinking inflects views of the Supreme Court and seeps into institutional legitimacy – fits roughly with historical patterns we can observe in the wake of cases such as *Brown* and *Green* and also tracks evidence surrounding more recent decisions such as *Windsor*. The normative implications are considerable. At the same time, we should be careful when considering the scope of the argument and the ultimate implications. In the coming sections, I review the main findings of the manuscript and explore in detail their limitations and the unanswered questions they raise. I also situate the findings in the context of broader literatures concerning public opinion, media coverage, institutional support, and strategic behavior on the Supreme Court. I pay special attention to this last point, since it carries with it the most considerable implications concerning the Supreme Court's role as a guarantor of fundamental rights in American society. I suggest that the group antipathy model highlights a tension between the perception of the Court as a counter-majoritarian institution and the instances in which concerns over popular support can cause the institution to eschew this responsibility.

SUMMARY OF FINDINGS

The findings of this book suggest that a dominant ingredient that drove opinion about the Supreme Court in the wake of *Brown* continues to have an influence in the modern era. Group-based thinking shapes how citizens perceive the political world, and its resonance is quite powerful when it comes to jurisprudence involving rights-claims. The consistent finding across each of the studies presented in the manuscript is that a component of institutional legitimacy derives from the public's group-based thinking about the Court.

To be sure, this represents only one antecedent of diffuse support. Other work in the literature on legitimacy has identified its complex, multidimensional roots, touching on fundamental democratic values as well as partisan and ideological support. These considerations hold here. But group-based thinking has prominent resonance and serious implications, particularly in the wake of high-profile rulings.

A second, related finding concerns the contexts in which group antipathy operates most powerfully. It is important to acknowledge that Americans pay little attention to most of what the Supreme Court does and, even when they do follow decisions, they may receive a distorted portrait (Zilis, Wedeking, and Denison 2017). The vast majority of rulings will not activate group antipathy for most citizens. However, when activated, it operates powerfully. It may involve a wide range of social groups and influence the attitudes of both conservatives and liberals. It shapes the views that many classes of citizens hold, although its effects appear to be a bit more potent among those with higher levels of political knowledge. Based on the best evidence we have available, it also tends to endure for a period of time, although certainly not indefinitely.

Next, it is interesting to note that group antipathy has significant substantive effects. Its influence compares favorably to other antecedents of institutional support when evaluated in conjunction with them. And when we do our best to hold constant other relevant factors – such as the legal and policy substance of a ruling, using the identical decision studies from Chapter 5 – group-based considerations have a meaningful impact.

As further evidence that Americans think in group-based terms about the Supreme Court, this manuscript demonstrates that it is not only institutional legitimacy that is affected when the Court protects minority rights. Citizens also update their perceptions of the institution's ideological preferences, a fact that has indirect implications when it comes to legitimacy orientations. The ideology finding is interesting for a few reasons. First, it helps to shed some light on how citizens make sense of the complex and often contradictory cues surrounding the judiciary when deriving their subjective perceptions of its policy direction (Bartels and Johnston 2013). Based on a conjoint analysis of multiple, competing considerations, only two pieces of information about rulings shape ideological perceptions: social group cues and the ideological direction of the majority author. The latter is intuitive albeit not particularly interesting, but the former points to the broader resonance of the social group model. Second, the finding also challenges popular wisdom that certain types of decisions – such as those that strongly protect free speech rights – indicate a liberal Court. Based on the analyses presented here, it would be more accurate to say that the public may perceive substantively identical decisions as either conservative or liberal depending upon the social groups they involve.

The final set of findings emphasizes how popular group animus alters the Supreme Court's strategic calculus. We already have some anecdotal evidence of this, for instance, from Earl Warren's drive for unanimity in *Brown* out of legitimacy concerns. But Chapter 7 adds a few findings from an analysis of seven decades worth of data, showing the Court's general reluctance to docket prominent cases concerning disliked social groups as well as its tendency to follow the public in salient cases that it elects to resolve. Ultimately, the manuscript demonstrates the important role that group antipathy plays in coloring assessments of the Supreme Court, with a host of substantive implications.

IMPLICATIONS REGARDING ATTITUDES TOWARD THE COURT, NOMINATIONS, AND POLITICIZATION

The most direct contributions of this manuscript concern the large and rapidly evolving body of literature on institutional support and Supreme Court legitimacy. They do not call for a wholesale reassessment of this concept, for I have detailed the reasons why many of the antecedents that other scholars identify continue to play a critical role in understanding diffuse support. However, the manuscript introduces a novel consideration into our models of popular legitimacy, which can be distinguished in both conceptual and empirical terms from others. Group considerations enrich and alter our existing understandings in a number of ways.

First, group antipathy has implications for the democratic values model of diffuse support (Gibson, Caldeira, and Spence 2003b; Gibson and Nelson 2014, 2015). Both approaches de-emphasize the part that policy agreement plays in shaping legitimacy; indeed, some of the studies presented here are able to hold policy implications perfectly constant and still demonstrate how group-based thinking influences legitimacy. Relatedly, then, both approaches highlight how more enduring attitudes, commitments, and orientations contribute to institutional support. This is important given the limitations of Americans' political awareness, particularly when it comes to an institution whose actions tend not to be as salient as those of the president or even Congress. It is crucial for models of diffuse support to recognize this fact when considering how perceptions and assessments of the institution take shape.

Group antipathy also has both direct and indirect implications when it comes to the literature that suggests legitimacy derives from a citizen's ideological support for the Court (Bartels and Johnston 2013; Johnston, Hillygus, and Bartels 2014). One contribution of this literature is to identify the importance of *subjective* institutional perceptions in order to understand public opinion about the judiciary. In this way, Americans' limited objective knowledge is not only transparent but also has substantive importance. A puzzle then becomes understanding how citizens derive their subjective perceptions. Group cues have a role to play. As a result, there appears to be a complex interaction between group-based thinking, ideological perceptions, and institutional legitimacy when it comes to the Court.

A final thread in the recent literature and popular debates concerning Supreme Court legitimacy involves the place occupied by politicization, or the belief that the institution operates not as a legally principled institution but an ordinary political actor (Christenson and Glick 2015; Gibson and Nelson 2017). One finding in existing work is that perceptions of politicization can undermine diffuse support, although their effects are more powerful in certain contexts (and may also be blunted by communications that emphasize the legitimacy of the institution; see Gibson, Lodge, and Woodson 2014). The experiments in Chapter 5 shed light on this important concept by demonstrating the implications of group antipathy when it comes to the lens through which citizens perceive the Court. Because antipathy helps Americans derive their politicized versus legalistic perceptions, competing implications are possible. On the negative side for the Court, it is possible that perceptions of politicization may increase over time, as more rulings favoring disliked groups become prominent. The pattern would lay the groundwork to further undermine diffuse support. However, consider the alternative, in which the Court strategically adjusts its behavior, eschewing divisive group-rights cases to blunt perceptions of politicization. If more citizens come to perceive the institution as apolitical or legally motivated, it helps safeguard the reservoir of diffuse support. The cost comes in terms of the robust protection of minority rights.

More broadly, popular discourse has increasingly grappled with the effects of politicized Supreme Court nomination battles, such as that involving Justice Brett Kavanaugh. One prominent concern involves the influence of polarization and partisanship on how Americans perceive the institution in this environment. Polarization has indirect implications when it comes to the group-based model of opinion in that the left and right tend to divide in their reactions to rulings depending on the groups involved. To take one example from the manuscript, the left evinces less support for the Court when it protects the free speech rights of prolife advocates than when it takes the identical action with respect to prochoice protestors. Increased politicization has the potential to magnify these divisions going forward.

RELATIONSHIP WITH THE SUPREME COURT MEDIA LITERATURE

While this manuscript does not make media coverage of the Supreme Court a primary focus, it does offer a handful of observations about how the press portrays the institution. In reviewing other literature and conducting brief analyses of coverage on *Windsor*, *Arizona*, and *Citizens United*, I suggest that group-rights cases and Equal Protection jurisprudence tend to receive a prominent place in the public eye. Moreover, it appears that these cases attract attention *because* they concern prominent groups about which citizens feel strongly.

We know from the media coverage literature that citizens often learn about Court activities through secondhand accounts. As a result, press portrayals have a large influence on support for rulings (Zilis 2015) and institutional perceptions (Johnston and Bartels 2010). But existing work has yet to pay attention to the prominence of social group cues in the media. This leaves some notable gaps both when it comes to understanding popular perceptions of the Supreme Court and news production as a more general phenomenon. On the latter point, existing research suggests that journalists value accuracy in coverage while emphasizing that they also tend to canvas available cues from the Court – such as final voting outcomes – to shape the tenor of their coverage.

Might group cues blunt accuracy? It is worth exploring, for example, whether substantively equivalent decisions receive similar types of coverage when they involve distinct social groups. Indeed, the judicial context is ideal for such a test, since we know that the Court tends to apply the same legal principles across cases. A fuller examination has the potential to contribute to enduring debates about media bias that extend beyond the Supreme Court literature (Gentzkow and Shapiro 2010; Groseclose and Milyo 2005; Ho and Quinn 2008).

GENERAL IMPLICATIONS REGARDING PUBLIC OPINION

Some of this manuscript's central insights fit within and reinforce longstanding traditions in the political behavior literature. First, consider the prominent role of group-based thinking when it comes to how Americans interpret the political world. Converse (1964) made one of the original and most influential statements of this argument at a time when the civil rights movement raged and *Brown* was fresh in the public's mind. Given the rise of polarization in the decades since, one might question whether partisanship has blunted this influence. Recent advancements suggest that this is not the case – Americans still tend to organize their opinions about the political world in group-based terms (Kinder and Kalmoe 2017). This manuscript provides some additional evidence in the context of the Supreme Court. While the 1950s and 1960s may have represented an apogee of rights-based jurisprudence, the remnants reverberate to this day. Citizens tend to think about the work of the judiciary based on the groups involved in high-profile controversies.

A second line of research in the behavioral literature recognizes the limits to Americans' awareness about politics and suggests how efficient information processing – including the ability to leverage heuristics and cues – can help to overcome these deficiencies. The issue is particularly worthy of attention given the modest levels of knowledge Americans have about Supreme Court jurisprudence. Fitting with some of the same insights in the behavioral literature, this manuscript demonstrates the prominent role of group cues when it comes to assessments of the institution.

An interesting extension of this work is unique to the Court context, where legally principled justifications accompany political cues. Put in different terms, scholars have little sense of whether a "legally principled" framing can blunt the influence of group-based cues. The manuscript suggests reasons for pessimism, which come through most clearly in the pair of identical decision experiments. Even if we supply citizens strong, legally principled arguments for a Court decision, their reliance on social group cues continues unabated, further polarizing attitudes between the left and right. Further, in highlighting the central role of heuristic-based processing, the manuscript offers novel insights about the conditional effects of political knowledge. This upends the conventional wisdom suggesting that knowledge uniformly buttresses diffuse support. While certainly true on average, the conventional finding overlooks a more nuanced story. Knowledge has the capacity to exacerbate the negative effects of group antipathy on legitimacy. The mechanism that underpins this relationship involves a citizen's ability to correlate group-based cues with institutional assessments, a task that may prove more difficult for citizens with limited knowledge of the Court and its political role.

The manuscript also advances the behavioral literature when it comes to the question of how citizens form ideological perceptions about political institutions. Much of the existing work on this question demonstrates that stereotypes and other cues influence perceptions of *individual actors*, including specifically in the campaign context. For example, one notable finding demonstrates that Americans cue from the race and gender of political candidates to infer their ideological orientations, typecasting women and minority candidates as more liberal (Hayes 2011; Hutchings and Valentino 2004; McDermott 1997, 1998). Perceptions of institutional ideology are of equal importance, but scholars tend to know much less about how they take shape, in part because it is difficult for citizens to interpret race and gender cues when it comes to collective bodies like collegial courts or legislatures. The manuscript shows that other cues have a role to play. Specifically, group-based cues provide an overarching yet easy-to-understand indication of an institution's collective preferences. For example, these cues may signal the tendency of the Supreme Court as a whole to favor African Americans, or immigrants, or big business. Extending this framework, we may surmise that citizens leverage *summative cues*, or indicators of the average or collective preference, for other collegial institutions. For instance, citizens also use the ideological preference of the majority opinion author to infer the Court's preferences (see Study H), whereas the summative cue may be distinct when it comes to other institutional actors. This represents a fruitful area for future research.

IMPLICATIONS REGARDING STRATEGIC BEHAVIOR AND MINORITY RIGHTS

A dominant approach in the judicial politics literature sees justices as strategic actors with a variety of goals in mind (e.g., Epstein and Knight 1997, 2000, 2013; Maltzman, Spriggs, and Wahlbeck 2000; Murphy 1964). The insight has numerous implications, including the fact that justices place a premium on preserving their legitimacy and institutional authority (Clark 2011; Hall 2011). Yet, scholarship rarely applies the insights from the existing approaches in the legitimacy literature (e.g., Gibson and Nelson 2014; Bartels and Johnston 2013) in a direct fashion to the study of strategic judicial behavior. Not only does this manuscript suggest theoretical implications when it comes to the effects of group antipathy on Court decision-making, it also conducts empirical examinations on this front in Chapter 7.

The group antipathy model has significant resonance. From the perspective of judicial behavior, it suggests a specific mechanism that can influence the Court's calculus when it comes to legitimacy maintenance. Not only that, this mechanism – the public's attention to social group cues – has direct implications for a very specific form of judicial behavior, which involves the Court's actions on "group-rights cases," or those high-salience disputes involving claims brought by prominent social and political segments in American society. Often, these cases concern equal protection and due process rights or the First Amendment. When it comes to the strategic model, then, there is an incentive for the justices to adjust their behavior in a high-salience subset of cases. In short, the manuscript suggests the potential for productive lines of research that can combine the literatures on popular legitimacy and strategic judicial behavior.

The normative consequences are of greater importance. In Chapter 1, I identified a basic tension: "because the Court lacks enforcement power, its ability to protect fundamental rights depends on the pillar of institutional legitimacy." Yet, empirical examinations strongly suggest that citizens condition their level of legitimacy in response to their feelings toward the groups involved in prominent cases, a finding that implies that when the Court rules in favor of a disliked minority, its legitimacy may suffer. This, then, represents the *rights paradox*, or the contradictions between two basic goals of the Supreme Court: protecting minority rights and maintaining institutional legitimacy.

Of course, it is far from novel to identify the tension the Court faces between the need to maintain majority support and the responsibility to act in a counter-majoritarian fashion (Bickel 1986). But this manuscript marries two well-developed literatures to identify a particular type of cases and set of minorities that are most vulnerable in the modern era. If we conceive of the Supreme Court as purely strategic, one implication is that equal protection may not prove "equal" in any real sense. Rather, a Court focused on safeguarding its legitimacy has reason to deny claims when they come from the most disliked, vulnerable minorities. Claims made by other groups, however, may meet with success.

It goes without saying that such behavior would prove problematic from a normative perspective. But it may also be an oversimplification to suggest that the Court operates on a purely strategic basis. After all, the institution was responsible for *Brown*, well aware of the potential for backlash that would result. A more realistic conceptualization sees the justices as balancing a sincere commitment to the principles in the Constitution – and, in some cases, a desire to draft strong equal protection guarantees – with a series of other goals, such as the maintenance of legitimacy, in a strategic fashion. Doing so suggests an interesting possibility: for future work to explore, both at the institutional and micro-level, how justices balance these goals.

LIMITATIONS, UNANSWERED QUESTIONS, AND FUTURE DIRECTIONS

There are a number of limitations and unanswered questions concerning the intersection of institutional legitimacy and minority rights. First and most basically, the manuscript necessarily offers but a snapshot of how group antipathy conditions legitimacy, limited to certain groups and cases in a narrow time frame. Anecdotally, some of these results square with what we can observe about past cases in the Supreme Court's history, but it is quite reasonable to question how the patterns may evolve in the coming decades. One thing that we know for certain is that the public's attitudes toward various groups and the cases available to the Court will change over time. In the middle of the twentieth century, for example, African American rights took center stage at the Court, as did controversies such as the Japanese internment in *Korematsu*. Things have changed quite a bit in the intervening decades, and now different groups and claims find themselves in the spotlight. Similarly, the Court's orientation toward various groups has also evolved, a fact that we can witness in its increasing conservatism on civil rights matters from *Brown* to *Bakke* to *Shelby County* (see also Gibson and Caldeira 1992). While the general principles of group antipathy hold even as the groups themselves may shift, it is worth considering whether citizens will continue to organize their opinions of the political world along group-based demarcations going forward. A sensible alternative, brought on by the increase in polarization, is that party and ideology may become the overwhelming behavioral cleavage when it comes to evaluations of the Court. At the same time, the rise of identity politics in the modern era suggests that group-based thinking may continue to play a prominent role.

A second, separate consideration that deserves further exploration involves the persistence of group-based effects over time. In particular, it is fruitful to explore the length of time that high-profile group cues reverberate in assessments of the Court. We have some indications that these effects may persist over a period of months or even years, but much less is known about how subsequent developments condition temporal effects. For example, the Court's statement in *Brown* was followed by other pro-integration rulings in the coming decades, supplying fairly clear and consistent cues that the Warren Court was a friend to African Americans. This has the potential to dramatically strengthen the effects of group antipathy over a long period. But in other instances, the Court may fail to establish a consistent line of jurisprudence with respect to a particular group. It may even issue complex or potentially contradictory rulings in short succession. Ultimately, these possibilities raise important questions about how multiple factors interact when it comes to the public's perceptions concerning the social groups that the Supreme Court tends to favor.

The preceding discussion raises a question regarding the effects of strategic elite communications. Given that diffuse support responds strongly to group cues, political elites have an incentive to manipulate their communications about the groups that the Court favors. To offer one recent anecdote, consider a tweet from President Trump in the aftermath of *Sessions v. Dimaya* (2018). The Court had struck down a statutory provision as unconstitutionally vague, but the president suggested that the ruling would benefit "violent criminal aliens" (Lafond 2018). It is not a stretch to see this as an effort to affect public responses to the decision.

Going forward, it may prove valuable for scholars to consider multiple questions regarding strategic communications: Under what conditions do

Limitations, Unanswered Questions, and Future Directions 135

political actors seek to manipulate group cues about the Court? What strategic adjustments do the justices make, in terms of opinion language or otherwise, to combat these portrayals? And how do citizens make sense of elite cues about the Court in an era of news and fake news, particularly in the wake of high-profile rulings? On this latter point, Nelson and Gibson (2019) provide interesting work demonstrating how elite credibility conditions the effectiveness of Court-focused communications.

A final extension of this work would broaden our focus beyond institutional legitimacy. While a critically important thread in the literature, diffuse support represents only one way to gauge the authority of the Supreme Court. Another interesting outcome is enforcement and compliance with rulings, the lack of which greatly undermines the institution. Indeed, in some of the book's motivating examples, it is not just the Court's legitimacy that suffered but also the enforcement of its decisions. In the Appendix, I have conducted supplementary analysis on what I call decision acceptance, or the extent to which citizens want the government to enforce rulings and believe that Americans should comply and recognize their legitimacy. The results suggest that the effects of group antipathy extend into acceptance, raising a set of broader concerns (see also Zilis in press). These initial analyses lay the groundwork for a much more interesting inquiry on observed non-compliance such as that which followed *Green* or the school prayer cases of the 1960s (McGuire 2009).

***

The legitimacy concerns raised by its civil rights holdings did not take the Supreme Court by surprise. In the year following the release of *Brown*, the justices grappled with how to minimize white animus. Justice Felix Frankfurter emphasized the need to "encourage moderate leadership" in the South. Justice Robert Jackson cautioned that the ruling would not be accepted if "the Northern majority of this Court should make a Pharisaic and self-righteous approach to this issue." Perhaps, as Chief Justice Earl Warren had advised, the Court needed to operate in a "tolerant" and "non-accusatory" manner?[1] These statements suggest an institution well aware that the equal protection holding could undermine its popular legitimacy. Yet, however exceptional *Brown* was, a similar line of thinking appears at other historical junctures.

Six decades after *Brown*, Justice Scalia sought to undermine the legitimacy of another landmark civil rights case. Scalia, who had previously criticized the Court majority for adopting a pro-same-sex rights agenda without considering the Framers' original intent, wrote that *Obergefell v. Hodges* (2015) was a "decree say[ing] that my Ruler, and the Ruler of 320 million Americans coast-to-coast, is a majority of the nine lawyers on the Supreme Court." He

---

[1] This account is drawn from Klarman (2006, 315–316).

mentioned the silenced majority: "With each decision of ours that takes from the People a question properly left to them – with each decision that is unabashedly based not on law, but on the 'reasoned judgment' of a bare majority of this Court – we move one step closer to being reminded of our impotence."

Scalia's framing is grounded in timeless legal and constitutional principles, and it raises questions about the majoritarian versus counter-majoritarian dichotomy that has long animated debates about the Supreme Court's proper role. But is this representative of how ordinary Americans tend to understand the institution's landmark rights decisions? Or are other ingredients at work? A basic paradox facing the US Supreme Court is that Americans today evaluate the institution's legitimacy based on their feelings toward the very groups that equal protection of the law is intended to serve.

Appendix

OVERVIEW OF STUDIES, EXTERNAL VALIDITY, AND QUESTION WORDING

Studies A and B: The American Panel Survey

The American Panel Survey (TAPS) is a monthly online survey administered by the Weidenbaum Center at Washington University (Smith 2013). TAPS recruits respondents as a national probability sample using an address-based sampling frame with replenishment. Specifically,

the sample of addresses was drawn from the U.S. Postal Service's computerized delivery sequence file (CDSF). The CDSF covers some 97% of the physical addresses in all 50 states including P.O. boxes and rural route addresses. Homes that are vacant or seasonal are identified as are other categories that help to refine the efficiency of the sample to be mailed. Using data from available U.S. Census files plus from a variety of commercial databases, such as White Pages, Experian, Acxiom, etc., MSG can add names to these addresses, match with landline telephone numbers, and – with some level of accuracy – tag on information regarding race/ethnicity, age of householder, whether there are people of a certain age in the household, presence of children, home ownership status, etc.

To counterbalance under-response tendencies, TAPS uses four mutually exclusive strata, including Hispanic aged 18–24, all other Hispanic, non-Hispanic aged 18–24, and all other adults. In order to observe over time change and the effects of the group-rights rulings, I focus on respondents who remained in the survey without missing data on key indicators during the course of 2012–2013, the time period necessary to construct the models presented in Chapter 3. The N's are thus lower than in any single wave. Demographic information about these respondents is included in the following sections. Further technical information is available at taps.wustl.edu.

Question Wording (Factor Loadings in Parentheses Where Appropriate)

LEGITIMACY
- If the Court started making decisions that most people disagree with, it might be better to do away with the Court. (0.79)
- The right of the Supreme Court to decide certain types of controversial issues should be reduced. (0.80)
- The US Supreme Court gets too mixed up in politics. (0.61)
- Justices who consistently make decisions at odds with what a majority of the people want should be removed. (0.84)
- The US Supreme Court ought to be made less independent so that it listens a lot more to what the people want. (0.85)
- It is inevitable that the Court gets mixed up in politics; we ought to have a stronger means of controlling the Court. (0.86)
- Justices are just like other politicians; we cannot trust them to decide court cases in a way that is in the best interests of our country. (0.80)

GAY ANTIPATHY
- Rate each group using the scale shown below ... [Gays]
- Rate each group using the scale shown below ... [Gay rights activists]

IMMIGRANT ANTIPATHY (REVERSED AS APPROPRIATE)
- Rate each group using the scale shown below. [Hispanics] (0.37)
- [How concerned are you about each of the following?] Illegal immigrants are putting an unfair burden on US schools and government services. (0.64)
- [How concerned are you about each of the following?] Taking strict measures against illegal immigrants would lead authorities to harass Hispanics living in the United States. (0.71)
- [How concerned are you about each of the following?] Taking strict measures against illegal immigrants would go against the American tradition of welcoming those who come to the United States to find a better life. (0.74)
- [How concerned are you about each of the following?] Illegal immigrants are the cause of crime. (0.49)
- [How concerned are you about each of the following?] Illegal immigrants who are sent back to their country of origin will face a life of poverty. (0.60)

BLACK ANTIPATHY
- Rate each group using the scale shown below. [African Americans]

RULE OF LAW
- It is not necessary to obey a law you consider unjust. (0.68)
- Sometimes, it might be better to ignore the law and solve problems immediately rather than wait for a legal solution. (0.64)
- The government should have some ability to bend the law in order to solve pressing social and political problems. (0.52)

Appendix

- It is not necessary to obey the laws of a government that I did not vote for. (0.67)
- When it comes right down to it, law is not all that important; what's important is that our government solve society's problems and make us all better off. (0.68)

MINORITY LIBERTY SUPPORT
- Society shouldn't have to put up with those who have political ideas that are extremely different from the majority. (0.71)
- It is better to live in an orderly society than to allow people so much freedom that they can become disruptive. (0.73)
- Free speech is just not worth it if it means that we have to put up with the danger to society of extremist political views. (0.69)

POLITICAL TOLERANCE
- [Selected disliked group] should be allowed to hold public rallies and demonstrations in my community.

POLITICAL KNOWLEDGE
- Which party holds a majority of seats in the US House of Representatives in Washington? [Republicans = correct]
- How many votes are required in Congress to override a presidential veto? [a two-thirds majority of both houses of Congress = correct]
- How long is one term for a member of the US Senate? [six years = correct]
- The ability of a minority of senators to prevent a vote on a bill is known as [a filibuster = correct]
- Who is the Vice President of the United States? [Joseph Biden = correct]
- A president may serve [two terms = correct]
- Members of the US Supreme court serve [life terms = correct]
- Who is the Chief Justice of the United States Supreme Court? [John Roberts = correct]
- Social Security is [the benefit program for senior citizens = correct]
- On which of the following federal programs is the most money spent each year? [Medicare = correct]

SUPREME COURT IDEOLOGY (PRE-MODEL)
- Where would you place each of the following on this liberal–conservative scale? [very liberal, liberal, moderate; middle of the road, conservative, very conservative]

SUPREME COURT IDEOLOGY (POST-MODEL)
- Thinking about the US Supreme Court in Washington and the decisions that it has been making lately, would you say that the Court is ... [a very liberal court, a somewhat liberal court, a somewhat conservative court, a very conservative court]

TABLE A.1 *Descriptive statistics for Study A*

	Mean	St. Dev.	Min.	Max.
Legitimacy	0.64	0.23	0	1
Gay antipathy	0.50	0.28	0	1
Immigrant antipathy	0.58	0.25	0	1
Black antipathy	0.36	0.23	0	1
Labor union antipathy	0.56	0.30	0	1
Political tolerance	0.61	0.28	0	1
Minority liberty	0.73	0.21	0	1
Rule of law	0.77	0.16	0.15	1
Ideological disagreement	0.39	0.26	0	1
Knowledge	0.77	0.20	0	1
Republican	0.31	0.46	0	1
Education	0.82	0.25	0	1
Income	0.43	0.24	0	1
Female	0.41	0.49	0	1
Black	0.06	0.23	0	1
Hispanic	0.09	0.28	0	1

From respondents analyzed in first model of Table 3.1.

Study C: Identical Decisions

This study consists of a large-scale survey experiment drawing a sample of respondents recruited by Survey Sampling International (SSI). SSI's participant pool is managed to allow the selection of samples to reflect the target population, in this case voting age US adults. SSI balanced respondents for this study by age, gender, ethnicity, and census region. Potential participants were contacted with multiple notifications, including by email, and once within SSI's system, participants were matched with an available survey using multiple points of randomization. Respondents were replaced for straight-lining and speeding as well as the failure of two attention check questions, which could harm data quality. The study was administered during August 2018.

Validity

Respondents were randomly assigned to read stories involving one of three legal policy areas (free expression, religious freedom, or campaign spending) concerning six possible groups (prochoice/prolife activists, Muslims/Christian fundamentalists, labor unions/big business). To maintain strong internal validity, I designed the stimuli so that identical rulings could be plausibly framed to benefit very different groups. To maximize verisimilitude, I modeled their text on actual coverage of the US Supreme Court from mainstream news outlets with large audiences. The following coverage served as a model:

Appendix

"Court Rejects Zone to Buffer Abortion Clinic." Adam Liptak and John Schwartz for the *New York Times*. June 26, 2014.
www.nytimes.com/2014/06/27/us/supreme-court-abortion-clinic-protests.html

"Supreme Court: Abortion 'Buffer Zones' Violate Freedom of Speech." Haley Sweetland Edwards for *Time*. June 26, 2014.
http://time.com/2927734/supreme-court-abortion-buffer-zones/

"Hobby Lobby's Win for Religious Freedom." Jennifer Rubin for the *Washington Post*. June 30, 2014.
www.washingtonpost.com/blogs/right-turn/wp/2014/06/30/hobby-lobbys-win-for-religious-freedom/?utm_term=.f77b0a030ea5

"How Citizens United Has Changed Politics in 5 Years." Gabrielle Levy for *U.S. News and World Report*. January 21, 2015.
www.usnews.com/news/articles/2015/01/21/5-years-later-citizens-united-has-remade-us-politics

"Supreme Court Ruling on Union Fees is a Limited Blow to Labor." Steven Greenhouse for the *New York Times*. June 30, 2014.
www.nytimes.com/2014/07/01/business/supreme-court-ruling-on-public-workers-and-union-fees.html

Question Wording (Factor Loadings in Parentheses Where Appropriate)

LEGITIMACY
- It is inevitable that the US Supreme Court gets mixed up in politics; therefore, we ought to have stronger means of controlling the actions of the US Supreme Court. (0.72)
- The US Supreme Court ought to be made less independent so that it listens a lot more to what the people want. (0.73)
- Judges on the US Supreme Court who consistently make decisions at odds with what a majority of the people want should be removed from their position as judge. (0.74)
- Supreme Court Justices are just like any other politicians; we cannot trust them to decide court cases in a way that is in the best interests of our country. (0.73)
- If the US Supreme Court started making a lot of decisions that most people disagree with, it might be better to do away with the Court altogether. (0.71)
- The US Supreme Court gets too mixed up in politics. (0.59)
- The right of the Supreme Court to decide certain types of controversial issues should be reduced. (0.77)

KNOWLEDGE
- On which of the following federal programs is the most money spent each year? [Medicare = correct]

TABLE A.2 *Descriptive statistics for Study C*

Characteristic	Proportion of sample
Age	
18–25	11.07
26–35	18.93
36–45	16.88
46–55	16.07
56–65	19.47
66 or over	17.58
Race	
White	70.52
Black	11.26
Asian/Pacific Isl.	5.26
Native American	0.96
Other/White	12.00
Ethnicity	
Hispanic	10.23
Non-Hispanic	89.77
Gender	
Male	46.13
Female	53.87

From respondents analyzed in Study C.

- Who is the Chief Justice of the United States Supreme Court? [John Roberts = correct]
- How many votes are required in Congress to override a presidential veto? [a two-thirds majority of both houses of Congress = correct]

Study D: Additional Identical Decision Study

This study uses a similar experimental design to Study C, administered to a convenience sample of respondents who were recruited through Amazon's mTurk interface in July 2017. The study advertisement invited respondents to take part in a short survey about their political opinions. Following best practices to ensure data quality, participation was restricted to individuals 18 years and older located in the United States who had successfully completed at least 1,000 mTurk tasks at a rate of greater than 95% approval.

Validity
Please see discussion for Study C, which used identical materials.

Appendix

Question Wording (Factor Loadings in Parentheses Where Appropriate)

LEGITIMACY

- It is inevitable that the US Supreme Court gets mixed up in politics; therefore, we ought to have stronger means of controlling the actions of the US Supreme Court. (0.78)
- The US Supreme Court ought to be made less independent so that it listens a lot more to what the people want. (0.77)
- Judges on the US Supreme Court who consistently make decisions at odds with what a majority of the people want should be removed from their position as judge. (0.79)
- Supreme Court Justices are just like any other politicians; we cannot trust them to decide court cases in a way that is in the best interests of our country. (0.77)
- If the US Supreme Court started making a lot of decisions that most people disagree with, it might be better to do away with the Court altogether. (0.74)
- The US Supreme Court gets too mixed up in politics. (0.61)
- The right of the Supreme Court to decide certain types of controversial issues should be reduced. (0.80)

KNOWLEDGE

- On which of the following federal programs is the most money spent each year? [Medicare = correct]
- Do you happen to know who has the last say when there is a conflict over the meaning of the Constitution – the US Supreme Court, the US Congress, or the President? [The US Supreme Court = correct]
- Who is the Chief Justice of the United States Supreme Court? [John Roberts = correct]
- The ability of minority senators to prevent a vote on a bill is known as ... [a filibuster = correct]
- How many votes are required in Congress to override a presidential veto? [a two-thirds majority of both houses of Congress = correct]

TABLE A.3 *Descriptive statistics for Study D*

	Mean	St. Dev.	Min.	Max.
Legitimacy	24.67	9.44	0	42
Predispositions	4.93	3.91	0	12
Age	39.83	13.47	19	81
Female	0.49	0.50	0	1
Black	0.07	0.25	0	1
Hispanic	0.08	0.27	0	1
Knowledge	3.55	1.26	0	5

From respondents analyzed in first model of Table 5.7.

Study E: Multiple Decisions

This study uses a convenience sample of respondents recruited through Amazon's mTurk interface in May 2016. The study advertisement invited respondents to take part in a short survey about their political opinions. Following best practices to ensure data quality, participation was restricted to individuals 18 years and older located in the United States who had successfully completed at least 1,000 mTurk tasks at a rate of greater than 95% approval.

Validity

Respondents were randomly assigned to read stories involving one of four social groups (African Americans, big business, immigrants, or Muslims). To maintain strong internal validity, I designed the stimuli so that the only information that changed about a group was the frequency with which the Court ruled in its favor. To maximize verisimilitude, I modeled the text on actual coverage of the US Supreme Court from mainstream news outlets with large audiences. The following coverage served as a model:

> "For Justices, Free Speech Often Means 'Speech I Agree With.'" Adam Liptak for the *New York Times*. May 5, 2014.
> www.nytimes.com/2014/05/06/us/politics/in-justices-votes-free-speech-often-means-speech-i-agree-with.html?mcubz=2
>
> "Corporations Find a Friend in the Supreme Court." Adam Liptak for the *New York Times*. May 4, 2013.
> www.nytimes.com/2013/05/05/business/%20%20pro-business-decisions-are-defining-this-supreme-court.html?mcubz=2
>
> "Playing Favourties." *The Economist*. May 13, 2014.
> www.economist.com/blogs/democracyinamerica/2014/05/judicial-bias

TABLE A.4 *Descriptive statistics for Study E*

	Mean	St. Dev.	Min.	Max.
Legitimacy	22.91	9.57	0	42
Predispositions	2.49	1.84	0	6
Age	38.47	12.98	19	79
Female	0.48	0.50	0	1
Black	0.07	0.25	0	1
Hispanic	0.07	0.26	0	1
Knowledge	3.33	1.41	0	5

From respondents analyzed in first model of Table 5.8.

Appendix

Study F: Pending Case

This study uses a convenience sample of respondents who were recruited through Amazon's mTurk interface during the fall of 2016. The study advertisement invited respondents to take part in a short survey about their political opinions. Following best practices to ensure data quality, participation was restricted to individuals 18 years and older located in the United States who had successfully completed at least 1,000 mTurk tasks at a rate of greater than 95% approval.

Validity

Respondents were randomly assigned to read stories concerning potential Supreme Court involvement in Donald Trump's proposals to ban immigration from majority Muslim nations and Muslims more generally. The study was administered just prior to the 2016 presidential election, when there was uncertainty as to whether Trump would win the election and whether, if he did, the immigration proposal would be implemented and its constitutionality reviewed. This uncertainty provided the opportunity to credibly manipulate information about potential judicial involvement in a group-rights controversy.

TABLE A.5 *Descriptive statistics for Study F*

	Mean	St. Dev.	Min.	Max.
Legitimacy	24.66	10.17	0	42
Predispositions	2.47	1.86	0	6
Age	41.06	13.15	18	79
Female	0.49	0.50	0	1
Black	0.07	0.25	0	1
Republican	0.77	0.80	0	2
Knowledge	3.68	1.30	0	5

From respondents analyzed in first model of Table 5.9.

Study G: Conjoint Analysis

This study uses a convenience sample of respondents who were recruited through Amazon's mTurk interface during the spring of 2018. The study advertisement invited respondents to take part in a short survey about their political opinions. Following best practices to ensure data quality, participation was restricted to individuals 18 years and older located in the United States who had successfully completed at least 1,000 mTurk tasks at a rate of greater than 95% approval. Respondents were tasked with learning about prominent First Amendment rulings from the US Supreme Court over the past five decades.

Validity

A primary benefit of the conjoint design is its ability to isolate the component-specific effects of many attributes through full randomization. For the purpose of this study, the component of interest was the social group that benefits from a Supreme Court ruling. This created the need to identify other attributes that could simultaneously vary. Drawing on research concerning Supreme Court media coverage (Zilis 2015), I identified five other high-profile attributes that tend to get referenced in coverage: ideology, the use of judicial review, the treatment of precedent, the legal issue, and the vote outcome in a case. This design helped to ensure that respondents received information that is often included in media coverage.

Outcome Question

Which Court do you believe to be more liberal?

The Court that issued Ruling A
The Court that issued Ruling B

EXPERIMENTAL MATERIALS

Randomly assigned treatments in [brackets]

Study C: Identical Decisions

[Note: Free expression condition]

Supreme Court Allows [Pro-Choice/Pro-Life] **Groups Leeway for Aggressive Protest**

Washington (AP) – In response to recent developments at the Supreme Court, some [pro-choice/pro-life] groups are vowing to use strong new protest tactics to exercise their First Amendment rights. In the past 5 years, the Court has issued two rulings that substantially broaden the ability of [pro-choice/pro-life] groups to stage aggressive demonstrations near clinics, churches, and other public spaces. The rulings are based on the premise that the constitution protects even the most offensive language when it is under the guise of political protest.

In one landmark ruling, the Court held that even language that may "inflict great pain" is entitled to strong First Amendment protections. The lone dissenter in the case wrote that the Court was protecting "outrageous conduct" that would "allow the brutalization of innocent victims" targeted by aggressive protestors. In a second case, the Court invalidated "buffer zone" areas that had been implemented to protect ordinary citizens from harassment from aggressive protestors. All nine justices agreed that these protections violated the First Amendment.

Taken together, the decisions offer greater legal protection for [pro-choice/pro-life] groups who engage in aggressive protest. In one recent case out of

Massachusetts, a small group of [pro-choice/pro-life] protestors blocked a sidewalk while shouting obscenities at counter-demonstrators. Three members of the group were arrested for breaching the peace, but a district court, applying recent Supreme Court standards, threw out the case.

As some [pro-choice/pro-life] groups consider new organizing strategies and aim to grow their bases of support, the Court's rulings have provided them a powerful tool. According to John James, the president of Americans for [Choice/Life], a [pro-choice/pro-life] lobbying group, "We now have the legal protection necessary to make sure the message of [choice / life] is heard, loud and clear."

[Note: Religious freedom condition]
Supreme Court Offers Legal Exemptions for [Muslim/Christian Fundamentalist] **Groups**

Washington (AP) – Recent developments at the Supreme Court have exempted [**Muslim/Christian fundamentalist**] organizations from federal law when compliance would raise a religious objection. In the past 10 years, the Court, under its religious freedom doctrine, has issued rulings that substantially broaden the ability of religious groups to ignore federal mandates. In response, some [**Muslim/Christian fundamentalist**] groups are vowing to seek exemptions from a wide variety of regulations.

In one landmark decision, issued in 2014, the Court ruled that even the most powerful religious organizations may object to federal law, including mandates to protect employee rights and prevent discrimination. These objections would then pave the way for exemptions so that the organizations do not have to comply with the law. The dissenting justices in the case argued that exemptions will allow religious groups with powerful lobbying organizations to gain special treatment. In an earlier case, a unanimous Court offered additional exemptions for religious groups.

Taken together, the decisions offer greater legal protection for [**Muslim/Christian fundamentalist**] organizations to flex their political muscle while enjoying immunity from some aspects of federal law. In one recent case out of Colorado, the owner of [an Islamic/a Christian] bookstore refused to answer questions posed by federal agents who were investigating child labor violations. After the owner cited a religious objection, a district court, applying recent Supreme Court standards, excused him from testifying.

As [**Muslim/Christian fundamentalist**] groups consider strategies to wield political influence, the Court's rulings have provided them a powerful tool. According to Jonathan Sharan, the head of [an Islamic/a fundamentalist] lobbying organization in Dallas, the rulings are "a shot in the arm for the often-overlooked rights of devout [**Muslims / Christians**]."

[Note: Campaign spending condition]

Supreme Court Further Expands Role of [Labor Union/Corporate] **Money in Campaigns**

Washington (AP) – In a ruling with profound implications for the role of money in American campaigns, the Supreme Court has punched an even bigger hole in the complex web of federal campaign finance regulations. The case concerned the ability for a [labor union/corporation] to support specific candidates for office. The Supreme Court's earlier decisions had permitted [union /corporate] spending on issue advertising, but the Court has now substantially extended the right to spend so that it includes candidate advertising. As a result, some [unions/companies] are vowing to take a much more aggressive approach in the upcoming elections.

Critics have warned that decision calls into question fundamental principles of equal access in American democracy. They fear that organizations will spend so much money they will be able to pick and choose who wins elections with little recourse from ordinary citizens. But the ruling has been cheered by those who said it returns the country to the core free speech precept that political speech should be protected, no matter who is speaking.

The Court argues it is returning to "ancient First Amendment principles." The stronger protections for [labor/corporate] influence in elections mean that a host of new legal issues may arise. In one recent case out of New York, a [union/corporate] board authorized spending over $20,000 to attack a judicial candidate as "unfit for office." The candidate, Melanie Taylor, sought an injunction, but a district court, applying the new Supreme Court standard, allowed the advertising campaign to go forward.

Now some [unions/corporations] are vowing an even more active role in politics. "The government may not suppress our right to speak on issues important to us," said John Davis, president of [**National Labor, an activist trade union/National Investing, a wealth management firm**]. "The ruling represents a shot in the arm for [workers/companies] whose voices had been suppressed."

Study D: Additional Identical Decision Study

See the free expression and religious freedom conditions in the previous sections, which used identical materials.

Study E: Multiple Decisions

Treatment:

> The Supreme Court has been increasingly in the public eye this campaign season and a recent academic analysis raises questions about its future direction. This study analyzed all rulings that involved big business organizations and found that, a few high-profile decisions notwithstanding, the current Court is strongly [**pro/anti**] GROUP, [**supporting/rejecting**] GROUP-rights claims in about 80% of the cases it has resolved since 2005.

Appendix

Study F: Pending Case

Respondents were randomly assigned to a control prompt, with no text, or a treatment prompt, in which they received items that referenced Donald Trump's proposed immigration ban and the Supreme Court's likely involvement in the case. These items read as follows:

- Republican presidential candidate Donald Trump has previously proposed banning all Muslims from entering the United States. According to Trump, "Until we are able to determine and understand this problem and the dangerous threat it poses, our country cannot be the victims of horrendous attacks by people that believe only in Jihad, and have no sense of reason or respect for human life." Please rate your support for a potential ban on Muslim immigration.
- If implemented, an immigration ban is likely to be reviewed by the Supreme Court. Please rate your agreement with the following statement: A ban on Muslim immigration is constitutional.

To satisfy the "objection precondition," respondents' answers to the first item were used to determine an additional item that would be shown:

- Many legal analysts believe that the Supreme Court is likely to [uphold/strike down] any ban on Muslim immigration as constitutional. Please rate your support for a ruling that would uphold a ban on Muslim immigration.

Study G: Conjoint Analysis

Instructions

In the following questions, we will show you information that will enable you to compare some prominent First Amendment rulings issued over the last 50 years. These rulings occurred at different points in time, meaning that they were issued by different groups of justices. Please read this information carefully. Then, we would like you to compare the rulings that have been described.

TABLE A.6 *Possible ruling profiles presented to respondents*

Attribute	Potential traits
Most prominent beneficiaries	Christian fundamentalists groups, Big business organizations, Prolife demonstrators, Immigrant advocacy organizations, Islamic organizations, Labor unions
Did the ruling strike down legislation?	Yes, No
Ideology of opinion author	Conservative, Moderate, Liberal
Legal area	Campaign contributions, Membership exclusions, Political speech
Prior precedent related to the ruling	Prior decisions were largely consistent with ruling, Prior decisions were largely inconsistent with ruling
Vote outcome in case	9–0, 7–2, 5–4

TABLE A.7 *Ruling-pairs presents to respondents*

	Ruling A	Ruling B
Most prominent beneficiaries		*All traits fully randomized*
Did the ruling strike down legislation?		
Ideology of opinion author		
Legal area		
Prior precedent related to the ruling		
Vote outcome in case		

ADDITIONAL ANALYSES

The Conditioning Effect of Political Knowledge

Political knowledge plays a central role in studies of Supreme Court legitimacy, as high-knowledge individuals are much more likely to express durable support for the institution (Caldeira and Gibson 1992). Knowledge also affects exposure to and interpretation of new information more generally (Zaller 1992), and cues tend to have greater impact among the politically knowledgeable. Group-rights rulings represent one such cue about Supreme Court behavior. While the models in the main manuscript thus control for knowledge, it is also worth exploring whether knowledge conditions the effects of group antipathy. The analyses that follow explore how knowledge interacts with antipathy across all studies. When combined with evidence from the main manuscript, they suggest that the influence of antipathy is more pronounced among those high in knowledge.

TABLE A.8 *Knowledge interaction, Study A*

	(1) May 2012	(2) July 2012	(3) Jan. 2013	(4) July 2013
Gay antipathy	0.03	−0.01	0.05	0.02
	(0.11)	(0.12)	(0.12)	(0.12)
Knowledge	0.17	0.13	0.17	0.30*
	(0.10)	(0.10)	(0.10)	(0.11)
*Gay antipathy * Knowledge*	0.01	−0.03	−0.11	−0.13
	(0.14)	(0.16)	(0.15)	(0.16)
Immigrant antipathy	−0.10	−0.29*	−0.23	−0.02
	(0.13)	(0.13)	(0.13)	(0.14)
*Immigrant antipathy * Knowledge*	0.06	0.21	0.17	−0.12
	(0.16)	(0.16)	(0.17)	(0.17)
Black antipathy	−0.01	0.00	−0.00	0.02
	(0.03)	(0.04)	(0.04)	(0.04)
Labor union antipathy	−0.03	0.01	−0.02	−0.00
	(0.03)	(0.03)	(0.03)	(0.03)
Political tolerance	0.10*	0.13*	0.12*	0.19*
	(0.03)	(0.03)	(0.03)	(0.03)
Minority liberty	0.25*	0.21*	0.27*	0.22*
	(0.04)	(0.04)	(0.05)	(0.05)

Appendix

	(1) May 2012	(2) July 2012	(3) Jan. 2013	(4) July 2013
Rule of law	0.21*	0.28*	0.22*	0.22*
	(0.05)	(0.05)	(0.06)	(0.06)
Ideological distance	−0.18*	−0.14*	−0.19*	−0.20*
	(0.03)	(0.03)	(0.03)	(0.03)
Republican	0.01	−0.05*	−0.05*	−0.05*
	(0.02)	(0.02)	(0.02)	(0.02)
Education	0.13*	0.18*	0.17*	0.12*
	(0.03)	(0.03)	(0.03)	(0.03)
Income	0.03	0.01	0.01	−0.00
	(0.03)	(0.03)	(0.03)	(0.03)
Female	−0.02	0.00	−0.00	−0.01
	(0.01)	(0.02)	(0.02)	(0.02)
Black	0.04	0.08*	0.04	0.01
	(0.03)	(0.03)	(0.03)	(0.04)
Hispanic	0.05	0.02	0.01	0.01
	(0.03)	(0.03)	(0.03)	(0.03)
R^2	0.366	0.410	0.404	0.379
N	704	699	698	672

Note: Results are estimated ordinary least squares (OLS) coefficients with standard errors in parentheses. *p < 0.05 (one-tailed).

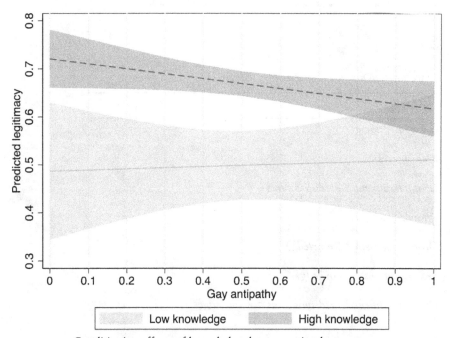

FIGURE A.1 Conditioning effects of knowledge, by gay antipathy
Note: Figure shows the predicted values and 95% confidence intervals from the final (post-ruling) model in the table above. Substantively, this shows stronger negative effects from gay antipathy on legitimacy among those highest in political knowledge.

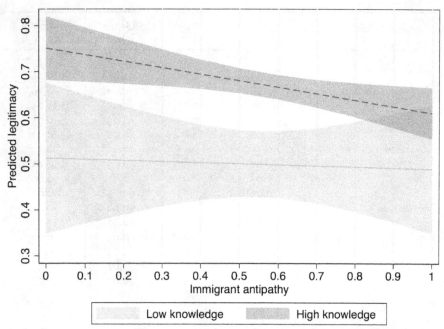

FIGURE A.2 Conditioning effects of knowledge, by immigrant antipathy
Note: Figure shows the predicted values and 95% confidence intervals from the final (post-ruling) model in the table above. Substantively, this shows stronger negative effects from immigrant antipathy on legitimacy among those highest in political knowledge.

TABLE A.9 *Knowledge interaction, Study D*

	(1) Study D
Group treatment	0.49
	(3.23)
Predispositions	−0.27
	(0.36)
Group treatment * Predispositions	0.14
	(0.50)
Knowledge	1.97*
	(0.59)
Group treatment * Knowledge	0.50
	(0.84)
Predispositions * Knowledge	0.06
	(0.09)
Group treatment * Predispositions * Knowledge	−0.16
	(0.13)

Appendix

	(1) Study D
Age	0.04
	(0.02)
Female	−1.43*
	(0.65)
Hispanic	−0.68
	(1.16)
Black	−1.36
	(1.26)
R^2	0.134
N	798

Note: Results are estimated OLS coefficients with standard errors in parentheses.
*p < 0.05 (one-tailed).

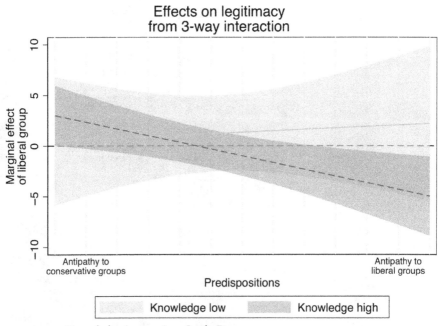

FIGURE A.3 Knowledge interaction, Study D
Note: The figure displays marginal effects and 95% confidence intervals from the experimental treatment when interacted with knowledge and predispositions using the model from the table above. Substantively, this shows that increased levels of political knowledge strengthen the effects of group considerations on Supreme Court legitimacy.

TABLE A.10 *Knowledge interaction, Study E*

	(1) **Study E**
Group treatment	3.11
	(2.99)
Antipathy	1.02
	(0.64)
*Group treatment * Antipathy*	−1.54*
	(0.92)
Knowledge	3.35*
	(0.57)
*Group treatment * Knowledge*	−0.38
	(0.83)
*Antipathy * Knowledge*	−0.31*
	(0.17)
*Group treatment * Antipathy * Knowledge*	0.27
	(0.25)
Age	−0.01
	(0.03)
Female	−0.13
	(0.66)
Black	−3.68*
	(1.29)
Hispanic	01.92
	(1.27)
R^2	0.177
N	759

Note: Results are estimated OLS coefficients with standard errors in parentheses.
*p < 0.05 (one-tailed).

Appendix

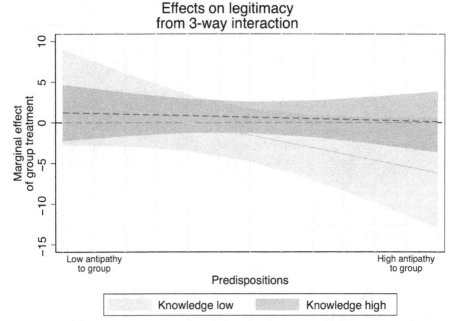

FIGURE A.4 Knowledge interaction, Study E
Note: The figure displays marginal effects and 95% confidence intervals from the experimental treatment when interacted with knowledge and predispositions using the model from the table above. Substantively, this shows no link between political knowledge and the effects of group considerations on Supreme Court legitimacy.

The Components of Legitimacy

TABLE A.11 *Legitimacy disaggregated, Study D*

	Legit item 1	Legit item 2	Legit item 3	Legit item 4	Legit item 5	Legit item 6	Legit item 7
Group treatment	0.46*	0.41*	0.25	0.35	0.24	0.30	0.33
	(0.18)	(0.20)	(0.19)	(0.18)	(0.18)	(0.19)	(0.18)
Predispositions	0.01	0.01	0.01	−0.01	0.01	−0.03	−0.03
	(0.02)	(0.02)	(0.02)	(0.02)	(0.02)	(0.02)	(0.02)
Group treatment * Predispositions	−0.09*	−0.06*	−0.05	−0.06*	−0.06*	−0.05*	−0.06*
	(0.03)	(0.03)	(0.03)	(0.03)	(0.03)	(0.03)	(0.03)
Age	0.00	0.01	0.01*	0.01	0.01	−0.00	0.01
	(0.00)	(0.01)	(0.00)	(0.00)	(0.00)	(0.00)	(0.00)

(*continued*)

TABLE A.11 (continued)

	Legit item 1	Legit item 2	Legit item 3	Legit item 4	Legit item 5	Legit item 6	Legit item 7
Female	-0.32*	-0.32*	-0.42*	-0.08	0.20	0.08	-0.15
	(0.12)	(0.13)	(0.12)	(0.12)	(0.11)	(0.12)	(0.12)
Hispanic	-0.04	0.01	-0.01	-0.36	-0.07	-0.12	-0.11
	(0.21)	(0.23)	(0.21)	(0.21)	(0.20)	(0.21)	(0.21)
Black	-0.58*	-0.67*	-0.04	0.00	-0.16	0.23	-0.19
	(0.23)	(0.25)	(0.23)	(0.23)	(0.22)	(0.23)	(0.22)
Knowledge	0.30*	0.39*	0.34*	0.25*	0.38*	0.11*	0.34
	(0.05)	(0.05)	(0.05)	(0.05)	(0.05)	(0.05)	(0.05)
R^2	0.103	0.119	0.110	0.066	0.134	0.034	0.119
N	798	798	798	798	798	798	798

Note: Results are estimated OLS coefficients with standard errors in parentheses. *p < 0.05 (one-tailed).

Group-Specific Effects

TABLE A.12 *Conditions disaggregated, Study D*

	(1) Free expression (Prochoice/Prolife)	(2) Religious freedom (Muslim/Christian)
Group treatment	3.09*	1.19
	(1.45)	(1.41)
Predispositions	-0.09	0.03
	(0.16)	(0.17)
Group treatment * Predispositions	-0.48*	-0.34
	(0.23)	(0.23)
Age	0.04	0.06
	(0.03)	(0.04)
Female	-0.55	-2.39*
	(0.91)	(0.95)
Hispanic	-1.24	-0.12
	(1.59)	(1.67)
Black	-0.00	-3.23
	(1.78)	(1.78)
Knowledge	1.77*	2.43*
	(0.36)	(0.40)
R^2	0.098	0.198
N	429	369

Note: Results are estimated OLS coefficients with standard errors in parentheses. *p < 0.05 (one-tailed).

TABLE A.13 *Conditions disaggregated, Study E*

	(1) Business	(2) Immigrant	(3) Muslim
Group treatment	−1.31	4.34*	1.52
	(2.49)	(1.75)	(1.80)
Antipathy	1.36*	−0.38	−0.95*
	(0.42)	(0.38)	(0.42)
Group treatment * Antipathy	0.17	−1.45*	−0.27
	(0.63)	(0.59)	(0.57)
Age	0.05	0.00	−0.00
	(0.05)	(0.04)	(0.04)
Female	−1.40	0.58	−0.62
	(1.21)	(1.08)	(1.08)
Black	0.64	−8.39*	−5.03*
	(2.38)	(2.24)	(1.97)
Hispanic	−2.37	2.65	−2.68
	(2.52)	(1.97)	(2.00)
Knowledge	1.81*	3.15*	2.96*
	(0.44)	(0.38)	(0.39)
R^2	0.175	0.259	0.284
N	231	279	249

Note: Results are estimated OLS coefficients with standard errors in parentheses. *$p < 0.05$ (one-tailed).

Additional Implications Regarding Legal Acceptance

In addition to institutional legitimacy, Study C included items that enable us to assess the effects of group antipathy on a wide range of rule of law attitudes. I utilize a multiple item index to measure *acceptance* of rulings: support for the rulings described, willingness to "challenge the rulings and get them changed," agreement with whether they "ought to be considered the final word on the matter," and agreement with whether "the government should refuse to implement the rulings." Responses to these items load strongly on a single underlying factor (eigenvalue 1.65), and the final summative index is scaled from 0 to 16 with higher values representing greater acceptance. The following table displays the full set of coefficient estimates from models that will be analyzed.

To explore the effects of group antipathy on acceptance, we can focus on the estimated coefficient for the interaction between treatment and predispositions, which is statistically significant and negative. This shows that legal acceptance is shaped by group-based considerations. Specifically, it depicts how predispositions interact with social groups in a predictable and substantively meaningful way. When we focus first on the left-hand side of the figure, we are homing in on strong liberals and Democrats, who possess the most negative feelings toward conservative groups (prolife protestors, Christian fundamentalists, big business organizations). In a legally principled model, these individuals should be most positively disposed toward Supreme Court rulings that favor the protection of free speech and political protest. But the results strongly belie this expectation. Rather than legal principles, it is the *specific groups* that benefit that affect acceptance. When liberal groups stand to benefit from a free speech ruling, the model predicts a significantly higher degree of acceptance than when conservative groups benefit (predicted support for compliance is 7.69 versus 5.28). This is the difference between approximately the 27th and 47th percentiles in acceptance, which equates in substantive to the difference between a "neutral" and a "disagree" position in response to more than two of the compliance items.

TABLE A.14 *Predicting rule of law attitudes, Study C*

	(1) Main	(2) Interactive
Group treatment	2.41*	1.31*
	(0.21)	(0.36)
Predispositions	0.31*	0.20*
	(0.02)	(0.04)
Group treatment * Predispositions	−0.39*	−0.26*
	(0.03)	(0.06)
Age	−0.19*	−0.19*
	(0.03)	(0.03)
Female	−0.22	−0.21
	(0.11)	(0.11)
Black	0.33	0.34
	(0.18)	(0.18)
Hispanic	0.27	0.25
	(0.19)	(0.19)
Knowledge	−0.02	−0.63*
	(0.06)	(0.16)
Group treatment * Knowledge	~	0.83*
		(0.22)
Predispositions * Knowledge	~	0.08*
		(0.02)
Group treatment * Predispositions * Knowledge	~	−0.09*
		(0.03)
R^2	0.076	0.082
N	3,117	3,117

Note: Results are estimated OLS coefficients with standard errors in parentheses. *$p < 0.05$ (one-tailed).

Appendix

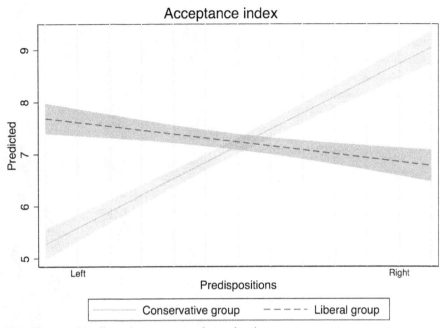

FIGURE A.5 The effect of group antipathy on legal acceptance
Note: Predicted values and 95% confidence intervals from the main acceptance model in the table above. Substantively, this shows how social groups polarize acceptance of the law.

References

Allen, Jody L., and Brian J. Daugherity. 2006. "Recovering a 'Lost' Story Using Oral History: The United States Supreme Court's Historic *Green v. New Kent County Virginia* Decision." *Oral History Review* 33(2): 25–44.

Arceneaux, Kevin. 2012. "Cognitive Biases and the Strength of Political Arguments." *American Journal of Political Science* 55(2): 271–285.

Arceneaux, Kevin, and Robin Kolodny. 2009. "Educating the Least Informed: Group Endorsements in a Grassroots Campaign." *American Journal of Political Science* 53(4): 755–770.

Armaly, Miles T. 2018. "Extra-Judicial Actor Induced Change in Supreme Court Legitimacy." *Political Research Quarterly* 71(3): 600–613.

Aronson, Eliot, Phoebe C. Ellsworth, J. Merrill Carlsmith, and M. H. Gonzales. 1990. *Methods of Research in Social Psychology*, 2nd ed. New York: McGraw Hill.

Badas, Alex. 2019. "The Applied Legitimacy Index: A New Approach to Measuring Judicial Legitimacy." *Social Science Quarterly* 100(5): 1848–1861.

Bailey, Michael A., and Forrest Maltzman. 2008. "Does Legal Doctrine Matter? Unpacking Law and Policy Preferences on the U.S. Supreme Court." *American Political Science Review* 102(3): 369–384.

Banks, Antoine J., and Heather M. Hicks. 2015. "Fear and Implicit Racism: Whites' Support for Voter ID Laws." *Political Psychology* 37(5): 641–658.

Banks, Antoine J., and Nicholas Valentino. 2012. "Emotional Substrates of White Racial Attitudes." *American Journal of Political Science* 56(2): 286–297.

Bartels, Brandon L. 2009. "The Constraining Capacity of Legal Doctrine on the U.S. Supreme Court." *American Political Science Review* 103(3): 474–495.

Bartels, Brandon L., and Christopher D. Johnston. 2013. "On the Ideological Foundations of Supreme Court Legitimacy in the American Public." *American Journal of Political Science* 57(1): 184–199.

2020. *Curbing the Court: Why the Public Constrains Judicial Independence*. New York: Cambridge University Press.

Bartels, Brandon L., and Andrew J. O'Geen. 2015. "The Nature of Legal Change on the U.S. Supreme Court: Jurisprudential Regimes Theory and Its Alternatives." *American Journal of Political Science* 59(4): 880–895.
Baum, Lawrence. 2017. *Ideology in the Supreme Court*. Princeton, NJ: Princeton University Press.
Baumeister, Roy F., Ellen Bratslavsky, Catrin Finkenauer, and Kathleen D. Vohs. 2001. "Bad Is Stronger than Good." *Review of General Psychology* 5(4): 323–370.
Berinsky, Adam J., Gregory A. Huber, and Gabriel S. Lenz. 2012. "Evaluating Online Labor Markets for Experimental Research: Amazon.com's Mechanical Turk." *Political Analysis* 20(3): 351–368.
Bickel, Alexander M. 1986. *The Least Dangerous Branch: The Supreme Court at the Bar of Politics*. New Haven, CT: Yale University Press.
Black, Ryan C., Ryan J. Owens, Justin Wedeking, and Patrick C. Wohlfarth. 2016a. "The Influence of Public Sentiment on Supreme Court Opinion Clarity." *Law and Society Review* 50(3): 703–732.
  2016b. *U.S. Supreme Court Opinions and Their Audiences*. Cambridge: Cambridge University Press.
  2020. *The Conscientious Justice: How Supreme Court Justices' Personalities Influence the Law, the High Court, and the Constitution*. Cambridge: Cambridge University Press.
Bobo, Lawrence, and Frederick C. Lacari. 1989. "Education and Political Tolerance: Testing the Effects of Cognitive Sophistication and Target Group Affect." *Public Opinion Quarterly* 53(3): 285–308.
Brader, Ted, Nicholas A. Valentino, and Elizabeth Suhay. 2008. "What Triggers Public Opposition to Immigration? Anxiety, Group Cues, and Immigration Threat." *American Journal of Political Science* 52(4): 959–978.
Brady, Henry E., and Paul M. Sniderman. 1985. "Attitude Attribution: A Group Basis for Political Reasoning." *American Political Science Review* 79(4): 1061–1078.
Brambor, Thomas, William R. Clark, and Matt Golder. 2005. "Understanding Interaction Models: Improving Empirical Analyses." *Political Analysis* 14(1): 63–82.
Brandenburg, Bert. 2004. "*Brown v. Board of Education* and Attacks on the Courts: Fifty Years Ago, Fifty Years Later." Brennan Center for Justice, www.brennancenter.org/sites/default/files/Brown%20v.%20Board%20of%20Education%20Attacks%20on%20the%20Courts%2C%2050%20Years%20Ago%2C%2050%20Years%20Later.pdf.
Buhrmester, Michael, Tracy Kwang, and Samuel D. Gosling. 2011. "Amazon's Mechanical Turk: A New Source of Inexpensive, Yet High-quality, Data?" *Perspectives on Psychological Science* 6(1): 3–5.
Caldeira, Gregory A., and James L. Gibson. 1992. "The Etiology of Public Support for the Supreme Court." *American Journal of Political Science* 36(3): 635–664.
Carrubba, Clifford J., Barry Friedman, Andrew D. Martin, and Georg Vanberg. 2012. "Who Controls the Content of Supreme Court Opinions?" *American Journal of Political Science* 56(2): 400–412.
Casillas, Christopher J., Peter K. Enns, and Patrick C. Wohlfarth. 2011. "How Public Opinion Constrains the U.S. Supreme Court." *American Journal of Political Science* 55(1): 74–88.

References

Chong, Dennis, and James N. Druckman. 2007. "Framing Theory." *Annual Review of Political Science* 10: 103–126.

Christenson, Dino P., and David M. Glick. 2015. "Chief Justice Roberts's Health Care Decision Disrobed: The Microfoundations of the Supreme Court's Legitimacy." *American Journal of Political Science* 59(2): 403–418.

2019. "Reassessing the Supreme Court: How Decisions and Negativity Bias Affect Legitimacy." *Political Research Quarterly* 72(3): 637–652.

Clark, Tom S. 2009. "The Separation of Powers, Court Curbing, and Judicial Legitimacy." *American Journal of Political Science* 53(4): 971–989.

2011. *The Limits of Judicial Independence*. Cambridge: Cambridge University Press.

Clark, John A. and Kevin T. McGuire. 1996. "Congress, the Supreme Court, and the Flag." *Political Research Quarterly* 49(4): 771–781.

Clark, Tom S., Jeffrey R. Lax, and Douglas Rice. 2015. "Measuring the Political Salience of Supreme Court Cases." *Journal of Law and Courts* 3(1): 37–65.

Clark, Tom S., Jeffrey K. Staton, Yu Wang, and Eugene Agichtein. 2018. "Using Twitter to Study Public Discourse in the Wake of Judicial Decisions: Public Reactions to the Supreme Court's Same-Sex Marriage Cases." *Journal of Law & Courts* 6(1): 93–126.

Cohen, Geoffrey L. 2003. "Party over Policy: The Dominating Impact of Group Influence on Political Beliefs." *Journal of Personality and Social Psychology* 85(5): 808–822.

Collins, Todd A., and Christopher A. Cooper. 2012. "Case Salience and Media Coverage of Supreme Court Decisions: Towards a New Measure." *Political Research Quarterly* 65(2): 396–407.

2015. "Making the Cases 'Real': Newspaper Coverage of U.S. Supreme Court Cases, 1953–2004." *Political Communication* 32(1): 23–42.

Conover, Pamela Johnston. 1988. "The Role of Social Groups in Political Thinking." *British Journal of Political Science* 18(1): 51–76.

Conover, Pamela Johnston, and Stanley Feldman. 1984. "The Origins and Meaning of Liberal/Conservative Self-Identifications." *American Journal of Political Science* 25(4): 617–645.

Continetti, Matthew. 2019. "Kavanaugh and the Crisis of Legitimacy." *National Review*. September 21, 2019, www.nationalreview.com/2019/09/brett-kava naugh-accusations-democratic-strategy/.

Converse, Philip E. 1964. "The Nature of Belief Systems in Mass Publics." In *Ideology and Discontent*, David Apter (ed.). New York: Free Press.

1970. "Attitudes and Non-attitudes: Continuation of a Dialogue." In *The Quantitative Analysis of Social Problems*, E. R. Tufte (ed.). Reading, MA: Addison-Wesley, 168–189.

Crawford, Jerome T., and Janet M. Pilanski. 2012. "Political Intolerance, Right and Left." *Political Psychology* 35(6): 841–851.

Cruz, Ted. 2015. "Constitutional Remedies to a Lawless Supreme Court." *National Review*. June 26, 2015, www.nationalreview.com/article/420409/constitutional-remedies-lawless-supreme-court-ted-cruz.

Dahl, Robert A. 1957. "Decision-Making in a Democracy: The Supreme Court as a National Policy-Maker." *Journal of Public Law* 6: 279–295.

Davis, Richard. 2014. "The Symbiotic Relationship between the U.S. Supreme Court and the Press." In *Covering the United States Supreme Court in the Digital Age*, Richard Davis (ed.). Cambridge: Cambridge University Press, 4–22.

Druckman, James N., Donald P. Green, James H. Kuklinski, and Arthur Lupia. 2011. "Experiments: An Introduction to Core Concepts." In *Cambridge Handbook of Experimental Political Science*, James N. Druckman, Donald P. Green, James H. Kuklinski, and Arthur Lupia (eds.). Cambridge: Cambridge University Press.

Drudge Report. 2013. "Gay Day at the High Court: DOMA Unconstitutional." Drudge Report. June 26, 2013, www.drudgereportarchives.com/data/2013/06/26/20130626_171231.htm.

Easton, David. 1965. *A Systems Analysis of Political Life*. New York: Wiley.

  1975. "A Re-Assessment of the Concept of Political Support." *British Journal of Political Science* 5(4): 435–457.

Edwards, Harry T. 1991. "The Judicial Function and the Elusive Goal of Principled Decisionmaking." *Wisconsin Law Review* 5: 837–866.

Eggen, Dan. 2010. "Large Majority Opposes Supreme Court's Decision on Campaign Financing." *Washington Post*, www.washingtonpost.com/wp-dyn/content/article/2010/02/17/AR2010021701151.html/02/17/AR2010021701151.html.

Engel, Stephen. 2011. *American Politicians Confront the Court: Opposition Politics and Changing Responses to Judicial Power*. Cambridge: Cambridge University Press.

Epstein, Lee, Daniel E. Ho, Gary King, and Jeffrey A. Segal. 2005. "The Supreme Court during Crisis." *NYU Law Review* 80: 1–116.

Epstein, Lee, and Jack Knight. 1996. "The Norm of Stare Decisis." *American Journal of Political Science* 40(4): 1018–1035.

  1997. *The Choices Justices Make*. Washington: Congressional Quarterly.

  2000. "Toward a Strategic Revolution in Judicial Politics: A Look Back, a Look Ahead." *Political Research Quarterly* 53(3): 625–651.

  2013. "Reconsidering Judicial Preferences." *Annual Review of Political Science* 13: 11–31.

Epstein, Lee, Christopher M. Parker, and Jeffrey A. Segal. 2018. "Do Justices Defend Speech They Hate? In-Group Bias, Opportunism, and the First Amendment." *Journal of Law and Courts* 6(2): 237–262.

Epstein, Lee, and Jeffrey A. Segal. 2000. "Measuring Issue Salience." *American Journal of Political Science* 44(1): 66–83.

Farganis, Dion. 2009. "Court Curbing in the Modern Era: Should Supreme Court Justices Really Worry about Attacks from Congress?" SSRN. July 12, 2009, https://papers.ssrn.com/sol3/papers.cfm?abstract_id=1430723.

Feldman, Stanley, and Karen Stenner. 1997. "Perceived Threat and Authoritarianism." *Political Psychology* 18(4): 741–770.

Flemming, Roy B., John Bohte, and B. Dan Wood. 1997. "One Voice among Many: The Supreme Court's Influence on Attentiveness to Issues in the United States, 1947–92." *American Journal of Political Science* 41(4): 1224–1250.

Franklin, Charles H., and Liane C. Kosaki. 1989. "Republican Schoolmaster: The U.S. Supreme Court, Public Opinion, and Abortion." *American Political Science Review* 83(3): 751–771.

Gawthorpe, Andrew. 2018. "The Cost of Kavanaugh's Victory? The Legitimacy of the U.S. Supreme Court." *The Guardian*. October 7, 2018, www.theguardian.com/commentisfree/2018/oct/07/brett-kavanaugh-victory-high-price-us-supreme-court-republicans.

Gentzkow, Matthew, and Jesse M. Shapiro. 2010. "What Drives Media Slant? Evidence from U.S. Daily Newspapers." *Econometrica* 78(1): 35–71.

References

Gibson, James L. 1989. "Understandings of Justice: Institutional Legitimacy, Procedural Justice, and Political Tolerance." *Law & Society Review* 23(3): 469–496.
  1992. "Alternative Measures of Political Tolerance: Must Tolerance Be 'Least-Liked'?" *American Journal of Political Science* 36(2): 560–577.
  2015. "Legitimacy Is for Losers: The Interconnections of Institutional Legitimacy, Performance Evaluations, and the Symbols of Judicial Authority." In *Motivating Cooperation and Compliance with Authority: The Role of Institutional Trust*, Brian H. Borstein and Alan J. Tomkins (eds.). New York: Springer, 81–116.
Gibson, James L., and Gregory A. Caldeira. 1992. "Blacks and the United States Supreme Court: Models of Diffuse Support." *Journal of Politics* 54(4): 1120–1145.
  2009. "Knowing the Supreme Court? A Reconsideration of Public Ignorance of the High Court." *Journal of Politics* 71(2): 429–441.
Gibson, James L., Gregory A. Caldeira, and Lester Kenyatta Spence. 2003a. "Measuring Attitudes towards the United States Supreme Court." *American Journal of Political Science* 47(2): 354–367.
  2003b. "The Supreme Court and the U.S. Presidential Election of 2000: Wounds, Self-Inflicted or Otherwise?" *British Journal of Political Science* 33(4): 535–556.
Gibson, James L., Milton Lodge, and Benjamin Woodson. 2014. "Losing, but Accepting: Legitimacy, Positivity Theory, and the Symbols of Judicial Authority." *Law & Society Review* 48(4): 837–866.
Gibson, James L., and Michael J. Nelson. 2014. "The Legitimacy of the U.S. Supreme Court: Conventional Wisdoms, and Recent Challenges Thereto." *Annual Review of Law and Social Science* 10: 201–219.
  2015. "Is the U.S. Supreme Court's Legitimacy Grounded in Performance Satisfaction and Ideology?" *American Journal of Political Science* 59(1): 1–13.
  2017. "Reconsidering Positivity Theory: What Roles Do Politicization, Ideological Disagreement, and Legal Realism Play in Shaping U.S. Supreme Court Legitimacy?" *Journal of Empirical Legal Studies* 14(3): 592–617.
  2018. *Black and Blue: African Americans and Legal Legitimacy*. New York: Oxford University Press.
Gibson, James L., Miguel M. Pereira, and Jeffrey Ziegler. 2017. "Updating Supreme Court Legitimacy: Testing the 'Rule, Learn, Update' Model of Political Communication." *American Politics Research* 45(6): 980–1002.
Giles, Micheal W., and Arthur S. Evans. 1985. "External Threat, Perceived Threat, and Group Identity." *Social Science Quarterly* 66(1): 50–66.
Giles, Micheal W., Bethany Blackstone, and Richard L. Vining. 2008. "The Supreme Court in American Democracy: Unraveling the Linkages between Public Opinion and Judicial Decision Making." *Journal of Politics* 70(2): 293–306.
Green, Donald P., Bradley Palmquist, and Eric Schickler. 2004. *Partisan Hearts and Minds: Political Parties and the Social Identities of Voters*. New Haven: Yale University Press.
Groseclose, Tim, and J. Milyo. 2005. "A Measure of Media Bias." *Quarterly Journal of Economics* 120(4): 1191–1237.
Hainmuller, Jens, Daniel J. Hopkins, and Teppei Yamamoto. 2014. "Causal Inference in Conjoint Analysis: Understanding Multidimensional Choices via Stated Preference Experiments." *Political Analysis* 22(1): 1–30.

Hall, Matthew E. K. 2011. *The Nature of Supreme Court Power*. Cambridge: Cambridge University Press.
　2014. "The Semiconstrained Court: Public Opinion, the Separation of Powers, and the U.S. Supreme Court's Fear of Nonimplementation." *American Journal of Political Science* 58(2): 352–366.
　2016. "Judicial Review as a Limit on Government Domination: Reframing, Resolving, and Replacing the (Counter) Majoritarian Difficulty." *Perspectives on Politics* 14(2): 391–409.
Hamilton, Alexander. 1788. "Federalist No. 78." Library of Congress. https://guides.loc.gov/federalist-papers/full-text.
Hannah-Jones, Nikole. 2019. "It Was Never About Busing." *New York Times*. July 12, 2019, www.nytimes.com/2019/07/12/opinion/sunday/it-was-never-about-busing.html.
Hansford, Thomas G., Chinita Intawan, and Stephen P. Nicholson. 2018. "Snap Judgment: Implicit Perceptions of a (Political) Court." *Political Behavior* 40(1): 127–147.
Harvey, Anna. 2013. *A Mere Machine: The Supreme Court, Congress, and American Democracy*. New Haven: Yale University Press.
Harvey, Anna, and Barry Friedman. 2009. "Ducking Trouble: Congressionally Induced Selection Bias in the Supreme Court's Agenda." *Journal of Politics* 71(2): 574–592.
Haven, Stefanie. 2013. "DOMA, Prop 8 Rulings Draw Favor from the Left, Fury from the Right." CBS News. June 26, 2013, www.cbsnews.com/news/doma-prop-8-rulings-draw-favor-from-the-left-fury-from-the-right/.
Hayes, Danny. 2011. "When Gender and Party Collide: Stereotyping in Candidate Trait Attribution." *Politics & Gender* 7(2): 133–165.
Hetherington, Marc J., and Joseph L. Smith. 2007. "Issue Preferences and Evaluations of the U.S. Supreme Court." *Public Opinion Quarterly* 71(1): 40–66.
Hitt, Matthew P., and Kathleen Searles. 2018. "Media Coverage and Public Approval of the U.S. Supreme Court." *Political Communication* 35(4): 566–586.
Ho, Daniel, and Kevin M. Quinn. 2008. "Measuring Explicit Political Positions of Media." *Quarterly Journal of Political Science* 3(4): 353–377.
Huddy, Leonie. 2001. "From Social to Political Identity: A Critical Examination of Social Identity Theory." *Political Psychology* 22(1): 127–156.
Hutchings, Vincent L., and Nicholas A. Valentino. 2004. "The Centrality of Race in American Politics." *Annual Review of Political Science* 7: 383–408.
Iyengar, Shanto, Guarav Sood, and Yphtach Lelkes. 2012. "Affect, Not Ideology: A Social Identity Perspective on Polarization." *Public Opinion Quarterly* 76(3): 405–431.
Iyengar, Shanto, and Sean J. Westwood. 2015. "Fear and Loathing across Party Lines: New Evidence on Group Polarization." *American Journal of Political Science* 59(3): 690–707.
Jardina, Ashley E. 2014. Demise of Dominance: Group Threat and the New Relevance of White Identity for American Politics. Ph.D. Dissertation. University of Michigan.
　2019. *White Identity Politics*. Cambridge: Cambridge University Press.
Johnston, Christopher D., and Brandon L. Bartels. 2010. "Sensationalism and Sobriety: Differential Media Exposure and Attitudes toward American Courts." *Public Opinion Quarterly* 74(2): 260–285.

References

Johnston, Christopher D., D. Sunshine Hillygus, and Brandon L. Bartels. 2014. "Ideology, the Affordable Care Act Ruling, and Supreme Court Legitimacy." *Public Opinion Quarterly* 78(4): 963–973.

Judd, John W. 1905. "The XIV Amendment – Its History and Evolution – Part One." *American Lawyer* 13: 338–342.

Klarman, Michael J. 2006. *From Jim Crow to Civil Rights: The Supreme Court and the Struggle for Racial Equality*. Oxford: Oxford University Press.

Kinder, Donald R. and Nathan P. Kalmoe. 2017. *Neither Liberal nor Conservative: Ideological Innocence in the American Public*. Chicago: University of Chicago Press.

King, Gary, Michael Tomz, and Jason Wittenberg. 2000. "Making the Most of Statistical Analyses: Improving Interpretation and Presentation." *American Journal of Political Science* 44(2): 341–355.

Lafond, Nicole. 2018. "Trump Grumbles that Gorsuch Is Too Liberal after Immigration Case Vote." *Talking Points Memo*. April 20, https://talkingpointsmemo.com/livewire/trump-grumbles-gorsuch-too-liberal.

Lau, Richard R. 1985. "Two Explanations for Negativity Effects in Political Behavior." *American Journal of Political Science* 29(1): 119–138.

Library of Congress. No date. *Congress Globe*. 39th Congress, 1st Session, Part Four, 2881–3840, https://memory.loc.gov/cgi-bin/ampage?collId=llcg&fileName=073/llcg073.db&recNum=2.

Linos, Katerina, and Twist, K. 2016. "The Supreme Court, the Media, and Public Opinion: Comparing Experimental and Observational Methods." *Journal of Legal Studies* 45(2): 223–254.

Liptak, Adam. 2013. "Corporations Find a Friend in the Supreme Court." *New York Times*, May 4, 2013, www.nytimes.com/2013/05/05/business/pro-business-decisions-are-defining-this-supreme-court.html?mcubz=2.

2014. "For Justices, Free Speech Often Means 'Speech I Agree With.'" *New York Times*, May 5, 2014, www.nytimes.com/2014/05/06/us/politics/in-justices-votes-free-speech-often-means-speech-i-agree-with.html?mcubz=2.

Lupia, Arthur. 1994. "Shortcuts versus Encyclopedias: Information and Voting Behavior in California Insurance Reform Elections." *American Political Science Review* 88(1): 63–76.

Madison, James. 1788. "Federalist No. 10." Library of Congress, https://guides.loc.gov/federalist-papers/full-text.

Maltzman, Forrest, James F. Spriggs, and Paul J. Wahlbeck. 2000. *Crafting Law on the Supreme Court: The Collegial Game*. Cambridge: Cambridge University Press.

Marcus, George E., John L. Sullivan, Elizabeth Theiss-Morse, and Sandra L. Wood. 1995. *With Malice toward Some: How People Make Civil Liberties Judgments*. Cambridge: Cambridge University Press.

Mark, Alyx, and Michael A. Zilis. 2019. "The Conditional Effectiveness of Legislative Threats: How Court Curbing Alters the Behavior of (Some) Supreme Court Justices." *Political Research Quarterly* 72(3): 570–583.

Martin, Andrew D., and Kevin M. Quinn. 2002. "Dynamic Ideal Point Estimation via Markov Chain Monte Carlo for the U.S. Supreme Court, 1953–1999. *Political Analysis* 10(2): 134–153.

Mason, Lilliana. 2015. "'I Respectfully Disagree': The Differential Effects of Partisan Sorting on Social and Issue Polarization." *American Journal of Political Science* 59(1): 128–145.
  2018. *Uncivil Agreement: How Politics Became Our Identity*. Chicago: University of Chicago Press.
Matthews, Richard K. 2005. "James Madison's Political Theory: Hostage to Democratic Fortune." *Review of Politics* 67(1): 49–67.
McDermott, Monika L. 1997. "Voting Cues in Low-Information Elections: Candidate Gender as a Social Information Variable in Contemporary United States Elections." *American Journal of Political Science* 41(1): 270–283.
  1998. "Race and Gender Cues in Low-Information Elections." *Political Research Quarterly* 51(4): 895–918.
McGuire, Kevin T. 2009. "Public Schools, Religious Establishments, and the US Supreme Court: An Examination of Policy Compliance." *American Politics Research* 37(1): 50–74.
McGuire, Kevin T., and James A. Stimson. 2004. "The Least Dangerous Branch Revisited: New Evidence on Supreme Court Responsiveness to Public Preferences." *Journal of Politics* 66(4): 1018–1035.
Miller, Erin. 2010. "Has the Supreme Court Been Mainly a Friend or Foe to African Americans?" *SCOTUSblog*. February 1, 2010, www.scotusblog.com/2010/02/has-the-supreme-court-been-mainly-a-friend-or-a-foe-to-african-americans/.
Mishler, William, and Reginald S. Sheehan. 1993. "The Supreme Court as a Countermajoritarian Institution? The Impact of Public Opinion on Supreme Court Decisions." *American Political Science Review* 87(1): 87–101.
Mondak, Jeffery J., and Shannon Ishiyama Smithey. 1997. "The Dynamics of Public Support for the Supreme Court." *Journal of Politics* 59(4): 1114–1142.
Murphy, Walter F. 1964. *Elements of Judicial Strategy*. Chicago: University of Chicago Press.
Murphy, Walter F., and Joseph Tanenhaus. 1969. "Public Opinion and the United States Supreme Court: A Preliminary Mapping of Some Prerequisites of Court Legitimation of Regime Changes." In *Frontiers in Judicial Research*, J. B. Grossman and J. Tanenhaus (eds.). New York: Wiley.
National Review. 2016. "In *Fisher*, Another Blow to Equal Opportunity." *National Review*. June 23, 2016, www.nationalreview.com/article/437047/fisher-v-ut-supreme-court-gets-it-wrong.
Nelson, Michael J., and James L. Gibson. 2019. "How Does Hyper-Politicized Rhetoric Affect the U.S. Supreme Court's Legitimacy?" *Journal of Politics* 81(4): 1512–1516.
  2020. "Measuring Subjective Ideological Disagreement with the U.S. Supreme Court." *Journal of Law and Courts* 8(1): 75–94.
Nelson, Thomas E., and Donald R. Kinder. 1996. "Issue Frames and Group-Centrism in American Public Opinion." *Journal of Politics* 58(4): 1055–1078.
Nelson, Michael J., and Patrick Tucker. In Press. "The Stability of the U.S. Supreme Court's Legitimacy." *Journal of Politics*, https://doi.org/10.1086/710143.
Nichols, Curt, Dave Bridge, and Adam M. Carrington. 2014. "Court Curbing via Attempt to Amend the Constitution: An Update of Congressional Attacks on the Supreme Court from 1955–1984." *Justice System Journal* 35(4): 331–343.

References

O'Callaghan, Jerome, and James O. Dukes. 1992. "Media Coverage of the Supreme Court's Caseload." *Journalism Quarterly* 69(1): 195–203.

O'Donnell, Michael. 2018. "Commander v. Chief." *The Atlantic*. April, www.theatlantic.com/magazine/archive/20182018/04/commander-v-chief/554045/.

Ohlheiser, Abby. 2015. "Kentucky Clerk Kim Davis on Gay Marriage Licenses: 'It Is a Heaven or Hell Decision.'" *Washington Post*. September 1, 2015, www.washingtonpost.com/news/acts-of-faith/wp/2015/09/01/kentucky-clerk-kim-davis-on-gay-marriage-licenses-it-is-a-heaven-or-hell-decision/?utm_term=.1e4df8163fe4.

Owens, Ryan J., Justin Wedeking, and Patrick C. Wohlfarth. 2013. "How the Supreme Court Alters Opinion Language to Evade Congressional Review." *Journal of Law and Courts* 1(1): 35–59.

Peffley, Mark, Marc L. Hutchison, and Michal Shamir. 2015. "The Impact of Persistent Terrorism on Political Tolerance: Israel, 1980–2011." *American Political Science Review* 109(4): 812–832.

Perlman, Matthew, Bill Hutchinson, and James Warren. 2013. "Edith Windsor, Center of Supreme Court's DOMA Ruling, Wins 'Everything We Asked and Hoped For.'" *New York Daily News*. June 26, 2013, www.nydailynews.com/new-york/edith-windsor-wins-hoped-article-1.1383602.

Perlstein, Rick. 2012. "Lee Atwater's Infamous 1981 Interview on the Southern Strategy." *The Nation*, www.thenation.com/article/exclusive-lee-atwaters-infamous-1981-interview-southern-strategy/.

"Playing Favourites." 2014. *The Economist*. May 13, 2014. No author, www.economist.com/blogs/democracyinamerica/2014/05/judicial-bias.

Popkin, Samuel L. 1991. *The Reasoning Voter*. Chicago: University of Chicago Press.

Reilly, Ryan J., and Sabrina Siddiqui. 2013. "Supreme Court DOMA Decision Rules Federal Same-Sex Marriage Ban Unconstitutional." *Huffington Post*. June 26, 2013, www.huffingtonpost.com/2013/06/26/supreme-court-doma-decision_n_3454811.html.

Richards, Mark J., and Herbert M. Kritzer. 2002. "Jurisprudential Regimes in Supreme Court Decision Making." *American Political Science Review* 96(2): 305–320.

Rosenberg, Gerald N. 2008. *The Hollow Hope: Can Courts Bring about Social Change?* Chicago: University of Chicago Press.

Ross, William G. 2002. "Attacks on the Warren Court by State Officials: A Cast Study of Why Court-Curbing Movements Fail." *Buffalo Law Review* 50: 483–612.

Sandalow, Terrance. 1977. "Judicial Protection of Minorities." *Michigan Law Review* 75: 1162–1195.

Sarratt, Reed. 1966. *The Ordeal of Desegregation*. New York: Harper.

Segal, Jeffrey A., and Harold J. Spaeth. 2002. *The Supreme Court and the Attitudinal Model Revisited*. Cambridge: Cambridge University Press.

1973. "Segregation Academies and State Action." *Yale Law Journal* 82(7): 1436–1461.

Sen, Maya. 2017. "How Political Signals Affect Public Support for Judicial Nominations: Evidence from a Conjoint Experiment." *Political Research Quarterly* 70(2): 374–393.

Sherman, Mark. 2017. "How Supreme Court Justices Could Avoid Issuing a Verdict on Trump's Travel Ban." *PBS*. September 19, 2017, www.pbs.org/newshour/politics/supreme-court-justices-avoid-issuing-verdict-trumps-travel-ban.

Silverleib, Alan. 2010. "Gloves Come Off After Obama Rips Supreme Court Ruling." CNN. January 28, 2010, www.cnn.com/2010/POLITICS/01/28/alito.obama.sotu/index.html?hpt=Sbin.

Slattery, Gram. 2014. "Public Confidence in Supreme Court at Historic Low, Poll Suggests." *Christian Science Monitor.* June 30, 2014, www.csmonitor.com/USA/Justice/2014/0630/Public-confidence-in-Supreme-Court-at-historic-low-poll-suggests.

Slotnick, Eliot E. 1991. "Media Coverage of Supreme Court Decision Making: Problems and Prospects." *Judicature* 75(3): 128–130.

Smith, Steven S. 2013. "The American Panel Survey." Weidenbaum Center at Washington University. Available at: taps.wustl.edu.

Sniderman, Paul M., Richard A. Brody, and Phillip E. Tetlock. 1991. *Reasoning and Choice: Explorations in Political Psychology.* Cambridge: Cambridge University Press.

Solberg, Rorie Spill, and Eric N. Waltenburg. 2014. *The Media, the Court, and the Misrepresentation: The New Myth of the Court.* New York: Routledge.

Soroka, Stuart N. 2014. *Negativity in Democratic Politics: Causes and Consequences.* Cambridge: Cambridge University Press.

Spaeth, Harold J., Lee Epstein, Andrew D. Martin, Jeffrey A. Segal, Theodore J. Ruger, and Sara C. Benesh. 2017. Supreme Court Database, version 2017, release 1, http://supremecourtdatabase.org.

Stancil, Will. 2018. "The Radical Supreme Court Decision that America Forgot." *The Atlantic.* May 29, 2018, www.theatlantic.com/education/archive/2018/05/the-radical-supreme-court-decision-that-america-forgot/561410/.

Stimson, James. 2018. *Public Opinion in American: Moods, Cycles, and Swings.* New York: Routledge.

Stohr, Greg. 2015. "Americans Want Supreme Court to Turn Off Political Spending Spigot." *Bloomberg Politics,* www.bloomberg.com/politics/articles/2015-09-28/bloomberg-poll-americans-want-supreme-court-to-turn-off-political-spending-spigot2015-09-28/bloomberg-poll-americans-want-supreme-court-to-turn-off-political-spending-spigot.

Strickler, Vincent James. 2014. "The Supreme Court and New Media Technologies." In *Covering the United States Supreme Court in the Digital Age,* Richard Davis (ed.). Cambridge: Cambridge University Press, 61–88.

Strother, Logan. 2017. "How Expected Political and Legal Impact Drive Media Coverage of Supreme Court Cases." *Political Communication* 34(4): 571–589.

Sullivan, John L., James Piereson, and George E. Marcus. 1993. *Political Tolerance and American Democracy.* Chicago: University of Chicago Press.

Sullivan, John L., and John E. Transue. 1999. "The Psychological Underpinnings of Democracy: A Selective Review of Research on Political Tolerance, Interpersonal Trust, and Social Capital." *Annual Review of Psychology* 50(1): 625–650.

Sunstein, Cass R. 2004. "Did *Brown* Matter?" *New Yorker,* www.newyorker.com/magazine/2004/05/03/did-brown-matter.

Tajfel, Henri, and John Turner. 1979. "An Integrative Theory of Intergroup Conflict." In *Organizational Identity: A Reader,* William G. Austin and Stephen Worchel (eds.). Monterrey, CA: Brooks/Cole, 33–47.

References

Totenberg, Nina. 2010. "Roberts Slams 'Pep Rally' Scene at State of the Union." *National Public Radio*, www.npr.org/templates/story/story.php?storyId=124537470.

Tushnet, Mark, and Katya Lezin. 1991. "What Really Happened in *Brown v. Board of Education*." *Columbia Law Review* 91(8): 1867–1930.

Tyler, Tom R. 2006. *Why People Obey the Law*. Princeton: Princeton University Press.

Ura, Joseph Daniel. 2014. "The Placement of Conflict: The Supreme Court and Issue Attention in the National Media." In *Covering the United States Supreme Court in the Digital Age*, Richard Davis (ed.). Cambridge: Cambridge University Press, 153–172.

Valentino, Nicholas A., Ted Brader, and Ashley E. Jardina. 2013. "Immigrant Opposition Among U.S. Whites: General Ethnocentrism or Media Priming of Attitudes about Latinos?" *Political Psychology* 34(2): 149–166.

Valentino, Nicholas A., Vincent L. Hutchings, and Ismail K. White. 2002. "Cues that Matter: How Political Ads Prime Racial Attitudes during Campaigns." *American Political Science Review* 96(1): 75–90.

Wedeking, Justin, and Michael A. Zilis. 2018. "Disagreeable Rhetoric and the Prospect of Public Opposition: Opinion Moderation on the U.S. Supreme Court." *Political Research Quarterly* 71(2): 380–394.

Zaller, John R. 1992. *The Nature and Origins of Mass Opinion*. Cambridge: Cambridge University Press.

Zilis, Michael A. 2015. *The Limits of Legitimacy: Dissenting Opinions, Media Coverage, and Public Responses to Supreme Court Decisions*. Ann Arbor: University of Michigan Press.

2018. "Minority Groups and Judicial Legitimacy: Group Affect and the Incentives for Judicial Responsiveness." *Political Research Quarterly* 71(2): 270–283.

In Press. "How Identity Politics Polarizes Rule of Law Opinions." *Political Behavior*, doi: 10.1007/s11109-020-09616-3.

Zilis, Michael A., Justin Wedeking, and Alexander Denison. 2017. "Hitting the 'Bullseye' in Supreme Court Coverage: News Quality in the Court's 2014 Term." *Elon Law Review* 9(2): 489–523.

Index

Abortion
  Prochoice groups, 8, 68, 70–71, 83, 130, 140, 146
  Prolife groups, 8, 28, 68, 70–71, 79, 83, 101, 104, 130, 140, 146, 149, 156–157
Affirmative action, 11, 37, 86, 112
African Americans, 1–3, 9–12, 15, 22–24, 28, 30, 37, 39–40, 43, 50, 55, 64, 66, 68, 74, 87, 94, 132, 134, 138, 144
American Civil Liberties Union, 69
The American Panel Survey, 39, 41, 55, 137
Arizona v. United States, 7, 31, 35–38, 43, 49–50, 66, 112, 124, 130

Bartels, Brandon, 3, 7, 13–15, 19, 25, 27, 30–31, 48–49, 52, 76, 98, 100, 105, 109, 128–130, 132
Baum, Lawrence, 19, 28, 98, 112, 114, 124
Bickel, Alexander, 2, 9, 108, 133
Big business, 8, 24, 33, 50–65, 68–69, 74, 87–88, 95, 99, 101, 104, 132, 140, 144, 148–149, 158
Bowers v. Hardwick, 21
Brown v. Board of Education, 1, 4, 11–14, 24, 30, 109, 111–112, 117, 126–128, 131, 133–135
Bush v. Gore, 13

Caldeira, Gregory, 3, 7, 13–16, 19, 25, 30–31, 37, 43, 50, 52, 57, 64, 76, 129, 134, 150
Campaign finance, 59–60, 62, 64, 68, 72, 148
Christenson, Dino, 3, 7, 13, 16, 18, 47, 81, 83, 129

Christian fundamentalists, 68, 70–71, 80, 83, 99, 101–102, 104, 140, 147, 149, 158
Citizens United v. F.E.C., 8, 24, 33, 50–59, 66, 97, 111, 130, 141
Civil rights, 2, 11, 18, 22–24, 28, 34, 37, 50, 64, 91, 131, 134–135
Compliance, 6, 14, 16, 71, 111, 135, 147, 158
Conjoint analysis, 98, 101, 104, 128, 146
Converse, Philip, 4–5, 7, 17, 19, 28–29, 131
Cooper v. Aaron, 11
Cues, 7–8, 18–19, 26, 30, 55, 67, 72, 84, 98, 104–107, 128–132, 134, 150

Defense of Marriage Act, 34
Diffuse support. *See* Legitimacy
Dred Scott v. Sandford, 21

Easton, David, 2, 6, 12
Eisenhower, Dwight, 126
Employment Division v. Smith, 66
Epstein, Lee, 5–6, 19, 28, 53, 97, 109, 114, 116, 132
Experiments, 7–8, 19, 26–27, 33, 50, 52, 58–65, 129, 131
  Treatments used in, 61, 67, 73–75, 99

Fisher v. Texas, 112
Fisher v. University of Texas, 86
Framing, 7, 38–39, 41, 53, 86, 88–89, 100, 105, 131, 133, 136
Free exercise. *See* US Constitution
Free speech. *See* US Constitution

173

Fundamental rights, 2, 5, 9, 51, 108–109, 127, 133

Gay rights, 7, 23, 27, 33–50, 58, 65, 95, 107, 113, 126, 138, 151
Gibson, James, 3, 7, 13–16, 19–20, 22, 25–26, 28–31, 37, 39, 43, 48, 50, 52, 57, 60, 64, 76, 129, 132, 134–135, 150
Glick, David, 3, 7, 13, 16, 18, 47, 81, 83, 129
Green v. New Kent County, 1, 3–6, 11, 17, 22, 24, 26, 110, 126, 135
Group antipathy, 5–6, 32, 35, 39, 44, 50, 52, 61, 64, 74, 76, 81, 86, 91, 94, 104, 107, 125, 127–129, 131–132, 134–135, 150
  Group antipathy hypothesis, 20, 23, 32, 41, 60, 69, 91
  Right limitation hypothesis, 21, 23, 43, 91
  Weak signal hypothesis, 22–23
Grutter v. Bollinger, 4

Hamilton, Alexander, 2, 9, 32, 34, 49
Heuristics, 74, 107, 131
Hollingsworth v. Perry, 7, 23, 34–36, 38, 43, 49–50, 107

Immigrants, 7, 10, 18, 27, 31, 33, 35, 37–38, 40–46, 48–50, 58, 66, 68, 87, 95, 101, 138, 144, 152
Implementation, 6, 9, 14, 30, 109

Jefferson, Thomas, 13, 32
Johnston, Christopher, 3, 7, 13–15, 19, 25, 27, 30–31, 48–49, 52, 76, 98, 100, 105, 128–130, 132
Judicial review, 2, 13–14, 94, 101–102, 104, 116, 146, 149

Kinder, Donald, 5, 7, 17, 19, 29, 98, 131
Knox v. Service Employees International Union, Local 23, 38–39, 43, 50
Korematsu v. United States, 4, 21, 24, 32, 134

Labor unions, 23, 34, 38–40, 43, 59–63, 68–70, 72, 74, 81, 99, 101–102, 113, 140–141, 148–149
Lawrence v. Texas, 31, 111, 126
Legitimacy, 2–3, 6, 9, 25, 32–33, 36, 38, 55, 59–60, 64, 69–70, 82–83, 86, 88–89, 92, 95, 98, 105, 110, 117, 120, 124, 131–133, 135, 157
  Democratic norms, 3, 5, 15, 25–26, 43–44, 48, 58, 96, 127, 129

Negativity bias and, 3, 16, 18, 47
Political knowledge, in relation to, 48, 58, 64, 70, 74, 83, 85–86, 88, 96, 127, 131, 151, 153, 155
Positivity symbols and, 25, 31
Positivity theory of, 3, 52
Subjective ideological disagreement model, 16–17, 27
Loving v. Virginia, 11

Madison, James, 4, 51
Marbury v. Madison, 13
Mechanical Turk, 68, 82–83, 86–87, 91, 99–101, 142, 144–145
Media coverage, 19, 65
  Bias in, 130
  Chicago Tribune, in the, 36, 53
  Los Angeles Times, in the, 36, 53, 114, 118
  New York Times, in the, 36–37, 53, 88, 114, 116, 118, 141, 144
  Salient cases, 5, 7–9, 16, 18–19, 21–24, 26, 31, 36, 38–39, 43, 50, 58, 61, 79, 81, 96, 112, 114, 118, 120, 122, 124, 128–129, 132–133
  Washington Post, in the, 36, 53, 114, 118, 141
Mediation analysis, 98, 105
Milliken v. Bradley, 2, 6
Minority rights, 1, 4, 6–7, 9, 21, 25, 32–34, 44, 49–50, 91, 95, 107–110, 128, 130, 133
Muslims, 66, 68, 70–71, 79–80, 83, 87–88, 91–95, 99, 101, 140, 144–145, 147, 149, 156

National Federation of Independent Business v. Sebelius, 13
National Organization of Marriage, 35
National Rifle Association, 69
Nelson, Michael, 3, 7, 13–17, 19, 25, 29–31, 39, 43, 48, 60, 129, 132, 135
Noncompliance. *See* Compliance

Obama, Barack, 30, 37, 51
Obergefell v. Hodges, 4, 6, 13, 24, 50, 135

Party identification, 2, 4, 32, 34, 41, 61, 70, 84, 94, 112–113, 134, 139
Polarization, 16, 63, 75, 130–131, 134
Political awareness, 17, 22, 26, 29, 129
Political elites, 3, 13–14, 17, 28, 30, 52, 65, 86, 98, 100, 126, 134
Political predispositions, 31, 61–62, 70, 75, 85, 88, 92, 94, 153, 155, 157

Index

Political tolerance, 5, 15, 26–27, 41, 48, 57, 139
Politicization, 14, 76, 81–82, 129–130
Public opinion, 4–6, 17–18, 20, 26, 32, 38, 43, 52, 64–65, 98, 105, 109, 117, 122, 124, 127, 129
  Group identity and, 18
  Group-centric nature of, 7, 17–21, 24
  Social identity and, 4

Reagan, Ronald, 97
Receive-accept-sample model, 26
Regents of the University of California v. Bakke, 11, 24, 134
Republican National Convention, 97
Resistance, 1–2, 11, 13, 15, 109
Rights paradox, 4, 25, 133

Same-sex marriage. See *Obergefell v. Hodges*
Segal, Jeffrey, 5, 19, 28, 53, 97, 109, 114, 116, 125
Segregation, 1, 4, 11, 113
Sessions v. Dimaya, 134
Shelby County v. Holder, 21, 23–24, 37, 39, 43, 91, 134
Shelley v. Kraemer, 4
Social groups, 4, 6–7, 12, 17–25, 30, 32–33, 35–36, 38, 40, 44, 48–49, 61, 74, 85, 87, 89, 95–96, 98, 108, 111, 114, 116–117, 123–124, 127–128, 130, 134, 144, 157, 159
  In-group, out-group considerations and, 18, 28, 97
Spaeth, Harold, 24, 109, 111, 125, 169
Specific support, 12–14, 16, 31, 41, 44–45, 49, 130
Supreme Court
  Attitudinal model of the, 55, 109
  Backlash to the, 1, 3–4, 6, 11, 109, 133
  Certiorari, 65–66, 68, 91–92, 95, 110, 117–118, 124
  Chief Justice of the, 4, 16, 51, 83, 114, 135, 139, 142–143
  Counter-majoritarian behavior of the, 9, 14, 19, 108–110, 127, 133, 136
  Curbing, 15, 108
  Docket of the, 9, 23–24, 66, 110, 114–115, 122, 124, 128
  Group rights rulings of the, 111, 114, 137
  Guardian role of the, 9, 11–12, 21, 108–110, 120, 124
  Ideological perceptions of the, 8, 29, 73, 96, 98–100, 105–107, 128–129, 131
  Legal constraints on the, 109
  Media coverage of, 19–20, 23–24, 30, 36–38, 52, 54, 58, 64, 101, 127, 130, 146
  Nominations to, 3, 6, 79, 130
  Republican schoolmaster role of the, 30
  Responsive behavior of the, 9, 25, 105, 108, 117–118, 120, 122, 124
  Strategic behavior of, 4, 6–7, 9, 12, 16–17, 19, 21, 28, 31–33, 105, 107–110, 117, 124, 127–128, 132–134
  Treatment of precedent, 50, 63, 101–102, 104, 109, 116, 146, 149
  Unanimous decisions of the, 114, 116
Supreme Court Database, 112–114, 116, 118
Supreme Court justices
  Burger, Warren, 115, 117
  Earl Warren, 126
  Frankfurter, Felix, 4, 135
  Ginsburg, Ruth Bader, 51
  Gorsuch, Neil, 85
  Jackson, Robert, 2, 135
  Kavanaugh, Brett, 3, 6, 12, 79, 130
  Kennedy, Anthony, 34, 49, 88
  Rehnquist, William, 23, 97, 115, 117
  Roberts, John, 16, 51, 58, 88, 97, 115, 117, 139, 142–143
  Scalia, Antonin, 2, 31, 35, 37, 88, 124, 126, 135
  Stone, Harlan Fiske, 4
  Vinson, Fred, 115, 117
  Warren, Earl, 4, 30, 35, 115, 117, 126, 128, 134–135
Survey Sampling International, 59, 68, 83, 99, 106, 140
Surveys, 7–8, 23, 32–33, 35, 39, 45, 52, 55, 58–59, 61, 63, 65, 67, 69, 76, 82, 87, 98, 137, 140, 142, 144–145
Swann v. Charlotte-Mecklenburg Board of Education, 11

Texas v. Johnson, 97
Trump v. Hawaii, 21, 66
Trump v. International Refugee Assistance Project, 66
Trump, Donald, 21, 66, 79, 91, 94–95, 100, 134, 145, 149
Travel ban signed by, 66, 91–95, 145, 149, 169

US Constitution, 2, 9, 13, 32, 34, 51, 126, 133, 143
  Civil War Amendments to the, 111
  Due Process Clause of the, 126

US Constitution (cont.)
  Equal protection and the, 11, 20–21, 107, 109, 111, 113, 121, 130, 132–133, 135–136
  Fifth Amendment to the, 126
  First Amendment to the, 5, 7, 14, 16, 18, 24, 27–28, 30, 33, 41, 43, 51–52, 59–60, 63, 91, 101, 116, 121, 124, 128–129, 131–133, 145–146, 148–149
  Fourteenth Amendment to the, 9–10, 35, 111

United States v. Carolene Products, 4, 109
United States v. Windsor, 4, 7, 23–24, 34–36, 38, 43, 49–50, 65, 107, 126, 130

Validity, 53, 59, 67, 69, 87–88, 112, 140, 144
Voting rights. *See Shelby County v. Holder*
Voting Rights Act. *See Shelby County v. Holder*

Zaller, John, 26, 52, 65, 150

CPSIA information can be obtained
at www.ICGtesting.com
Printed in the USA
LVHW111224030821
694401LV00002B/101